ILLUSTRATED
ENGLISH SOCIAL HISTORY

Works by
George Macaulay Trevelyan, O.M.

I   Queen Anne and the Knights of the Garter (1713)

ILLUSTRATED
ENGLISH SOCIAL HISTORY

VOLUME THREE

The Eighteenth Century

by

G. M. TREVELYAN, O.M.

Master of Trinity College, 1940–1951
Formerly Regius Professor of Modern
History in the University of Cambridge

ILLUSTRATIONS SELECTED BY
RUTH C. WRIGHT

1724

LONGMANS, GREEN AND CO
LONDON · NEW YORK · TORONTO

LONGMANS, GREEN AND CO LTD
6 & 7 CLIFFORD STREET LONDON W I

ALSO AT MELBOURNE AND CAPE TOWN

LONGMANS, GREEN AND CO INC
55 FIFTH AVENUE NEW YORK 3

LONGMANS, GREEN AND CO
215 VICTORIA STREET TORONTO I

ORIENT LONGMANS LTD
BOMBAY CALCUTTA MADRAS

BIBLIOGRAPHICAL NOTE
First published in U.S.A. and Canada 1942
First published in Great Britain 1944
This volume first published 1951

Photogravure plates printed by
JARROLD & SONS LTD. NORWICH

Colour plates printed by
EDMUND EVANS LTD. LONDON

Text printed in Great Britain by
SPOTTISWOODE, BALLANTYNE & CO. LTD.
London & Colchester

PREFATORY NOTE TO THE ILLUSTRATIONS

ALTHOUGH the broad principles of selection from English sources contemporary with the scenes represented have governed my choice of illustrations for Volume III as for Volumes I and II, a basic difference in the artist's or illustrator's approach is visible when one reaches the Eighteenth Century.

In the mediaeval period such social scenes as exist are, as it were, incidental, occurring mainly in decorative borders, or as miniatures or as seasonal or zodiacal representations in the calendars of liturgical MSS. With the rise of printing comes a crude and often stereotyped kind of woodcut to illustrate such educational books as the *Stans Puer ad Mensam* or romances and legends such as Caxton and Wynkyn de Worde produced.

But in the later Sixteenth Century, book illustration includes engraved maps and bird's eye views of towns, and moves besides into the field of technical woodcuts (with explanatory keys) of mine workings or methods of glass blowing, as well as into that of the deliberate recording of foreign scenes and peoples as in de Bry's *Virginia*. These various classes of illustration continue and develop throughout the Seventeenth Century, but there appear also the road map, the battle plan, outdoor sporting scenes —racing or hunting—or fashionable amusements such as taking the waters at Bath, side by side with the popular broadsheet 'cuts' of gamesters or milkmaids, of marvels and wonders of all kinds.

It is not until the Eighteenth Century, however, that there appears for the first time the artist with his sketch book jotting down either for his own pleasure, or for antiquarian record, or simply as an illustrative accompaniment to a tour undertaken with a patron, scenes of any and every kind, the interior of a Northumbrian kitchen, a cricket match, a picnic party, the passers-by in Edinburgh High Street or the frequenters of a coffee house.

Besides the formal conversation piece, the painter contributes records of a rural ale-bench or the stage-coach on the Dover road, while the engraver and book illustrator, besides representing noblemen's houses and ancient castles, are now interested in depicting the latest cotton mill or brass foundry, and the satirist makes himself responsible for calling attention to the social evils of the new age.

It is thus possible to see life in the Eighteenth Century at many levels through contemporary eyes in a way which had not been possible before that date. For instance, a row of poor dwellings has become of sufficient interest in itself to catch the sketcher's eye, as the colliers' houses on the Newcastle road caught Grimm's, but we can search in vain in an earlier age to find a contemporary representation of the interior of a mediaeval peasant's hut. The illuminator of the Smithfield Decretals had not hesitated to censure ecclesiastical laxity or rapacity, but this is something entirely different from the harsh realism of Gillray's satire on the press gang or Hogarth's gin sodden London slum.

Documentary record, social criticism, antiquarianism and topographical interest all play their part in Eighteenth Century illustration, actuated sometimes by an instinct for the decorative and picturesque, sometimes by the desire for savage caricature, sometimes by the mere delight of setting down things seen and enjoyed.

It has thus been possible to illustrate in this volume more sides of life than previously in that the extant records are themselves fuller and more diversified, and I have therefore allowed the artist and illustrator to speak out more fully for the new industrial age that was just beginning, for the rural life of the south and north not yet smothered or standardised, for town development and the ways in which men and women were expressing themselves, and have cut down to a minimum the better known and more formalised conversation pieces, which have been used so often to emphasise the elegance of Eighteenth Century manners and settings.

As previously, full notes of the sources from which these illustrations have been drawn, together with details of anything noteworthy in their content or history, will be found at the end of the book.

I must again record my gratitude to the late Sir Henry Hake and to his assistant (now Director) at the National Portrait Gallery, Mr. C. K. Adams, for their advice on the dating and authenticity of the portraits illustrated.

RUTH C. WRIGHT
Illustrations Editor

CONTENTS

Prefatory Note to the Illustrations

Introduction

ILLUSTRATIONS

INTRODUCTION

THIS third volume of the Illustrated Edition of my *English Social History* covers the Eighteenth Century. It describes first the period of English civilization known as the Age of Anne. It is natural to compare and contrast it with the Age of Elizabeth, described in the previous volume, noting the changes, some loss and some gain, in the character of civilization that had taken place between Queen and Queen.

The next section of this volume is the age of Dr. Johnson, the early and middle years of George III. Here the reader is presented with two pictures: first the peculiar civilization of the period, highly favourable to arts, crafts and letters, aristocratic but much broader and more liberal than the contemporary *ancien régime* on the Continent; and secondly the earlier stages of those fundamental economic and social changes known as the Industrial Revolution. Finally a chapter is appended indicating some of the social consequences to both countries of the closer union of England and Scotland.

ACKNOWLEDGMENTS

THE publishers' grateful thanks are due to all those who have given permission for photographs to be taken of the MSS., printed books, pictures or antiquities in their care or ownership, or have allowed photographs in their possession to be reproduced. Full details of such ownership, etc., will be found in the descriptive notes for each item.

Chapter One

DEFOE'S ENGLAND[1]

Queen Anne, 1702–1714—George I, 1714–1727—The Marlborough Wars, 1702–1712.—Parliamentary and economic union with Scotland, 1707.

WHEN a survey is demanded of Queen Anne's England and its everyday life, our thoughts turn to Daniel Defoe, riding solitary and observant through the countryside. It was one of his tasks to traverse Britain on such tours of reconnaissance; after his day's journey, in the inn of some market town, he wrote his report on local opinion to his employer, Robert Harley, a mystery-man like himself, and a lover of exact information secretly given. On Sundays he would attend the Dissenters' Chapel, observant of his fellow-worshippers and inquisitive as to their business affairs. For besides being a trader, he was a Nonconformist, not indeed of the type laden with the proverbial conscience, for Defoe could be all things to all men, but a Puritan in his preference for solid work and homespun to fashionable display. Like Cobbett, who rode and wrote about England a hundred years after him, he was a realist and a man of the people, but he was not, like his successor, half blinded by rage against the powers that be. For the age of Anne was the prelude to a long era of content, and Defoe, more than Swift, was the typical man of his day. Defoe, the trader, hailed the advent of the era of business prosperity as heartily as Cobbett, the disinherited yeoman, bewailed the rural past. He first perfected the art of the reporter; even his novels, such as *Robinson Crusoe* and *Moll Flanders* are imaginary 'reports' of daily life, whether on a desert island or in a thieves' den. So then, the account that this man gives of the England of Anne's reign is for the historian a treasure indeed. For Defoe was one of the first who saw the old world through a pair of sharp modern eyes. His report can be controlled

---

[1] Only a few years ago I wrote some chapters on the social life of England under Queen Anne, in my history of her reign, published, like this volume, by Messrs. Longman. As I cannot improve on them now, I have laid them under contribution.

and enlarged by great masses of other evidence, but it occupies the central point of our thought and vision.[1]

Now this picture of England, drawn by Defoe in much wealth of prosaic detail, leaves the impression of a healthy national life, in which town and country, agriculture, industry and commerce were harmonious parts of a single economic system. Much indeed of the administrative machinery of government, particularly of the 'poor decayed borough towns' which Defoe despised, was antiquarian lumber too religiously preserved. But for many years to come no cry was raised for Reform, because the principle of freedom then peculiar to England enabled individual enterprise to flourish, and new shoots to push through the old jungle. The Bumbledom of that day could not suppress the economic initiative native to the island soil.

The England so ordered was prosperous and in the main contented even in time of war, partly owing to good harvests and cheap food in the first half of Anne's reign. Only during the last three years of a decade of hostilities with France (1702–1712) were there signs of distress and discontent due to war conditions. Otherwise industry, agriculture and commerce all continued to expand; society moved forward unconsciously towards the Industrial Revolution, which grew in the next hundred years out of the conditions described by Defoe. Oversea trade; water-carriage on the rivers, particularly of coal; sheep-farming and the cloth trade; the national marketing of agricultural produce by wholesale dealers—on these things he lays stress, and it was these things that enabled many landowners to pay the land tax, the mainstay of the Marlborough Wars. They grumbled but they paid, till the war was won, when they sent the Whigs about their business and made peace.

It is true that rural squires over their October ale cursed the moneyed men and traders as economic parasites, war-profiteers and Dissenters, would-be intruders into political life which was the proper sphere of the landed interest alone. But economically the activities of these undesirables doubled the rent of many a squire, as indeed he was partly aware. And the Act of Toleration,

---

[1] He published his *Tour through Great Britain* in the reign of George I, but the tours on which he based his observations were largely taken in the early and middle years of Anne. The first edition of the Tour (1724–27) has been edited and republished by Mr. G. D. H. Cole in 1927.

though scarcely to be mentioned without a groan over degenerate times, gave riches as well as quiet to the land.

In the reigns of Anne and George I the old way of life for peasant and craftsman was still carried on, but under conditions peculiarly favourable. The enterprise of trader and middleman was finding new markets for the products of the peasant's and craftsman's toil, and had already done much to relieve their mediaeval poverty without as yet destroying their rustic simplicity of manners. Money made in trade was more and more frequently put in the land by improving landlords, who had won or enlarged their fortunes as mercantile investors. This interplay of the activity of town and country, not yet subversive of the old social order, gave to Queen Anne's England a fundamental harmony and strength, below the surface of the fierce distracting antagonisms of sect and faction.

While religion divided, trade united the nation, and trade was gaining in relative importance. The Bible had now a rival in the Ledger. The Puritan, sixty years back, had been Cromwell, sword in hand; thirty years back, Bunyan, singing hymns in gaol; but now the Puritan was to be found in the tradesman-journalist Defoe. The Quaker, too, had ceased to prophesy in public against steeple houses, and had become a thrifty dealer, studying to be quiet. For old sake's sake, Puritans and Quakers were still called 'fanatics' in common parlance. But if there were 'fanatics' at large, one of them surely was Justice Bradgate, who 'rode a horseback into the Meeting House' at Lutterworth and told the preacher he lied. Yet that angry zeal of the High Churchmen was perpetually being tempered by patriotic and economic considerations that worked strongly in the minds of the Moderate Tories, led by Harley, whose secret servant was this same Defoe. Here then was an island which, with luck and good leading, might in wartime display enough unity, wealth and vigour to bring to his knees the mighty Louis of France, the undisputed lord of nobles and poor peasants, who had got rid of his Nonconformists once for all by revoking the Edict of Nantes.

Already English agriculture had improved so far that more wheat was grown than in mediaeval times. Wheat was reckoned at thirty-eight per cent. of the bread of the whole population;

rye came next, barley and oats a good third and fourth. Prices were therefore quoted in terms of wheat and rye.

But wheat formed a much smaller proportion of the actual corn grown than of the bread baked, because enormous crops of barley were produced all over the island to make malt for ale and beer. For example, Cambridgeshire south of Ely was 'almost wholly a corn country' and, as Defoe observed, 'of that corn five parts in six is barley, which is generally sold at Ware and Royston and other great malting towns of Hertfordshire.' Except in the cider counties of the West, ale had been unchallenged in former ages as the native drink of English men, women and children at every meal, and it was only beginning to feel the rivalry of strong spirits on the one hand and of tea and coffee on the other. It was still the drink of ladies. In 1705 Lady Carnarvon imputed the fact that Miss Coke was 'extremely fallen away and her voice weak and inward' to 'her having had stale beer all this summer.' Children still drank very small beer and it was in many cases better for them than the impure water which was too often the only alternative.

Not only did barley everywhere provide the staple drink, but in some districts it provided the staple food. The small farmers of the Welsh hills supplied themselves with an excellent barley bread. The peasantry of the northern counties consumed oats and rye in various forms; and in Scotland, oats 'supported the people' as Dr. Johnson was still able to assert many years later. In the central districts of England, rye and barley divided honours with wheat, and only in the drier climate of the south-east could wheat be said to preponderate.

But already in the reign of Anne a great interchange of agricultural products was going on between one district and another, especially where river traffic was available. Largely for this reason the deepening of rivers and the making of locks was a movement specially characteristic of the period, two generations before the era of the Duke of Bridgewater's artificial canals.[1] The

---

[1] The *Statutes* and the *Commons Journals* for Anne's reign, as well as local histories, afford abundant evidence of this. One case may be quoted for all: in 1699 the inhabitants of Wisbech petition the House of Commons to have the River Lark made navigable, as the roads are impracticable, and their district which itself produces only butter, cheese and oats, is supplied with wheat, rye and malt from Suffolk. Among the rivers at this period deepened and supplied with proper locks were the Bristol Avon, the Yorkshire Derwent, the Stour and the Cam 'from Clayhithe Ferry to the Queen's Mill' in Cambridge.

Thames all the way down from Oxford, and its affluents the Wey, the Lea and the Medway, were the scenes of an animated and crowded traffic—food, drink and timber going down to London, and Tyneside coal and overseas products towed up-country in return. Abingdon and Reading were each the emporium of a great agricultural district, of which they dispatched the produce by water to the capital. The coasts of Sussex and Hampshire sent their corn, Cheshire and other western counties sent their cheese, by sea to London, running the gauntlet of the French privateers from Dunkirk. The roads were at many times of year too soft for wagons, but in most weathers the sheep and cattle, the geese and turkeys of the northern and midland shires could be driven to the capital, grazing as they went on the broad grass of the roadside. Even before the Union of 1707, Scotland sent 30,000 head of cattle a year into England: the strange speech of the Welsh drovers was familiar on the roads near London; only the Irish cattle-trade had been killed by an Act of the reign of Charles II, a sacrifice to the jealousy of English breeders.

England and Wales already formed the most considerable area in Europe for internal free trade, to which Scotland was added half way through the reign of Anne. 'Tis our great felicity in England,' wrote Defoe, 'that we are not yet come to a *gabelle* or tax upon corn, as in Italy, and many other countries.' The shrewd Venetian envoy, Mocenigo, at the end of his residence in our island, reported to his masters in 1706 that freedom from internal *douanes* was one reason why 'industry was further advanced in England than in any other part of the world.' London and every provincial city was an open market for provisions, with no toll taken at the gate. Favoured by this freedom, the corn-factors and middlemen of agriculture pervaded the whole island, buying up on speculation the farmers' crops as they grew in the field, or as they lay unthreshed in the barn; penetrating to the most unlikely places, even to dangerous Highland straths, amid claymores and Jacobites, in search of cattle to be fattened in English parks; everywhere forwarding the movement towards agricultural progress by opening new markets for the produce of remote estates and hamlets.

Under this regime of enterprise and improvement England was sending corn oversea on a large scale, helped by the bounty on export. In the middle of Anne's reign the employees of the

Gloucestershire coal trade rose in revolt against the high price of corn, due to the scale on which the Bristol merchants shipped the local supply abroad. And even north of Trent, homely squires were calculating on sales abroad as an important item in their own and their tenants' fortunes.[1]

Nevertheless, this cheerful picture of agricultural and distributive activity must not delude us into imagining that England was already the land of improved agriculture and reformed traffic that it became by the end of the century. The busy life of the rivers was a measure of the badness of the roads. Corn-lands potentially the best in England—in the midlands, and northern East Anglia—were still for the most part unenclosed. In those regions the vast and hedgeless village field was still being cultivated by mediaeval methods that would have won the approval of a Doomsday commissioner, but were destined to shock the modern intelligence of Arthur Young. [See § 4.]

The initiative of improving landlord or farmer was closely circumscribed on these village fields, wherein the scattered strips of individual owners had perforce to be cultivated on the plan laid down for the whole community. A man could not profitably grow turnips or artificial grasses on his unfenced strips; for the whole 'field,' as soon as the corn was carried, was opened as pasture to the cattle of the village, which would eat his clover and turnips and he would be without redress. The open field was cultivated on a uniform plan. A small country town like Godmanchester, for example, still employed its bailiffs to summon all the farmers to appear, according to old custom, at the Court Hall, where they 'did agree that none should sow barley in the commonfield before Friday, 21st March' (1700), 'and that day only headlands.'

More initiative and therefore more progress was possible, though by no means inevitable, on newly enclosed farms which were constantly increasing in number, and in the regions of old enclosure in southern, western and northern England. But the

[1] In July 1709 Robert Molesworth writes to his wife from Edlington, near Doncaster: 'If God sends good harvest weather, there will be a very great store of corn in the kingdom, and yet such are the wants abroad that it is likely to bear a very good price for several years to come. This must enrich our farmers.' And next year he writes: 'Corn must certainly rise in price and that very suddenly, for the plague, which is got into the Baltic, will make soon both us and the Dutch to prohibit all trade there and then the Dutch must be furnished with corn from us.'

districts where enclosure was commonest were on the average the less productive parts of the island, with the worst climate. It is true that Kentish hop-fields and west country orchards and fruit gardens must be reckoned among the lands of early enclosure, but so must the intakes amid the weather-beaten moorlands of west and north. Most of the best cornlands of the midlands were still unenclosed.

Since many of the sheep and cattle were fed on stubble-fields, heaths and commons, and without the aid of roots or artificial grasses for winter feed, they were pitifully small and thin. Their weight at Smithfield market in 1710 was less than half that of ordinary sheep and cattle in 1795. At the beginning of the century the difficulty of keeping beasts alive in winter was still so great that, when they came off the summer grass, all save the breeding stock were slaughtered and salted, and the survivors were kept on short rations till spring. When the price of salt rose in 1703, the House of Commons was petitioned, on the ground that it was 'a grievance to the poorer sort of people who mostly feed on salted provisions.'

The days of Lord Townshend's turnip-fields and Coke of Norfolk's fat sheep and cattle were still in the future. But already the Wiltshire and Cotswold uplands, that bred sheep for the western wool-clothiers, were a wonder to behold. 'On the pleasant downs' within a six-mile radius of Dorchester, Defoe was informed that more than half a million sheep were feeding; and he noted that on Salisbury Plain and the Dorset Downs the land was becoming so much enriched by the folding of sheep with pens in a new place every night, that the chalk lands thus manured, though hitherto fit only for pasture, were rapidly coming under the plough.

Ever since Tudor times, and more particularly since the Restoration, there had flowed from the press an ever broadening stream of books on improved methods of agriculture. [See § 3.] The spirit of scientific inquiry emanating from the regions of the Royal Society into the walks of common life, was a constant stimulant but often a sore puzzle to the practical farmer. For the experts and modernizers were so seldom agreed. Jethro Tull, the great improver who introduced the drill and the horse-hoe into his own farming operations in the course of Anne's reign, was quite wrong on many other points, as subsequent experience showed.

7

But men were on the look-out to adopt new methods as soon as their value had been proved, especially where enclosed ground gave liberty for change.

With the idea of agricultural improvement thus in the air, the enclosure of commons and heaths was not only frequently practised as it had been for centuries, but was preached by modern theorists as a duty to the commonwealth. In Tudor times controversialists had been almost all on the side of the commons and the commoners against the enclosures. But when Anne came to the throne the agricultural writers were denouncing the commons as 'seminaries of a lazy, thieving sort of people,' whose sheep were 'poor, tattered and poisoned with rot,' and whose heath-fed cattle were 'starved, todbellied runts, neither fit for the dairy nor the yoke.' Here was another phase of the perennial controversy as to the social value of rights on the common, in which Cobbett a hundred years later was protagonist of the defeated commoners. On the merits of that dispute the historians of our own day are still divided. In Anne's reign there was not yet much enclosure done by Act of Parliament, but enclosure was going forward under the common law by agreement or otherwise.[1]

The age of Defoe was still a period of prosperity for English freehold yeomen, and it was no ill time for the still rising fortunes of the tenant farmers. The freehold yeomen and their families were reckoned at about one-eighth of the population of the country, and the substantial tenant farmers at a little less; at the time of the Revolution it had been calculated that the freehold yeoman was on the average a richer man than the tenant farmer. A hundred years later the opposite was probably the case, in so far as the freehold yeoman any longer existed. For in the Georgian era of agricultural improvements, the tenant farmer had the benefit of his landlord's capital poured into his land, while the small freeholder had no financial resources save his own with

[1] In the summer when Marlborough was marching to Blenheim, a Yorkshire squire was writing to his wife:

'The law in England is (as I know now by experience) that every freeholder can enclose so much of his common as lies upon him (much more a lord of a considerable land), provided he leaves out as much common as is sufficient for those that have rights, and disclaims any further title to put beasts on the rest of the common which he leaves out. This is the instance of Mr. Frettwell, of Hellaby, our neighbour, who carried it even against the Lord Castleton, who is lord of the manor, upon trial. And this is our case between us and Gunsborough.'

which to keep abreast of the times. But Anne's reign was perhaps a moment of no very marked economic difference between the two classes.

The difference was political and social. The freeholder had a vote for Parliament and was often in a position to use it as he liked. The tenant farmer had no vote, and if he had, he would have been obliged to cast it as his landlord wished. Even the ideal landlord, Sir Roger de Coverley, was represented by Addison to an approving world as exercising over his tenants an absolute patriarchal sway.

But the independence of the freehold yeoman was deeply cherished and stoutly maintained. In the election correspondence of country gentlemen in the reign of Anne we meet such expressions as 'the freeholders do not stick to say they will show their liberty in voting.' The squire, who had everyone else under his thumb, was all the more anxious to buy out the freehold yeoman for political and game-keeping reasons; and, as the century went on, many freeholders, whether yeomen or small gentry, were ready on fair terms to quit the countryside, in which their old importance was threatened by the increasing wealth of the large landlord and his tenant farmers. The process of buying out the small freeholder to form large compact estates for the grandees, began after the Restoration and continued during the next hundred years and more.

But the distinction between the class of freeholders and the class of tenants was never absolute, because a man often farmed one piece of land as a tenant and another piece as its owner.

The squalor of the mediaeval village had long been in retreat before the homely dignity and comfort of the rural middle class. In Anne's reign men were everywhere building or enlarging farmhouses, in stone, brick or half-timber according to the tradition or material of the district. The architectural results of rustic prosperity were most evident in those favoured regions where the cloth-manufacture made a great demand for the local wool, as in the magnificent stone farms of the Cotswolds dating from the Fifteenth to the Eighteenth Century, or in the dwellings of the Cumbrian and Westmorland mountaineers whose fortunes had more recently risen with the improvement of the local cloth trade. Besides the fine old farmhouses familiar to the traveller in the

9

Lake District to-day, there were then many cottages, since fallen to ruin, wherein the poorer dalesmen brought up large and sturdy families. The children were kept at their mother's knee, spinning for the clothiers, until they were old enough to go up on to the fells to drive the sheep and to pile those great stone walls up the sides of the precipices, which are the wonder of our less industrious age. It was only in the course of the Eighteenth Century that the beauty of Wordsworth's homeland attained the moment of rightful balance between nature and man. In previous centuries the valleys were 'choked, tangled, swampy and feature-less'; in our day man is all too successfully regulating the face of nature with the machine. But in the reign of Anne the dales were just beginning to take on their brief perfection of rural loveli-ness, ordered but not disciplined, in contrast with the mountain magnificence above and around.

Nevertheless visitors were extremely rare in the Lake District, 'the wildest, most barren and frightful' in England, as it appeared to Defoe and his contemporaries. The few strangers whom business or curiosity caused to ride up the steep stony tracks beyond Windermere and over Hardknot, complained of the bread of the Lake Valleys as 'exceedingly black, coarse and harsh,' and the houses as 'sad little huts' of unmortared stone, more fit for cattle than for men. But already 'here and there was a house plastered' and sometimes the 'oat clap bread' was cunningly baked and delicious. And already the famous Windermere delicacy, 'the fish called charrs came potted to London.' We may conclude from these travellers' impressions that the great improvement in the prosperity of this happy pastoral region (with its well-drained valley bottoms, its solid farm buildings and their oak furniture) was by no means complete in the reign of Anne, although it had been in rapid progress since the Restoration, thanks to the manu-facture of cloth at Kendal.

In the neighbouring county of Northumberland, recently so warlike and barbarous, the travellers along the coast and in the valley of the South Tyne, found 'plenty of good bread and beer' as well as hens and geese, and famous stocks of claret, no doubt on account of the neighbourhood of Scotland where the gentry im-ported claret from France in spite of the war. When Anne came to the throne there was still a 'County Keeper' for Northumber-land, who drew a salary of £500 in return for making good out of this sum all cattle stolen and not restored. Although the wild moorlands between Redesdale and the Roman Wall still had a bad name, the County Keeper had the best of his bargain, and 'was able to inform travellers that the moss-trooping trade is very much laid aside, and that a small sum will recompense all the robberies that are yearly committed in the County.' Peace with Scotland, the wealth of the Tyneside mines, and the trade of Newcastle were factors already raising the standard of life along the Border. But the more outlying rural districts of Northumberland, Cumberland and Durham were still very poor, though more thickly inhabited than they afterwards became. In many a 'township' that to-day consists of a single prosperous sheep farm, half a dozen cottages of the crofter type clustering round a peel tower then maintained a hardy population of borderers, unused to comfort, and tilling the moorland for a meagre harvest of oats.

Throughout the Stuart period, particularly since the Restoration, fine country houses were rising in place of the castles wherein the gentry of the Border had been forced to live in the turbulent times gone by. Some of these Stuart mansions, like Chipchase, Capheaton, Wallington and the first Fallodon, already existed in the reign of Anne. But the work of making the roads, and enclosing and draining the moorland farms of Northumberland, the planting of its beech woods, and the making of its spacious brick-walled gardens, was chiefly the work of the Hanoverian age that followed. These great changes in the appearance and productivity of a region that had so long been backward and barbarous, were carried out in the course of the Eighteenth Century, favoured by free trade with Scotland after the Union of 1707, and paid for by Tyneside money, made in coal and invested in land. Political events, such as the Rising of 1715, assisted the economic tendency for industrial and mercantile families to oust old Jacobite and Catholic lords of the soil, as in the case of the Osbaldistones in *Rob Roy*. The newcomers brought with them their industrial wealth and poured it into the estates they had bought, to increase the rent of their farms, the prosperity of their tenants and the amenity of their new country homes.

In the more southerly districts of England, where civilization was of older date, peace unbroken since the Civil War was multiplying the comforts of life. Everywhere that perfectly beautiful equilibrium between man and nature, which marked the Eighteenth Century landscape, was in process of being established. While hedgerow and orchard were gaining on the wild, the multiplication and improvement of cottages, farm-buildings and Halls was going on, either in old traditional styles, or in that dignified but simple manner which we know as 'Queen Anne.' [See § 1.] That style, which seems to us to-day native English, in its origin owed something to Dutch influence. Nor was the internal decoration unworthy of the architecture: in 1710 a foreign visitor noted that 'now in England tapestry is no longer in fashion, but all is panelled at great cost.' Spacious panels, five feet high and broad in proportion, were now preferred to the small pattern of earlier Stuart wainscoting. Big sash-windows with large panes of glass replaced Gothic and Elizabethan lattices. High well-lighted rooms were the new fashion.

China-ware, brought to Europe by the Dutch and English East India Companies, had become a passion with ladies, and we may conceive the scheme of decoration in many Queen Anne mansions in town and country, as blue and white jars in panelled recesses, and tall grandfather clocks decorated with lacquered work from the East. Grinling Gibbons was still executing his marvels in woodwork. Mahogany was beginning to come in from the American Indies, and with it the lighter and finer furniture that we associate with Eighteenth Century taste. Already foreign art dealers were amazed by their opportunities over here, and 'fleeced the English rarely, selling for great sums what they imported for a trifle from France and Italy.' Foreign artists declared that the nobility and gentry over whom Anne reigned held secluded in their country Halls as many pictures by renowned Italian masters as were to be found in all the Palaces and museums of Rome itself.

Vanbrugh's Blenheim House, with its magnificent conception and doubtful detail, is by no means characteristic of the architecture of Anne's reign. [See § 9.] Usually a purer taste prevailed in the realm of ecclesiastical, academic and public buildings, while in ordinary domestic structure the note of the day was 'simple in elegance.' Wren was still alive and active over his London churches and his Hampton Court, and Gibbs was learning that skill which was soon to produce the Radcliffe Camera at Oxford.

[See § 5, 6, 38.] Together they taught the succeeding generations to effect 'the fusion of classic grace with vernacular energy.' The rules of proportion which these great men laid down, filtering into the text-books commonly used by local architects and builders, prepared for the Eighteenth Century a long and happy period of common English building in hamlet and country town. It was only when, in the Nineteenth Century, men attempted to restore the architecture of ancient Athens or of the Middle Ages, that the English tradition was lost, and was succeeded by a hideous anarchy of amateur fancies and exotic modes.

The country gentlemen were of many different grades of wealth and culture. At the top of the social hierarchy stood the Dukes, who would in any other land have been styled Princes, and whose manner of life outdid in magnificence the courts of allied monarchs drawing England's pay. At the lower end of the scale was the squire reckoned to be worth two or three hundred a year, farming a part of his own land, speaking the broadest provincial dialect, but distinguished from the yeomen, among whom he mingled almost on equal terms, by a small sporting establishment, by a coat of arms, and by the respect which all paid to him as a 'gentle-man.' If once in his life he went to London on business, he was noticeable in the City crowds for his horse-hair periwig, his jockey belt and his old-fashioned coat without sleeves. His library, traditionally at least, consisted of the Bible, Baker's *Chronicle*, *Hudibras* and Foxe's *Martyrs*, and, whether he read these works or not, his view on Puritans and Papists usually coincided with those expressed in the last two.

But this type of old-fashioned small squire was beginning to feel the pressure of the times. The heavy land tax of four shillings in the pound to pay for Whig Wars, hit him hard and added to the zeal of his Toryism. The style of living even in rural parts was becoming more expensive as it became less homely, more elabo-rate and more influenced by town example. And if the small squire found it more difficult to make two ends meet, it was easier for him to sell out at a good price, for many large landowners were on the watch to buy out their neighbours and consolidate their own great estates.

It may seem remarkable that the land-hunger among the wealthier members of the community should still have been so eager, now that so many other forms of investment were available, depriving land of the quasi-monopoly value which it had previously enjoyed as the most obvious use for capital. Plain merchants who would in Tudor times have settled land, or rents or tithe on their children, now invested in the Funds. But for the purposes of social and political ambition, the attractions of land-owning were greater than ever. Mr. Habakkuk, who has closely investigated changes in land-ownership in Northamptonshire and Bedfordshire between 1680 and 1740, writes:

People bought land who were peculiarly susceptible to considerations of social prestige and political power. Among them were a few large merchants, mainly chairmen of the East India Company, who went in for politics; but most of the newcomers were either connected in some way with government or were Judges, who desired to have that significance in society which only the possession of land could give. They bought up blocks of land in different parts of the country, bought out some of the surrounding gentry, bought advowsons and, in many cases, the manorial rights of Parliamentary Boroughs. They were not so much investing their money in land as buying up the perquisites of a social class, the undisturbed control of the life of a neighbourhood. When they looked over the fields they wanted to see their own land and nothing but their own land. The hatred of the small squires and gentry for the great lords, whether old or new, who were buying them out is the theme of many contemporary plays. (*Ec. Hist. Rev.*, p. 12, Feb. 1940, *English Landownership 1680-1740*.)

In picturing to ourselves the country house life of that time, we think first of the grandees, filling rural palaces with pictures from Italy, furniture from France, and editions of Italian, French or Latin authors which they not only collected but read—the men whom young Voltaire during his visit to England in 1726-1729, contrasted favourably with the French nobles as patrons of letters and science. [See § 10, 11, 12.] There were philosopher lords like the Third Earl of Shaftesbury; scholar statesmen like Somers and Montagu; and the greatest of all antiquarian collectors, Robert Harley, who when too much engaged as 'the nation's great support' to hunt books and manuscripts himself, still had his private agents everywhere on the look-out. The lords of the Whig Junto and their followers and foes at Westminster and St. James's prided themselves on being country gentlemen, whether self-made or to the manner born, each with his rural seat to which the careworn statesman was ever anxious, at least in theory, to return. [See Plate I.]

The London season was over by the first week in June, when people of fashion dispersed to their country homes or adjourned to Bath. A longer residence in town would have ruined many families who had strained a point to bring their daughters to the London marriage-market, while their neighbours were fain to be contented with a county capital, or with the round of such rural visits as ladies could accomplish in the coach in summer, and on the pillion behind their brothers in the muddy lanes at Christmas.

Lady Mary Wortley Montagu, a brilliant blue-stocking, in a letter of which the dullest part is a quotation from Tasso, condemns the squires of a certain southern county as 'insensible to other pleasures' than the bottle and the chase. 'The poor female part of the family were seldom permitted a coach, their lords and masters having no occasion for such a machine, as their mornings are spent among the hounds, and their nights with as beastly companions—with what liquor they can get.' Yet in the same letter she regrets and praises the society of the squires of Northamptonshire. No less real, if more rare, than boorish Squire Western was the learned country gentleman, celebrated in Somerville's sententious lines:

> A rural squire, to crowds and courts unknown
> In his own cell retired, but not alone,
> For round him view each Greek and Roman sage,
> Polite companions of his riper age.

Nevertheless, the impression left by turning over many hundreds of letters to the better-to-do gentry of the reign of Anne, is neither that of country scholar nor of country bumpkin. We read the actual thoughts of squires, anxious about their account books, their daughters' marriages and their sons' debts and professions; attending to their own estates, and to the county business on the bench of magistrates, as well as to their hounds and horses; devoted to their gardens and their ponds a little more than to their books; living, as we should expect, a wholesome and useful life, half public, half private, wholly leisured, natural and dignified. Many of the better-to-do gentry, as their letters and diaries show, were getting several thousands a year from their estates.

The expenditure required of a country gentleman, rich or poor, was in one respect very small. It was not then considered obligatory that his sons should be sent at great cost to exclusively patrician schools. At the nearest local grammar school, the squire's children sat beside those sons of yeomen and shopkeepers who had been selected for a clerical career; otherwise the young gentlemen were taught at home by a neighbouring parson, or in wealthier families by the private chaplain. Where a tutor was specially employed, he was often a Huguenot refugee, for the land was full of educated men of this type, welcomed by careful parents for their French, and doubly welcome in Whig families for their sufferings and their principles. Eton, Winchester and Westminster were indeed patronized by many, but not by most, of the aristocracy. And even at Westminster there could be found at the end of Anne's reign 'houses at which boys pay but £20 a year for boarding, and the schooling but five or six guineas.' Harrow, founded under Elizabeth to meet local and plebeian needs, began to rise into the rank of the fashionable schools in the reign of George I.

It followed that, whereas a gentleman of moderate means in our day often thinks himself obliged to spend a sixth part of his income on the schooling of one boy, he could in those days be satisfied to spend a hundredth. Thus squire Molesworth, at a time when he was drawing a rental of just under £2,000 paid £20 a year for each of his sons—including board, instruction, clothes and all charges. His heavy parental liabilities only began when the two lads left school, and the younger went into the army. Then indeed 'Dick must be furnished with a hundred pounds or he cannot stir a step. He has both horses, clothes and equipage to buy.' As 'he was not in the list of officers slain in the late glorious battle of Blenheim,' which would have been a sad economy, nor yet 'in any of desperate attacks on Lille,' Dick continued for many years to be an increasing source of expenditure and pride to his Yorkshire home. The elder, Jack, had chosen diplomacy, a no less costly method of serving the State. In 1710 the father writes: 'I verily believe these two sons of ours have spent between them £10,000 within the last seven or eight years; they and the daughters are all money-bound. It is well they have a good father's house to tarry in.' Five years later Dick's zeal for his regiment caused him to

§1 Bradbourne House, Kent (1713)

§2 London street scene in 1716

§3 Model husbandry in 1727

§4 Leicester cornfields still unenclosed in 1743

ANNO   A Perspective View of the outside
        of the RADCLIFFE LIBRARY.   1747

§5 The Radcliffe Camera, Oxford

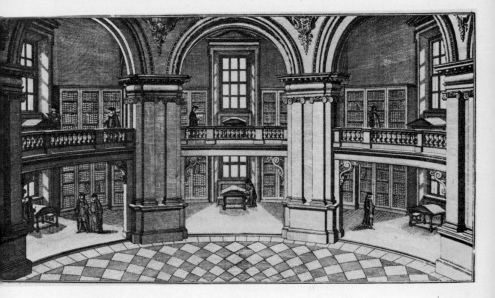

§6 The interior of the Radcliffe Camera, Oxford

§7　The Mall (c. 1735)

58 A musical party (c. 1731)

§9 Blenheim Palace

§10 Houghton, the palatial Norfolk home of Sir Robert Walpole

§11 Section of the hall and salon at Houghton

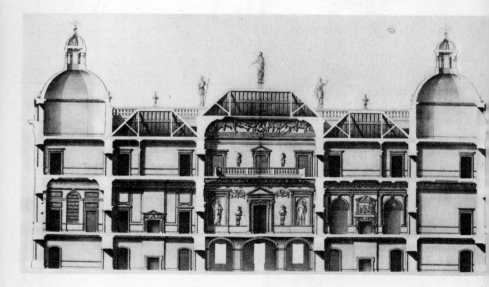

§12 Section of the east front, Houghton

§13 Bank House, Wisbech

§14 A house at Blandford

§15 Cockfighting in 1759.

"All classes shrieked their bets round the little amphitheatre"

§16. A game of Hazard

§17 A duel

§18 Joseph Addison

§19 Richard Steele

§20 A game of draughts

§21 Examining a watch

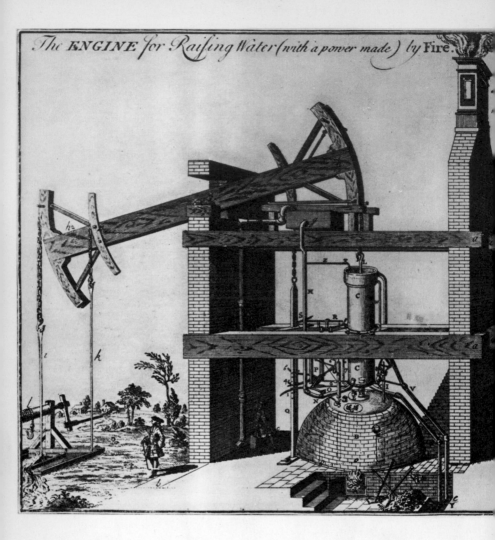

§22 The Newcomen engine

'lay out £600 above what was allowed him, so well he loves the service.'

Smaller squires paid equally little for their sons' schooling, and then prenticed them to cheaper trades than the army or diplomatic service. In the plays of Congreve and Farquhar the younger son of the manor may still expect to be 'bound prentice,' perhaps 'to a felt-maker in Shrewsbury'; and Steele declares that 'younger brothers are generally condemned to shops, colleges and inns of court.' On these terms the gentry could afford to have large families, and although a great proportion of their children died young, they kept England supplied with a constant stream of high-spirited young men, who led her along the forward path at home and oversea. For the younger sons were willing, as the cadets of the continental nobility were not, to mingle in the common avocations of mankind and not to stand upon their gentry. The fact that the younger son went out to make his fortune in the army or at the Bar, in industry or in commerce, was one of the general causes favouring the Whigs and their alliance with those interests, as against the desire of the High Tories to keep the landed gentry an exclusive as well as a dominant class. Dominant it remained for another century, but only on condition of opening its doors wide to newcomers, and fostering in a hundred different ways close alliance with interests other than agriculture, in scenes far remote from the manor-house and the village church. The country gentlemen ruled Eighteenth Century England, but they ruled it largely in the interest of commerce and empire.

The common schooling of the upper and middle classes was already being criticized for its rigidly classical curriculum. It was even declared by some that 'a girl which is educated at home with her mother is wiser at twelve than a boy at sixteen' who knows only Latin. Yet the second classical language was so ill taught at school and college that the excellent Latinists of Christ Church had not enough Greek to be aware that Bentley had proved them dunces over the *Letters of Phalaris*. It was only in the Nineteenth Century that the typical English scholar was equally at home with Aristophanes and with Horace.

Even so, Greek scholarship in the England of Bentley had not fallen as low as in the rest of Europe. In the Germany of that day not only was classical Greek no longer studied, but the names and stories of the mythology and history of Hellas were unknown.[1] But they were familiar to educated people in England, if not through Greek then through Latin and English authors. Every man of fashion in the reign of George I had at least to pretend an acquaintance with Pope's rendering of Homer. Milton was now rising to a place only a little lower than Shakespeare in the hierarchy of English literary reputations, and the use that he made of classical ideas and mythology set an example to the poets of this later age, though few were scholars of his calibre. In architecture and its ornaments, the 'Gothic' had disappeared, and had been replaced by ideas suggested directly or indirectly by the temples and statues of the ancient world.

But it would be a mistake to suppose that nothing was anywhere taught but classics; there was considerable variety in the type of school patronized by gentlemen. Thus Robert Pitt, father of a mighty son, writes in 1704 to his own scarcely less formidable father, Governor Pitt of Madras:

My two brothers are at Mr. Meure's Academy, near Soho Square, esteemed the best in England. They learn Latin, French and accounts, fencing, dancing and drawing. I think of settling them in Holland for their better education next summer: and should my wife's father-in-law, Lt. Gen. Stewart, accompany the Duke of Marlborough, of placing them under his care to see a campaign.

Among the critics of our educational methods were the wise Locke and the good-natured Steele, who both urged that perpetual flogging was not the best method of imparting knowledge and maintaining discipline. Upper-class education was admitted on all hands to need reform, yet nothing was done to reform it. Swift, for all his hatred of the Scots, agreed for once with Burnet that the lairds gave their sons more sound book-learning than the wealthier and idler English.

Yet the Eighteenth Century, in spite of its educational defects, produced a larger proportion of remarkable and original Englishmen from among those who passed through its schools than our highly educated and over-regulated age is able to do. And in spite of cruel flogging by 'those licensed tyrants the school-

[1] In 1718 Burckhard declared that the majority of University Students in Germany did not even know the names of Plato, Aristotle, Homer, Thucydides or Euripides. Such a statement would have been utterly absurd if made about England. *The Popular Background of Goethe's Hellenism,* Humphry Trevelyan, 1934, p. 8 and *passim.*

masters,' and cruel bullying by the unlicensed tyranny of ill-disciplined school-fellows, there was also much happiness in boyhood, that still had leisure and still spent it in the free range of the countryside. Nor was severity universal: a young lord, newly arrived at Eton, writes home, 'I think Eaton a very easy scholl. I am shure one cannot offend without they be meare rakes indeed.'

Women's education was sadly to seek. Among the lower classes it was perhaps not much worse than men's, but the daughters of the well-to-do had admittedly less education than their brothers. It was before the days of 'ladies' academies,' and though there were 'boarding schools' for girls, they were few and indifferent. Most ladies learnt from their mothers to read, write, sew and manage the household. We hear of no fair Grecians, like Lady Jane Grey and Queen Elizabeth in days of old. But a few ladies could read the Italian poets and were therefore held in some awe by their swains. And at least two women could meet Swift on terms of something like intellectual equality. Yet it was he who lamented 'that not one gentleman's daughter in a thousand should be brought to read her own natural tongue, or be judge of the easiest books that are written in it.' The want of education in the sex was discussed as an admitted fact, one side defending it as necessary in order to keep wives in due subjection, while the other side, led by the chief literary men of the day, ascribed the frivolity and the gambling habits of ladies of fashion to an upbringing which debarred them from more serious interests.

Nevertheless, country-house letters of the period show us wives and daughters writing as intelligent advisers of their menfolk. Such correspondents were something better than brainless playthings or household drudges. A whole class of the literature of the day, from the *Spectator* downwards, was written as much for ladies as for their fathers and brothers. And it was observed that the ladies took a part, often too eager, in the Whig and Tory feuds that divided town and country. As to rural pastimes, the prototype of Diana Vernon in *Rob Roy* is to be found in Belinda of Farquhar's play, who tells her friend 'I can gallop all the morning after the hunting horn and all the evening after a fiddle. In short I can do everything with my father but drink and shoot flying.'

In the upper and middle classes, husbands were often found for girls on the principle of frank barter. 'As to Cloky,' writes her father, squire Molesworth, 'we shall not have money enough to dispose of her here,' so she must be sent to Ireland to seek there a husband at a cheaper rate. Another squire, named Guise, who is in search of a wife for himself, writes 'Lady Diana sent a very venerable person to view my estates, and was well satisfied with the report and I think did sincerely desire I might have her daughter.' But the daughter had other views, so Guise found consolation elsewhere:

Being on the Bench at the quarter Session, a Justice of the Peace took me aside and asked me whether I would marry a woman worth twenty-thousand pounds. The lady I had seen but never spoke to, and upon the whole readily accepted his offer.

A Cornet of Horse writes with equal frankness:

Not expecting anything this campaign I had taken thoughts another way, to try my fortune under Venus, and accordingly about a fortnight ago was (by some friends) proposed to a lady of a very good fortune: but how I shall speed (farther than a favourable interview already) I can't tell.

Since almost everyone regarded it as a grave misfortune to remain single, women did not account it a universal grievance that their hands should often be disposed of by others. They were no doubt usually consulted as to their destiny, much or little according to character and circumstance. Swift, in writing 'to a very young lady on her marriage,' speaks of 'the person your father and mother have chosen for your husband,' and almost immediately adds, 'yours was a match of prudence and common good liking, without any mixture of the ridiculous passion' of romantic love. And this description would probably have covered a vast proportion of the 'arranged' marriages of the day. But since the 'ridiculous passion' often asserted itself, runaway matches were common enough, as in the case of Lady Mary Wortley Montagu. And even without that desperate expedient, an ever-increasing proportion of ordinary marriages were the outcome of mutual affection.

Divorce was almost unknown. It was obtainable only through Church Courts, and then only if followed by a special Act of Parliament; not more than six divorces were thus legalized during the twelve years of Queen Anne.

Both sexes gambled freely, the fine ladies and gentlemen even more than the country squires. In London, Bath and Tunbridge Wells the gaming-table was the central point of interest, while in the manor-house it was of less account than the stables and the kennel. The expenses of gambling and of sport, as well as a noble zeal for building and for laying out gardens and planting avenues, burdened estates with mortgages which proved a heavy clog on agricultural improvement and domestic happiness. Immense sums of money changed hands over cards and dice. [See § 16.]

Drunkenness was the acknowledged national vice of Englishmen of all classes, though women were not accused of it. A movement for total abstinence was out of the question, in days before tea or coffee could be obtained in every home and when the supply of drinking water was often impure. But tracts in favour of temperate drinking were freely circulated by religious bodies and anxious patriots, setting forth with attractive detail the various and dreadful fates of drunkards, some killed attempting to ride home at night, others seized by a fit while blaspheming, all gone straight to Hell. Among the common folk, ale still reigned supreme; but ale had a new rival worse than itself in the deadly attraction of bad spirits. The acme of cheap spirit-drinking was not indeed reached till the reign of George II, in the days of Hogarth's 'Gin Lane,' but things were already moving in that direction.

Meanwhile the upper class got drunk sometimes on ale and sometimes on wine. It is hard to say whether the men of fashion or the rural gentry were the worst soakers. But perhaps the outdoor exercise taken by the fox-hunting, sporting and farming squire made him better able to absorb his nightly quantum of October, than the gamester and politician of St. James's Square to escape the ill effects of endless Whig toasts in port and Tory toasts in French claret and champagne. Magistrates often appeared on the bench heated with wine; Courts Martial, by a prudent provision of the Mutiny Act, might only take place before dinner.

Tobacco was still taken in long churchwarden pipes. A 'smoking parlour' was set aside in some country houses. But Beau Nash forbade smoking in the public rooms at Bath as disrespectful and unpleasant to ladies. Among the common people of the south-western counties, men, women and even children smoked pipes of an evening. When in 1707 the Bill for the

Security of the Church of England was passing through Parliament, Dr. Bull, the High Church Bishop of St. David's, being suspicious of the Whig proclivities of some of the Episcopal Bench, kept watch 'sitting in the lobby of the House of Lords, all the while smoking his pipe.' Swift describes how his brother parsons pull his character to pieces at their favourite resort at Truby's Coffee House,

> And pausing o'er a pipe, with doubtful nod
> Give hints that poets ne'er believe in God.

The taking of snuff became general in England during the first year of Anne's reign, as a result of the immense quantities thrown on to the London market after the capture of Spanish ships loaded with snuff in the action of Vigo Bay.

The drinking and gambling habits of society, and the fierceness of political faction, led to frequent duels of which many ended ill. The survivor, if he could show there had been fair play, was usually convicted of manslaughter and imprisoned for a short term; or haply 'pleaded his clergy,' was 'touched with cold iron' and so set free. It was the privilege of all gentlemen, from a Duke downwards, to wear swords and to murder one another by rule. As soon as men were well drunk of an evening they were apt to quarrel, and as soon as they quarrelled they were apt to draw their swords in the room, and, if manslaughter was not committed on the spot, to adjourn to the garden behind the house, and fight it out that night with hot blood and unsteady hand. [See § 17.] If the company were not wearing swords, the quarrel might be slept upon and forgotten or arranged in the sober morning. The wearing of swords, though usual in London, as being like the full-bottomed wig a part of full dress, was fortunately not common in the depths of the country, among the uncourtly but good-natured rural squires, whose bark was often worse than their bite. And even at Bath, Beau Nash employed his despotic power to compel the fashionable world to lay aside their swords when they entered his domain: in this he did as good service to the community as in teaching the country bumpkins to discard their top boots and coarse language at the evening assemblies and dances. During his long supremacy as Master of Ceremonies, nearly covering the reigns of Anne and the first two Georges, Nash did perhaps as much as any other person even in the Eighteenth Century to civilize the neglected manners of mankind. But he encouraged public gambling and took for himself a percentage on the winnings of the bank.

London and the county capitals were the commonest scenes of such duels as Thackeray has immortalized in *Esmond*. Even more often than Leicester Fields, the open country behind Montagu House, the site of the present British Museum, was selected by duellists as being at that time on the edge of the new London. It was no unusual thing for the town to be disturbed by such a double event as the following:

Ned Goodyear has killed Beau Feilding as is reported, and made his escape. The quarrel began at the Play House in Drury Lane. The same night a captain here did the like friendly office for young Fullwood, so that there will be two Warwickshire beaus the fewer. The captain is in Newgate.

Ever since the Restoration, foreigners had admired the English bowling greens, 'which are so even, that they bowl upon them as easily as on a great billiard table. And as this is the usual diversion of gentlemen in the country, they have thick rowling-stones to keep the green smooth.' In Anne's reign a primitive kind of cricket was just beginning to take its place among village sports alongside of the far more ancient football. Kent was the county most renowned at the new game, and, 'among the Kentish men, the men of Dartford lay claim to the greatest excellence.'

At cockfighting all classes shrieked their bets round the little amphitheatre. If a foreigner should by chance come into these cockpits, we are told, 'he would certainly conclude the assembly to be all mad, by their continued outcries of Six to Four, Five to One, repeated with great earnestness, every Spectator taking part with his favourite cock, as if it were a party cause.' [See § 15.] Horse-racing presented much the same spectacle in a more open arena: the spectators, most of them on horseback, galloped up the course behind the race, yelling with excitement. The meetings were still regional or county gatherings. The only national meeting was at Newmarket. There indeed 'the vast company of horsemen on the plain at a match contains all mankind on equal footing from the Duke to the country peasant. Nobody wears swords, but are clothed suitable to the humour and design of the place for horse sports. Everybody strives to out-jockey (as the phrase is) one another.' Queen Anne, out of the secret service money, gave plates to be run for at Newmarket, and at Datchet near Windsor. Arab and Barb blood was being introduced by Godolphin and other noble patrons of the sport—a change fraught with great future consequence to the character and appearance of horseflesh in England.

When we try to imagine how the generality of our ancestors disported themselves out-of-doors, we must remember that most of them lived widely scattered and in the country. For most men the village was the largest unit of their intercourse. A village cricket match, or hurly-burly at football, or races on the green were very different from the 'organized athletics' of the modern arena. But most people took their 'exercise' as a matter of course in doing their work, in tilling the soil, or in walking or riding to and from their daily task. Among the upper and middle classes riding was the commonest act of the day.

The most usual sports that lay at many men's doors were taking fish, and shooting and snaring birds of all kinds, particularly but not exclusively game. England was alive with game and with many birds now rare or extinct, from the Great Bustard of the Downs and the eagle of Westmorland and Wales down to many smaller friends that survived to be recorded by Bewick. Much of the land was strictly preserved and religiously shot by the owners, but great tracts were open to any man who could procure a net or gun or who was clever at setting a springe. In Anne's reign, and indeed for the rest of the century, the fens and uncultivated lands round Cambridge were the common shooting grounds of the undergraduates, whence they returned with pheasants, partridges, duck, snipe, bitterns and ruffs, with none to say them nay. And in every part of the lovely island the uncared-for heaths, coppices and marshes, destined ere long to be drained, ploughed up or built over, were still the cover for abundance of wild life of every kind. The Englishman had only to move a few yards from his door to be in contact with nature at its best; and his love of field-sports led him to wander wide.

Few villagers had seen anything of town life. Most people remained all their lives under the influence of Pan and his magic. The mental food of English children was just such cottage fireside tales of 'the hall-house being haunted, of fairies, spirits and witches,' perhaps only half believed but pleasantly shuddered at.

Now that the witch could be pointed out but no longer hanged or ducked, such earth-born legendary lore was no unwholesome fare. For the common people, untouched by the scepticism of the town, the fairies still danced in the woods, though when the way-farer came round the bush they had always vanished.[1] Books in the village were few. The ordinary farmer and cottager saw no printed matter of any kind except Bible, Prayer Book and

> The ballads pasted on the wall,
> Of Joan of France and English Moll,
> Fair Rosamund, and Robin Hood,
> And the little children of the Wood.

And therefore even at the end of the 'Century of reason' and of artificial poetry among the governing class, the faculty of wonder was not dead in the English people. Wordsworth attributed the growth of imagination in his own mind partly to the fairy-tales and ballads of the rustic North that he heard in childhood, in contrast to the rationalism of the Nineteenth Century schoolroom. (*Prelude*, Bk. V, l. 205, *et seq.*) No city-made newspapers or magazines stamped a uniform mentality on the nation. In this isolation from the world at large, each shire, each hamlet had its own traditions, interests and character. Except for some unusual event like the Battle of Blenheim or the trial of Dr. Sacheverell, country folk had little to think or talk about except their own affairs. Their shrewd rustic comment on things that they knew and understood was expressed in the pithy dialect of their own countryside. For gossip and sensation they were satisfied with the daily human drama of their own village, with its poaching affrays and smuggling adventures, its feuds and loves, its ghosts and suicides, its quarrels of miller and innkeeper, of parson and squire.

The still unremedied badness of the roads was due to the want of any adequate administrative machinery for their reconstruction or repair. Every parish through which a road passed was legally bound to maintain it by six days a year of unpaid labour given by

---

[1] The educated upper class had generally ceased to believe in the real existence of fairies. In 1707 the philosopher Lord Shaftesbury, in his *Letter concerning Enthusiasm*, writes to Lord Somers, 'I could put your Lordship in mind of an eminent, learned and truly Christian Prelate you once knew who could have given you a full account of his belief in Fairys.' As if such a belief was unusual and obviously absurd.

the farmers, under no outside supervision; one of themselves was chosen as surveyor. The unfairness of laying the burden of repair not on the users of the great roads, but on the parishes through which they happened to pass, was equalled by the folly of expecting farmers, who had no interest in the matter, to act gratuitously as skilled makers of highways. The result was that a very inadequate number of hard roads had been made or kept up since the Romans left the island. In the Middle Ages, when there was little commerce, this had mattered less. Under the later Stuarts, when commerce was large and rapidly increasing, it mattered much; it was beginning to be felt as a national disgrace. The new system of turnpikes to make the users of the road pay for its upkeep was therefore enforced in a few of the worst sections by Acts of Parliament. When Anne came to the throne the usual machinery of local Justices of the Peace was employed to manage the turnpikes, but towards the end of the reign special bodies of Turnpike Trustees were sometimes established by Statute. It was not, however, till the House of Hanover had been some time on the throne that anything approaching a general reform was effected by this means. Defoe thus describes a main road in Lancashire:

We are now in a country where the roads are paved with small pebbles, so that we both walk and ride upon this pavement which is generally about one and a half yards wide. But the middle road where the carriages are obliged to go is very bad.

In winter and bad weather wheeled traffic did not attempt to take the road, and riders started early in the morning to get in front of the pack-horse trains which it was difficult to pass on the narrow causeway.

Under such conditions, sea and river traffic, however slow, held a great advantage over road traffic, especially for heavy goods. Fish could be sent up from Lyme Regis to London by relays of fast trotting horses; but coal came there by sea. Even so, while it cost but five shillings per chaldron at the Tyneside pit's mouth, it cost thirty shillings in London, and anything up to fifty shillings in the towns of the Upper Thames. This was partly because sea-borne coal was taxed, both to pay for the rebuilding of St. Paul's and to pay for the French war. Coal was cheaper in those towns of Yorkshire, Lancashire and the west Midlands to which it could be floated from the pit's mouth on rivers like

Calder or Severn. For coal carried on inland rivers was not taxed, like the coal carried by sea, neither was it exposed to the attacks of the Dunkirk privateers, nor harassed by the consequent restrictions of an inadequate convoy system supplied by the Royal Navy between Tyne and Thames.

The ownership of mines and an interest in their working was not deemed beneath the dignity of the greatest noblemen of the land, for in England, unlike most countries of Europe, all minerals except gold and silver have been treated as the property of the owner of the soil. Among the aristocratic coal owners of that time was Lord Dartmouth, to whom belonged many of the Staffordshire mines near his country house at Sandwell. He had a rival in a country gentleman named Wilkins, who was said to have 'engrossed the coalworks of Leicestershire to himself.'

It was then usual to leave pillars of coal to support the roof of the mine, rather than to use timber props. Shafts were sunk to a depth of 400 feet and more, and in Lancashire the science of the engineers had devised in the year 1712 a machine for pumping water out of the mine which has been described as 'the first genuine steam-engine.' [See § 22.] On Tyneside, wooden rails were used to run the trucks down to the river for loading the keels; twenty thousand horses were employed in the transport of coal in the environs of Newcastle alone. [See § 63.] Since the larger mines were deeper below the surface than in the Middle Ages, explosions due to fire-damp were already frequent, as at Gateshead in 1705, and at Chester-le-Street in 1708, when a hundred miners perished 'besides great damage to many houses and persons for several miles round. One man was blown quite out of the mouth of the shaft, which is fifty fathom, and found at a prodigious distance from the place.' Two years later another explosion at Bensham, in the same North Durham district, killed eighty more. But the amount of surface mining was still considerable; in the west there were many scores of small workings, each conducted by two or three colliers and sometimes by a single man.

The miners of all kinds and the quarrymen of every county form an important exception to the statement that in old England the method of industry was domestic. Other exceptions there were, but they are harder to specify and define. Many workshops had premises so large, and contained so many apprentices and paid journeymen, that they may be reckoned as standing half-way between the domestic and the factory system. The normal basis of industry still was apprenticeship, the only legal doorway to a trade whether for boys or girls. The apprentice system was often abused by cruel masters and mistresses; and pauper apprentices were at least as badly treated as children in the worst days of the subsequent factory system. There were no inspectors and no checks on ill usage. On the other hand, the apprentice was part of his master's 'family,' and the average man does not like to see unhappy faces at his own board and in his own household. Moreover, apprenticeship was invaluable for the discipline and skilled training that it provided during that important 'after-school age' so much neglected in our own day. It largely compensated for the deficiency of school education. Apprenticeship was the old English school of craftsmanship and of character.[1] [See § 28, 29.]

Before they were old enough to be apprenticed, small children were sometimes set to work in their parents' cottages at an age full as early as the factory children of later times. Especially was spinning for the cloth industry conducted in this fashion: Defoe noticed with approval at Colchester and in the Taunton clothing region, that 'there was not a child in the town or in the villages round it of above five years old, but, if it was not neglected by its parents and untaught, could earn its bread.' Again, in the clothing dales of the West Riding he found 'hardly anything above four years old but its hands were sufficient for its support.' Poor little mites! But at least, whenever their parents let them go to play, they had fields near at hand, instead of the boundless wilderness of slums.

Spinning was done chiefly in country cottages by women and children, and weaving chiefly in towns and villages by men. Both processes, though conducted under domestic conditions, required capitalist organization and supervision, either by employers, or by middlemen who bought the goods manufactured by the cottager. The methods by which the cloth trade was organized differed in the many different regions of England where it flourished.

---

[1] Already in Anne's reign there were complaints that apprenticeship was not made as universally obligatory as the laws dictated. In 1702 the Corporation of Kendal petitioned for a new and stricter law, because 'although there are laws against persons setting up any trade without having received seven years' apprenticeship, when such persons come to be prosecuted they meet with such favour that very few have been punished of late.' (H. M. C. Bagot, R. 10, pt. iv., p. 336.)

The cloth trade was the typical industry of the time. Two-fifths of English exports consisted of cloth woven in England. Many of our domestic laws and many measures of our economic and foreign policy were aimed at the great national object of promoting the manufacture of cloth and pushing its sale at home and abroad. It was felt that here lay our real advantage over Dutch rivals in the carrying trade of the world, for we had this great staple manufacture with which to load our outgoing ships, whereas they had little to export except herrings, and acted mainly as carriers between other nations.

The desire to keep open the great markets of the world for English cloth was a chief incentive to taking up arms in 1702 against the Franco-Spanish Power, which was at that moment, at the command of Louis XIV, proceeding to close Spain, the Netherlands, South America and the Mediterranean to our goods. The taking and keeping of Gibraltar in 1704 was symptomatic of more than military and naval ambition: a free entrance to the Mediterranean and Turkish trades was vital to the cloth industry. Not only were great quantities of our cloth sold in those parts, but our merchants brought back from Spain and Southern Italy oil used here in the manufacture of cloth. Spanish merino wool was worked up in England and sold back as cloth to Spain herself, whose native industry was in the last stages of decline. Of late years the fine quality and great quantity of English-grown wool had been yet further increased by means of 'clover and other grass seeds' to feed the sheep. Our American Colonies were valued largely as markets for our cloth. In Russia, too, a great demand for it was growing up in the new century.

Only in the Far East was it impossible to sell the heavy English cloth, and this was the most damaging argument which the East India Company had to meet in pleading its cause before Parliament. But the tea and silk it brought to England sufficed to condone the high economic crimes of failing to sell English cloth and daring to export bullion to buy cloth substitutes. In vain the merchants of the rival Turkey Company pleaded that 'if silk be brought from India where it is bought cheap with bullion, it will ruin our trade with Turkey, whither we send cloth for their silk.' The demands of fashion and luxury outweighed the arguments of clothiers, Turkey merchants and orthodox economists. 'Our stately fops admire themselves better in an Indian dressing gown

29

than in one made at Spitalfields.' The ladies, besides, were all drinking 'tay.' So the Indian Trade was permitted to flourish, and in spite of that the Cloth Trade flourished as well. [See Plate II.]

Thanks to the East India Company's great ships, not only tea but coffee was now a usual drink at least among the wealthier classes. From the reign of Charles II to the early Georges, the London Coffee House was the centre of social life. It afforded a much needed relaxation of the severe drinking habits of the time, for alcohol was not to be had on the premises. A list of some of the Coffee Houses in Queen Anne's time runs to nearly five hundred names. Every respectable Londoner had his favourite house, where his friends or clients could seek him at known hours.

'Remember, John,
'If any ask, to th' Coffee House I'm gone,'

says the citizen to his apprentice as he leaves the shop.

Then at Lloyd's Coffee House he never fails
To read the letters and attend the sales.[1]

The *beau monde* assembled at White's Chocolate House in St. James's Street, where, as Harley bitterly complained to Swift, young noblemen were fleeced and corrupted by fashionable gamblers and profligates. Tories went to the Cocoa Tree Chocolate House, Whigs to St. James's Coffee House. Will's, near Covent Garden, was the resort of poets, critics and their patrons; Truby's served the clergy, and the Grecian the world of scholarship; nor were there lacking houses for Dissenters, for Quakers, for Papists and for Jacobites. The 'universal liberty of speech of the English nation' uttered amid clouds of tobacco smoke, with equal vehemence whether against the Government and the Church, or against their enemies, had long been the wonder of foreigners; it was the quintessence of Coffee House life. [See § 18, 19.]

The Coffee House filled the place now occupied by the Club,

---

[1] In Ned Ward's *Wealthy Shopkeeper* (1706) his day is thus apportioned: rise at 5; counting-house till 8; then breakfast on toast and Cheshire cheese; in his shop for two hours then a neighbouring coffee house for news; shop again, till dinner at home (over the shop) at 12 on a 'thundering joint'; 1 o'clock on Change; 3, Lloyd's Coffee House for business; shop again for an hour; then another coffee house (not Lloyd's) for recreation, followed by 'sack shop' to drink with acquaintants, till home for a 'light supper' and so to bed, 'before Bow Bell rings nine.'

II   English Family at tea (c.1720)

but in a more cheap and informal manner, and with a greater admission of strangers. [See § 20, 21.] In days when men stood much on their rank, it had a levelling influence: at the Coffee House 'you will see blue ribbons and stars sitting familiarly with private gentlemen as if they had left their quality and degrees of distance at home.' But that was not all. In days before telegrams and effective journalism, news could be most easily obtained at the Coffee House. The Windsor, at Charing Cross, advertised itself as supplying the 'best chocolate at twelve pence the quart and the translation of the *Harlem Courant* soon after the post is come in.' Not only was news sought for its political, military and general interest, but for the strictly business purposes of commerce, particularly at Lloyd's. Edward Lloyd, whose surname instantly rises to men's lips when they speak of shipping to-day, was, when he walked the earth, nothing more nor less than a Coffee House keeper in Lombard Street in the reign of Queen Anne. To his house merchants came for the latest information and for the personal intercourse and advice necessary for all transactions. Newspapers had then no commercial column and no details of shipping. The spoken word did many things that print does to-day, and for merchants the word was spoken at Lloyd's. Before the end of the Queen's reign, Lloyd had set up a pulpit for auctions and for reading out shipping news.

The feud of High Church against Low Church and Dissent was the chief theme of political and ecclesiastical anger and eloquence. Nevertheless, in another aspect, the reigns of William and Anne were a period of purely religious activity and revival, which left a permanent mark on the life of the country, and sowed the seed of great developments in the future. An age to which we owe the Charity Schools and the Society for Promoting Christian Knowledge was not wholly absorbed in the quarrels of High Church and Low. [See § 23, 24.] In some of these better activities, members of the two parties co-operated with each other and with the Dissenters.

The religious revival had its origin in the brief and stormy reign of James II. The Tory pamphleteer, Davenant, in the early years of Anne, thus recalled how those times had stirred men's souls:

The measures King James the Second took to change the religion of the country, roused up fresh zeal in the minds of all sorts of men; they

A
Weekly Review
OF THE
Affairs of *FRANCE*:

Purg'd from the Errors and Partiality of *News-Writers* and *Petty-Statesmen*, of all Sides.

𝔖𝔞𝔱𝔲𝔯𝔡𝔞𝔶, Feb. 19. 1704.

The INTRODUCTION.

THIS Paper is the Foundation of a very large and useful Design, which, if it meet with suitable Encouragement, *Permissu Superiorum*, may contribute to Setting the Affairs of *Europe* in a Clearer Light, and to prevent the various uncertain Accounts, and the Partial Reflections of our Street-Scriblers, who Daily and Monthly Amuse Mankind with Stories of Great Victories when we are Beaten, Miracles when we Conquer, and a Multitude of Unaccountable and Inconsistent Stories, which have at least this Effect, That People are possest with wrong Notions of Things, and Nations Wheedled to believe Nonsense and Contradiction.

A   As

An Eighteenth Century Newspaper. Defoe's *Review* (1704)

32

Mercure Scandale :

O R,

ADVICE from the Scandalous CLUB:

BEING,

A Weekly History of Nonsense, Impertinence, Vice *and* Debauchery.

THis Club having been very full of Business for a Month or two past, we are oblig'd to refer the Abstract of their Proceedings to a Short Abridgement, which shall Supply the Place of long Particulars, because we are not willing to omit the Case of the *News Writers,* as it stands in the Journals of the Society according to our promise in our last.

The Writer of the *Gazette* being first in Quality, was Call'd in and Examin'd: He was Charg'd with Reproaching the Government, for that he who Writes by Authority should presume to Write Nonsense, was a Reflection upon that Authority that Employ'd him ; and to make out the Charge, he was Ordered to make Sence of the following Paragraph.

[*Count* Staremburgh *marching through the* Milanese *to join the Duke of* Savoy, *met* 200 *French Horse near* Brono, *whom they either kill'd or took Prisoners, except* 43 *who escaped, and all the rest were kill'd upon the spot.*] [Gazette, *Feb.* 14. 1703.]

The Gentleman would ha' laid the Fault upon the Printer, but it was plain 'twas no Errour of the Press, so he was oblig'd to Answer one of these two Questions.

1. If the whole Sentence were put into *Latin,* Which would be the principle Verb ?
2. If the Matter of Fact be true, How many of the *French* Horse were taken Prisoners?

But being not able to give a satisfactory Answer to either of these Questions, he withdrew ; and the Court considered that being a Publick Officer, he should be Civilly us'd, he was Ordered to receive a Reprimand from the Director of the Club, and be Dismiss'd on his Parole of Amendment. The embraced more straitly what they were in fear to lose. Courtiers did thrust themselves into the presence to quit their offices, rather than be brought to do what might prejudice the Church of England. Nor had the licentious ways of living in fleets and armies shaken our seamen and soldiers in their principles. They all stood firm. The clergy showed themselves prepared to die with their flocks and managed the controversial parts of Divinity with primitive courage and admirable learning. The Churches were everywhere crowded, and the prospect of persecution, though peradventure at some distance, begot devotion.

The symptoms of this moral and religious revival did not wholly subside with the crisis that gave it birth. In the first instance it gave an immense impetus to the work of the already existing Religious Societies inside the Church of England. These Societies were groups of 'serious young men,' who came together, usually under the influence of some active clergyman, to strengthen each other in religious life and practice. The original idea of John Wesley, many years later, was merely to form such 'societies' within the Church resembling those which that zealous Churchman his father had helped and defended in the reigns of William and Anne. The first object of these groups was to promote a Christian life in individuals and families, to encourage church attendance, family prayers and Bible study. But more public activities soon grew out of the impulse thus given. Of these activities some were carried on in rivalry to the Dissenters, others with their co-operation.

The Dissenters, who were excluded from both the Universities by law, and from many schools either by law or by custom, had started all over the country a number of excellent schools and academies of their own, covering the whole field of primary, secondary and higher education. These caused much jealousy, and at the end of Anne's reign the High Churchmen at last succeeded in passing the Schism Act to suppress them—an act of persecution repealed under George I. But the Church also reacted to the challenge of the Nonconformist schools in a more generous fashion. In the reign of Anne, Charity Schools were founded by hundreds all over England, to educate the children of the poor in reading, writing, moral discipline, and the principles of the Church of England. They were much needed, for the State did nothing for the education of the poor, and the ordinary parish had no sort of endowed school, though in many villages 'dames' and other unofficial persons taught rustics their letters in return for small fees; here and there an endowed Grammar School gave secondary education to the middle class.

The able men at the head of the Charity School movement introduced the principle of democratic co-operation into the field of educational endowment. They did not depend merely on the support of a few wealthy founders. The policy at headquarters was to excite the local interest of a parish in the setting up of a school. Small shopkeepers and artisans were induced to subscribe and to collect subscriptions, and were taught to take a personal interest in the success, and a personal part in the control of the school for which they helped yearly to pay. The principle of 'joint-stock enterprise' was being applied to many sides of life in that era, among others to the cause of philanthropy and education. By the end of Anne's reign there were 5000 or more boys and girls attending the new Charity Schools in the London area, and some 20,000 in the rest of England. The movement was already being taken up in Presbyterian Scotland by the General Assembly of the Church. Essential parts of the scheme were to clothe the children decently while at school, and to apprentice them to good trades afterwards. In 1708 a 'poor boy' could be clothed at nine shillings and twopence, and a 'poor girl' at ten shillings and three-pence in one of the London Schools. [See § 23, 24.]

Another characteristic organization of this period was 'The Society for the Reformation of Manners.' In its open ranks Churchmen and Dissenters co-operated against the licence of the age. Scores of thousands of tracts were issued against drunkenness, swearing, public indecency and Sunday trading. We know not what success attended the *Kind cautions against swearing* distributed among the hackney coachmen of London, and the similar *Kind cautions to watermen* distributed among the West Country bargees! More effective, perhaps, were the innumerable prosecutions instituted. Magistrates were shamed into enforcing laws which had become obsolete. These activities aroused furious opposition. Some of the High Churchmen, like Sacheverell, clamoured for the 'ancient discipline of the Church' to suppress vice, immorality, heresy and schism, instead of this newfangled Society for the Reformation of Manners in which laymen and even Dissenters were allowed to take a part, appealing to lay magistrates instead of to Church Courts. Some prudent Bishops like Sharp,

A ſhort Warning, or Reproof,

TO ALL
DESPERATE and PROPHANE
Swearers, Curſers, Damners, &c.

Whoſo loveth Inſtruction, loveth Knowledge; but he that hateth Reproof, is Brutiſh, Prov. 12. 1.

IF you are of thoſe that profeſs your ſelves to be *Chriſtians*, and are found in the Practice aboveſaid, Conſider what a great Diſhonour and Reproach you bring upon that worthy Name, and Jeſus Chriſt, the Author of it, by ſo doing: And altho' you may eſcape the Penalties and Puniſhment belonging to ſuch Offenders, made and provided by King and Parliament, in that Caſe; yet know for a certain, and remember, that it is impoſſible for you to eſcape the Judgment and Vengeance of the Great and Almighty GOD, if you perſiſt, without Repentance, in ſo henious and deſperate Courſe of Life; for ſuch a Practice doth even Defy and Dare the Great and Juſt GOD to pour down and Execute his Fierce Wrath and Indignation upon you, who certainly is able to cut you off in a Moment; and, in that great Day of Judgment, (wherein an Account muſt be given *of every Idle Word*, Mat. 12. 36.) paſs that Dreadful Sentence upon you, *Depart from me, ye Curſed*, &c. Mat. 25. 41.

O the Senſe and Conſideration of your Manifold and Great Provocations, with which the Lord hath been provoked on the one hand, and his great Mercy and long Forbearance in ſparing of you, on the other hand, work that Remorſe, and have that Effect upon your Conſciences, whereby you may come, in true Humility, to ask and beg for Pardon and Forgiveneſs of Him you have ſo greatly Offended; and withal, take up a Conſtant and Firm Reſolution (deſiring his Aſſiſtance) never to provoke him in like manner again.

So if this Caution ſeems worth taking notice of by you, you are deſired, for further Information, ſeriouſly to peruſe the following places in Scripture, in order, as they are here quoted: But if you ſlight it, yet remember you have been Warned

By **Philaletus.**

Firſt, How Swearing, Curſing, &c. is Forbidden and Reproved: See *Exod.* 20. 7. *Levit.* 19. 12. & 22. 32. *Mat.* 5. 33, 34. *James* 5. 12. *Pſal.* 10. 4, 6, 7. & 109. 17, 18. *Jer.* 23. 10. *Ezek.* 21. 23. *Hoſ.* 4. 2, 3. *Rom.* 2. 24. & 3. 13, to 18. & 1. 18.

Secondly, How God ſees and beholds all our Thoughts, Words, and Actions: See *Prov.* 15. 3. & 5. 21. *Job* 34. 21. & 31. 4. & 42. 2. *Pſal.* 139. 4. 2 *Chron.* 16. 9. *Pſal.* 7. 9. & 44. 21. *Eccleſ.* 12. 14. *Jer.* 17. 10. & 16, 17. *Luke* 8. 17. *Heb.* 4. 12, 13.

Thirdly, How God's Juſtice will overtake the Guilty, except they Repent: See *Pſal.* 7. 11, 12, 13. & 11. 6. *Iſai.* 3. 10. & 5. 14. *Zach.* 5. 3. *Levit.* 24. 14. *Mat.* 12. 36, 37. *Eph.* 6. 8. 2 *Theſſ.* 1. 7, 8, 9. *Mat.* 16. 27. 2 *Cor.* 5. 10. *Job* 34. 11. *Pſal.* 62. 12. *Jer.* 32. 19. *Heb.* 10. 31. *Ezek.* 7. 27. *Rev.* 20. 13. & 22. 12. & 21. 8. *Job* 21. 30. *Pſal.* 9. 17.

Fourthly, How God's Call is to Repent, Forſake, and Return, that he may ſhew Mercy, and forgive: See *Joel* 2. 12, 13. *Ezek.* 18. 21, 32. *Iſa.* 1. 16, 17. & 55. 7. *Acts* 17. 30. & 3. 19. *Mat.* 11. 29, 30. *Pſal.* 34. 13. 1 *Pet.* 3. 10, 11. *Rev.* 2. 7, 11, 17, 26. & 3. 5, 12, 21

Fiſthly, Of the Uncertainty of Time, therefore Repentance ought not to be delayed: See *Prov.* 27. 1. *Heb.* 3. 13. *James* 4. 14. *Job* 8. 9. & 14. 12. & 24. 22. *Pſal.* 39. 5, 6. & 144. 4. & 103. 15, 16. *Iſa.* 40. 6. 7.

Sixthly, How the Lord is in (or near) all Men, by his Light, to manifeſt Evil; by his Spirit, to reprove for it; and by his Grace, to teach to deny it; and, through Faith in Chriſt, to give Power to overcome it: See *Iſai.* 45. 22. *Amos* 4. 13. *Mic.* 6. 8. *John* 10. 30. & 15. 4, 5. & 14. 6. & 12. 46. & 1. 9. & 3. 19, 20, 21. *Eph.* 5. 13. *Prov.* 1. 23. *Rom.* 1. 19. *John* 14. 26. & 16. 8. 1 *John* 2. 27. *John* 6. 45. *Titus* 2. 11, 12. 1 *Cor.* 12. 7. *Rom.* 8. 14. *Luke* 17. 21. 2 *Cor.* 6. 16. *Prov.* 1. 31. *Iſa.* 40. 29. *John* 1. 12. *Mark* 9. 23. *John* 3. 17. *Acts* 10. 35. *Heb.* 2. 9. 1 *John.* 2. 12. 2 *Pet.* 3. 9. *Acts* 20. 32.

London, Printed and Sold by *T. Sowle* in *White-Hart-Court* in *Gracious-ſtreet,* 1702.

'Tracts were issued against . . . swearing'

and Judges like Holt, feared that organized delation would lead to ill-feeling, corruption and blackmail. Many magistrates positively refused to receive the evidence of the philanthropic informers. The mob in some places was dangerous, and at least one active member of the Society was murdered outright.

Nevertheless there were tens of thousands of successful prosecutions. It was said that no one but a person of quality could safely swear in a public place. There was, indeed, a strong body of opinion that supported these proceedings. Many quiet citizens had found the magistrates, ever since the Restoration, scandalously lax in restraining drunkards from annoying the sober, in protecting women from insult, and in preserving any show of decency and order. Nor was Sunday trading really desired by the bulk of the community. The Mayor of Deal, a courageous and energetic man, undertook single-handed a crusade against the behaviour of the town, carried most of his points and was re-elected Mayor in 1708. It is indeed probable that many of the prosecutions, especially for swearing and for travelling on Sunday, were vexatious, and the time came under the Georges when the Society was doing quite as much harm as good, and could disappear. But its activities in the reign of Anne helped to make the streets and taverns less unpleasant for decent people, to reduce drunkenness and to secure Sunday as a day of rest from business and labour.

The more gloomy side of the English Sunday struck a German visitor in 1710:

In the afternoon to St. James's Park, to see the crowds. No other diversion is allowed on Sunday, which is nowhere more strictly kept; not only is all play forbidden, and public-houses closed, but few even of the boats and hackney coaches may ply. Our hostess would not even allow the strangers to play the *viol di Gamba* or the flute, lest she be punished.

He added, rather sourly, that Sunday observance was the only visible sign that the English were Christians at all.

But the most important and lasting impression of the religious revival was made by the Society for Promoting Christian Knowledge, and its off-shoot, the Society for the Propagation of the Gospel in Foreign Parts. The self-same men were the supporters of both, above all the indefatigable Dr. Thomas Bray. The

37

spirit afterwards characteristic of the movement that abolished the Slave Trade and Slavery, inspired these voluntary societies of evangelists, lay and clerical, High and Low Church, Nonjuror and Nonconformist. The last years of William's reign and the first of Anne's saw them fully at work. The diffusion of Bibles and of other religious literature was their chief object. They were therefore great advocates of the Charity Schools where the poor could be taught to read them; the two movements went side by side. The Society's publications were welcomed by Marlborough in the army, and by Benbow and Rooke in the fleet. Cheap Bibles and Prayer Books were furnished in the country districts. And a supply of Bibles and other books to America was begun on a large scale, and to the rest of the world on a scale, modest indeed as compared to the gigantic work of the Society in later years, but ever growing with the growing power and wealth of England oversea. These activities betokened an instinctive movement of the English religious world to get away, on one side at least, from the denominational and political feuds in which it was entangled, into a field of broader vision, where zeal might produce something better than hate.

In the reign of Anne, as also long before and long after, religious differences were the motive force behind political passions. It is doubly impossible, therefore, for the English historian to ignore religion, if he would explain other phenomena. But he must not be tempted to forget that there was more in the religious sense of the nation than the feuds out of which, incidentally, our political liberties in large part arose. The religious life of many quiet parishes and humble families moved on its way, little concerned with partisanship of High and Low Church; English religion was, in the main, a free and healthy function of that old-world life, nicely guiding itself between superstition and fanaticism on the one side and material barbarism on the other.

And in spite of bitterness of party warfare, the prevalent frame of mind among educated persons already partook of that calm, broadminded optimism characteristic of the Eighteenth Century Briton. It has been well said:

Addison's England was fortunate in having behind it not only the Glorious Revolution of 1688, but such a poet as Milton, such a physicist as Newton, and such a philosopher as Locke.

All the dearest ambitions of men and of Britons had been realised;

the Constitution had been established and 'freedom' secured; Homer and Vergil had been equalled if not outdone, the law which preserves the stars from wrong, had been made manifest, and the true workings of the mind had been revealed. All these things had been done not only by Englishmen but by Christians. The brilliant explanations of Newton and Locke had not only removed the strain of living in a mysterious universe, but confirmed the principles of religion. (Basil Willey, *Seventeenth Century Background*, p. 264.)

Two miles away from the Parliament at Westminster and the Queen's Court at St. James's lay the centre of the greatest City in the world, less amenable to the jurisdiction of Court and Parliament than any other portion of English soil. London was governed by her own freely elected magistrates; policed, in so far as she was policed at all, by her own constables; guarded by her own militia; and rendered formidable to the neighbouring seat of government by the largest and least manageable mob in the island. With only a tenth part of her present population, and much less than a tenth of her present area, London had more than her present relative importance. She surpassed her nearest English rivals, Bristol and Norwich, at least fifteen times in number of inhabitants. Her merchants and her markets controlled the larger business operations of the towns and villages of England, 'sucking the vitals of trade to herself.' It was the peculiar boast of the men of Bristol that they alone kept their trade independent of London, bringing American goods to their own port and disposing of them in the west through their own carriers and agents. Everywhere else the strings of trade were pulled from the capital. 'Norwich buys Exeter serges, Exeter buys Norwich stuffs, all at London.' Every county joined in the great national business of supplying London with food, coal or raw material. In return she sent to every county the finished goods of her own luxury trades, and the distant products of her foreign merchandise. To the port of London belonged practically all the East India trade of the country, most of the European, Mediterranean and African, and much of the American.

The lower strata of the population of the capital, the dockers and unskilled casual labour of a great mart and port, lived under the most filthy conditions of overcrowding, without sanitation, police or doctors, and far beyond the range of philanthropy, education and religion. Such was their state both in the City proper and in the liberties beyond, in the days of Defoe. The death-rate among them was appalling, and was still going up because they were learning to drink spirits instead of ale. The privileged sanctuary of outlaws in 'Alsatia,' so outrageous to the dignity of the neighbouring lawyers at the Temple, had indeed been abolished a few years before Anne came to the throne, but the fraternity of thieves, highwaymen and harlots had only been scattered thence to spread themselves more thickly over the whole metropolitan area. Their secret organizer, the great Jonathan Wild, flourished at this period, ostensibly as a zealous magistrate, really as a receiver of stolen goods on an immense scale. Some of his methods of preserving discipline among his subordinates are ascribed to Peachum in the opening scene of the *Beggar's Opera*, which was written immediately after Wild's belated exposure, trial and execution in 1725. [See § 31, 33.] His life's story argues an inefficiency on the part of magistrates and constables that only began to be remedied in the middle of the century, when the famous brothers Fielding set up their office in Bow Street.

Even honest workmen in the ranks of unskilled labour in London were totally without education: Jonathan Brown, a leading personality among the bargemen, confessed to Calamy, the dissenting preacher, that he and his companions 'had never so much as heard who or what Christ was,' though they could easily be set on by their betters to burn Meeting Houses or Popish Chapels according to the political requirements of the hour. It was to combat this state of things that the Charity Schools were being founded by public subscription, and that in 1711 Parliament voted the taxpayers' money to build fifty new churches in the suburbs, to seat several hundred thousand persons unprovided for by the Established Church; the Dissenters, whom the Parliamentary Committee reckoned at 100,000 in that district, had already provided their own chapels.

But London was above all a city of contrasts. The port and mart where the goods of England and the world were exchanged, required not only the muscular efforts of unskilled labour, but a supervising army of foremen, clerks, shopkeepers and middlemen of every variety. Moreover, London was not only a mart; she was also the seat of manufactures, of finishing processes and luxury trades, employing the most skilled workmen in the island.

Many thousands of Huguenot silk manufacturers had recently settled in Spitalfields, and other skilled trades previously conducted in France were now practised in Long Acre and Soho by refugees who were rapidly becoming Englishmen and were already voting Whig to secure the toleration that they precariously enjoyed for their Calvinist worship. The finest native craftsmanship was also concentrated in London. In the best shops of the City the apprentices were sons of country gentlemen, likely to die richer than their elder brothers, and dressing in full-bottomed wigs when off duty. Greater London was the centre of English literary and intellectual life, and of fashion, law and government. For all these reasons the capital contained, alongside the most brutal ignorance, an immense and varied stock of skill and intellect. London wits were sharpened, not only by the processes of national and world commerce, but by daily contact with the lawyers and politicians of Westminster, and with the noblemen and persons of fashion of St. James's. During the season, the leaders of society lived in private mansions or in boarding-houses west of Temple Bar, and were as much Londoners as the annually returning swallow is English.

Such a city, containing more than a tenth of the population of England and a good half of its trained thinking power, placed beside the seat of government at Westminster in juxtaposition so close as to form a single metropolis, could not fail to exercise a decisive influence on the course of English history in the days when the difficulties of travel still isolated Court and Parliament from the other towns and shires of the land. At no time, indeed, did London seek to govern England as Rome had governed Italy or as Athens sought to govern Greece. She accepted the government of England by the Monarchy or by Parliament, so long as the rulers of the land remained at Westminster outside her gates, leaving her ancient municipal liberties undisturbed, and so long as they conducted the religious and foreign affairs of the country in the main in accordance with principles that were popular in London. The Kings and Queens whom she favoured—Henry VIII, Elizabeth, William III and Anne—left behind them political structures that survived. Those who quarrelled with her built for the day—Mary Tudor, the two Charleses and Jameses, and the Protector—though Oliver and the second Charles each owed his rise to power largely to her support.

The Tower of London, which was to have overawed the citizens, had been built by William the Conqueror on the side of the City away from Westminster. Partly for that reason, it had not overawed them long. In Stuart times it could not, in its isolated position, serve to protect Westminster and Whitehall from the insults of the London mob. In Anne's reign the Tower still served as the great arsenal whence cannon and gunpowder were shipped to the wars oversea; it also contained the Mint and its machinery for coining the money of the Realm, presided over by Newton himself as Master. The outer walls enclosed a network of streets inhabited by the officers of these two establishments. On occasion it was still a State prison. But already it had its lighter side, for it served as the Zoo and the Museum of the capital. Visitors were taken to see the Crown Jewels, and the newly finished Armoury where a line of English Kings sat mounted in battle array. The stock of lions and other wild beasts had been maintained ever since the days when the Tower had been a favourite residence of mediaeval kings; it was finely replenished by presents to Queen Anne from the monarchs of North African 'Barbary,' with whom the English merchants traded, and with whom the captors of Gibraltar made treaties of alliance against France and Spain.

Between the Tower and Temple Bar stretched the length of the City proper; its meagre breadth extended northwards from the river only as far as the bars of Smithfield, Holborn and Whitechapel.[1] But the march of bricks and mortar had burst the municipal bounds, chiefly in a westerly direction, attracted towards the seat of national government at Westminster. At the Strand began the jurisdiction of that City. But the municipal privileges of Westminster were no rival to those of London. Neither London nor the Court nor Parliament had ever wished to have to deal with a Lord Mayor of Westminster. So Westminster was never permitted to enjoy self-government, or to acquire a corporate sense. It was ruled by twelve burgesses appointed for life by the High Steward, and even their powers were being rapidly superseded by those of the Justices of the Peace and of the Vestries of the different parishes. It is true that the parliamentary franchise in Westminster was democratic, and in the days when most boroughs

[1] These 'bar' boundaries, were, of course, more extensive than the original City bounded by the wall and gates, *e.g.* Temple Bar was farther west than Ludgate.

had a narrow franchise, the election of a Member of Parliament for Westminster caused unusual political excitement long before the time of Charles Fox, as when General Stanhope stood in 1710 in the Whig interest and was defeated after a fierce contest and a hot canvass. But Westminster's local government was a mere bureaucracy, so far as it was anything better than an anarchy of rival jurisdictions.

On the other hand, the City of London enjoyed complete self-government in an unusually democratic form. At that time very few boroughs in England were so free of the element of oligarchy, unless it were Ipswich and Norwich. In London as many as 12,000 ratepaying householders voted in their respective Wards to elect the 26 Aldermen and 200 Common Councillors. These rate-payers of the Wards were almost identical with the Liverymen of the 89 Gilds and Companies: in their double capacity they controlled by their votes the antique and complicated machinery of London self-government.

The electorate of shopkeepers chose men of their own class to represent them on the Common Council, rather than the great merchant princes known in the world of high finance and politics. The City magnates were more often chosen as Aldermen. Common pride in the privileges and power of London, and jealous care for her independence, prevented a serious breach between the great men of the Exchange and the shopkeeping democracy. But there was sometimes friction, and in the course of Anne's reign a tendency became apparent for the democratic Common Council to be Tory, and for the Mayor, Aldermen and wealthy City magnates to be Whig.

The jurisdiction of London's elected magistrates was not confined to the area of their own City. Their power stopped short of Westminster, but they clipped it in on every side. They possessed the Shrievalty of Middlesex and the Bailiwick of Southwark. They administered and taxed the port of London. The Lord Mayor was Conservator of the river from Gravesend and Tilbury up to a point just above Staines Bridge—a course of over sixty miles. London levied coal duties in a radius of twelve miles, and enforced her monopoly of markets in a radius of seven.

The City proper was the most densely populated acreage in England. It was not, as in later times, abandoned to 'cats and caretakers' at nightfall; the merchant prince and the shopkeeper slept, each with his family, over his place of business—servants and prentices above in the garrets, and porters and messengers packed away anywhere in cellarage and warehouse. Old Jewry and Basinghall Street, in particular, were reputed to contain the homes of some of the richest men in England. But the nobility of the realm had already deserted their ancestral palaces in the crowded City and the Strand, whence gardens were vanishing apace; the grandees resided, during the season, round Covent Garden, Piccadilly, Bloomsbury or St. James's Square, or in some part of Westminster. [See § 39.] And gentlemen from the country, civil servants, Members of Parliament and professional men had smaller houses in these same regions, clustering round the mansions of the nobility. Such is the origin of many famous London 'Squares.'[1]

But the rich merchants still inhabited their beloved City for reasons alike of business and sentiment. They had also their country houses and villas among the woods, fields and pleasant villages within a twenty-mile radius of London. In their suburban and riverside retreats—in Hampstead, West Ham, Walthamstow, and below Epsom Downs, and especially along the green shores of the Thames from Chelsea upwards—there was perhaps as much good eating and drinking done by Londoners as in the City itself. The poorer sort walked out for a holiday in the country to favourite spots like Dulwich.

The river was the most crowded of the London highways. Passengers in boats were perpetually threading the heavy commercial traffic, to the accompaniment of volleys of traditional abuse and chaff exchanged between boatmen and bargees. On the north bank, between London Bridge and the Parliament Stairs were at least thirty landing-places, where boats waited by the steps to carry people along or across the river. Statesmen and parsons going over to Lambeth, or prentices and budding barristers on lighter errands to Cupid's Garden hard by, one and all crossed by

---

[1] Thus Bloomsbury Square, originally called Southampton Square, was a new fashionable quarter, built after the Restoration. The 'Square' was the first piece of properly planned development on the Bloomsbury estate of the last Earl of Southampton, on whose death it passed to his daughter Rachel and her 'dear lord,' the Whig hero executed in 1683. It was one of the earliest of the London squares, and was given that form in order to leave open the view from the front of the great mansion, Southampton (later Bedford) House that occupied its north end. A century passed before Russell Square was similarly developed out of the fields to the north of the great House. (*The Russells in Bloomsbury*, Scott Thomson, chaps. II and III.)

boat. There were ferries with platforms to take a coach and horses. For until Westminster Bridge was built in 1738, London Bridge was the only road over the river. The street that stood upon it had been rebuilt in a more modern style since the ravages of the Great Fire, but the projection of its ancient piers still hindered and endangered traffic. To 'shoot the bridge' was still an adventure; it was said that London Bridge was made for wise men to go over and fools to go under. [See § 40, 41.]

The big shipping, therefore, came no higher than the Bridge. [See § 42.] Below it, a forest of masts covered the Pool of London, with which no scene in the world save Amsterdam could compare. The fairway was the more crowded because scarcely any of the great docks had then been dug out, except those at Deptford, and the single dock at Blackwall used for the vessels of the East India Company.

Amid the hayfields on Thames bank stood Chelsea Hospital in solitary grandeur, inhabited by four hundred red-coated pensioners of Sedgemoor, Landen and the Boyne, discussing the weekly news of Marlborough's doings with the professional earnestness of Corporal Trim. A little way off lay the village of Chelsea, where a few persons of fashion had taken the fancy to build themselves retreats, as far removed from the turmoil of London and Westminster as Kensington Palace itself.

Since coal was burnt on almost every London hearth, the air was so infected that a foreign scholar complained 'whenever I examine London books I make my ruffles as black as coal.' On days when the north-east wind carried the smoke-cloud, even Chelsea became dangerous to the asthmatic, as the mild philosopher Earl of Shaftesbury had reason to complain. There is no wonder that King William with his weak lungs had lived at Hampton Court when he could, and at Kensington when he must. Anne, on her accession, could safely move the royal residence from country to town, from Kensington to St. James's Palace. But that was all the satisfaction she would give to her loving subjects; not only was she often at Bath and yet more often at Windsor, but even when she came to town, the doors of St. James's were open only to her Ministers and her female favourites, and to those whom Ministers or favourites introduced by the front stairs or the back. Throughout her reign she was an invalid. What asthma was to William, gout or dropsy was to Anne. To be jolted in a coach to Westminster to open Parliament, or to St. Paul's to give public thanks for some famous victory, was a penance that she could only occasionally consent to endure.

Queen Anne therefore kept Court as little as William. Metaphorically as well as literally, the Whitehall of the Merry Monarch lay in ruins, never to rise again. Except the Banqueting House of tragic memory, the whole Palace had been burnt in 1698, and its roofless walls still cumbered the river bank. Buckingham House was still the residence of a subject. The fashionable world parading in sedan chairs and six-horse coaches in the Mall, or sauntering in the more private garden immediately below the windows of St. James's Palace, had to be content with remembering that they were near the invisible Queen. [See § 7.] It was more to the point that in the other direction the Houses of Parliament were but a few minutes' walk away.

'The Court' had been the microcosm and throbbing heart of England ever since the days of Alfred, through Norman and Plantagenet times, through the spacious days of Henry and Elizabeth down to Charles II; his Court was not only the scene of much pleasure, liberty and scandal, it was also the centre of patronage for politics, fashion, literature, art, learning, invention, company-promoting, and a hundred other activities of the King's eager subjects seeking notoriety or reward. But after the Revolution the glory of the Court grew dim. Neither the political position of the Crown, nor the personal temperament of those who wore it was the same as of old. Stern William, invalid Anne, the German Georges, farmer George, domestic Victoria, none of them desired to keep a Court like Queen Elizabeth's. Henceforth the Court was the residence of secluded Royalty, pointed out from afar, difficult of access save on formal occasions of proverbial dullness. Patronage was sought elsewhere, in the lobbies of Parliament, in the ante-chambers of Ministers, in the country houses of the pleasantest aristocracy in the world—finally in an appeal to the educated public. This decline of the Court had many consequences, direct and indirect, on English life. It had no analogy in contemporary France, where Versailles still drew men like a magnet, and impoverished the life of château and province.

Chapter Two

DR. JOHNSON'S ENGLAND [*circa* 1740–1780][1]

1. *Population—Medicine and Philanthropy—Justice—Local administration
—Religion—Education—Universities—Wales*

THE first forty years of the Eighteenth Century, the reign
of Anne and the rule of Walpole, constitute an age of transition, during which the feuds and ideals of the Stuart era, lately a
lava flood scouring the land with devastating heat, were being
channelled and congealed into fixed, durable Hanoverian forms.
In this way the age of Marlborough and Bolingbroke, of Swift and
Defoe, was the meeting-point of two epochs. It is only in the
years that followed (1740–1780) that we find a generation of men
wholly characteristic of the Eighteenth Century ethos, a society
with a mental outlook of its own, self-poised, self-judged, and self-approved, freed from the disturbing passions of the past, and not
yet troubled with anxieties about a very different future which was
soon to be brought upon the scene by the Industrial and the
French Revolutions. The gods mercifully gave mankind this
little moment of peace between the religious fanaticisms of the past
and the fanaticisms of class and race that were speedily to arise
and dominate time to come. In England it was an age of aristocracy and liberty; of the rule of law and the absence of reform; of
individual initiative and institutional decay; of Latitudinarianism
above and Wesleyanism below; of the growth of humanitarian
and philanthropic feeling and endeavour; of creative vigour in
all the trades and arts that serve and adorn the life of man.

It is a 'classical' age, that is to say an age of unchallenged
assumptions, when the philosophers of the street, such as Dr.
Johnson, have ample leisure to moralize on the human scene, in
the happy belief that the state of society and the modes of thought
to which they are accustomed are not mere passing aspects of an
ever-shifting kaleidoscope, but permanent habitations, the final

---

[1] George II, 1727–1760. George III, 1760–1820. Dr. Johnson, *b.* 1709, *d.* 1784.
Seven Years' War, 1755–1761. War of American Independence, 1776–1782.

outcome of reason and experience. [See § 34.] Such an age does not aspire to progress though it may in fact be progressing; it regards itself not as setting out but as having arrived; it is thankful for what it has, and enjoys life without 'deep questioning which probes to endless dole.' And therefore the men of this 'classical' age looked back with a sense of kinship to the far-off Ancient World. The upper class regarded the Greeks and Romans as honorary Englishmen, their precursors in liberty and culture, and the Roman Senate as the prototype of the British Parliament. The mediaeval period, with its 'gothic' aspirations and barbarisms, sank for a while below the horizon of study and sympathy, so that the eye of taste could range back without hindrance across the gulf of time, and contemplate on its further shore the only civilization which could claim to be as classical, as poised, as enlightened and as artistic as the fortunate present.

Compared to the self-complacency of the mid-Eighteenth Century, the proverbial self-complacency of the Victorians is modesty itself, for the Victorians were, within certain limits, ardent and successful reformers, and admired themselves for the improvements they made. But to the typical men of the period of Blackstone, Gibbon and Burke, England appeared to be the best country possible in an imperfect world, requiring only to be left alone where Providence and the Revolution of 1688 had so fortunately placed her. Their optimism about England was based on a general pessimism about the human race, not on a belief in perpetual and world-wide 'progress' such as cheered simple hearts in the Nineteenth Century.

It is true that the men who were least content were those who looked closest at the realities of English life—Hogarth, Fielding, Smollett and the philanthropists [see § 35]; they indeed exposed particular evils as unsparingly as Dickens himself. But even their strictures kept within the limits of the classical and conservative philosophy of the time. Nor was the self-complacency of that age altogether unjustified, though it was unfortunate because it sustained an atmosphere inimical to any general movement of reform. It was a society which, with all its grave faults, was brilliant above and stable below.

In the course of the Eighteenth Century the population of England and Wales rose from about five and a half millions when

§§23 & 24 Charity-school children in Queen Anne's reign

§25 Captain Coram, the founder of the Foundling Hospital

§26 St. Thomas's Hospital in 1746

§27 The Foundling Hospital by 1746

§28 Apprentices at their silk looms in Spitalfields (*c.* 1747)

§29 A workshop in Spitalfields (*c.* 1747)

§30 The Bench

§31 The condemned cell

§32 The Fleet Prison Committee of 1729

§33 Scene from *The Beggar's Opera*

§34 Dr. Johnson in 1756

§35 Hogarth's self-portrait (1758)

§36 Beer Street

§37 Gin Lane

§38 St. Mary-le-Strand (Built 1714–17)

§39 Covent Garden in 1749

§40 Vauxhall Gardens in 1765

§41 London Bridge in the mid-eighteenth century

§42 The Thames near London in the mid-eighteenth century

§43 The spirit of
scientific enquiry (1768).

Queen Anne came to the throne, to nine millions in 1801. This unprecedented increase, the herald of great changes in the life of our island, was not caused by immigration: the entry of cheap Irish labour which now first became an important feature of our social and economic life, was counterbalanced numerically by English emigration oversea. The advance in population represented a rather larger birth-rate and a very much reduced death-rate. The survival of many more infants and the prolongation of the average life of adults mark off modern times from the past, and this great change began in the Eighteenth Century. It was due mainly to improved medical service.

In the first decades of the Century the death-rate had risen sharply and passed the birth-rate. But this dangerous tendency was reversed between 1730 and 1760, and after 1780 the death-rate went down by leaps and bounds.

Both the rise of the death-rate and its subsequent fall have been attributed in part to the growth and decline of the habit of drinking cheap gin instead of beer. The dire consequences of that change in the habits of the poor have been immortalized in Hogarth's famous delineation of the horrors of 'Gin Lane' contrasted with prosperous 'Beer Street.' In the third decade of the Century, the epoch of the *Beggar's Opera*, statesmen and legislators had deliberately encouraged the consumption of gin by throwing open the distilling trade and by placing on spirits far too light a tax. Distilling, said Defoe, consumed corn and was therefore

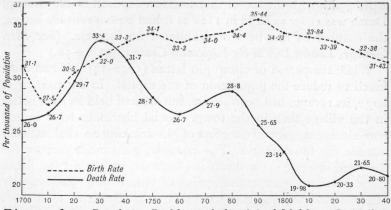

Diagram from *Population Problems of the Age of Malthus.* G. Talbot Griffith. Cam. Press, 1926.

good for the landed interest, and so thought the Parliament of landlords. But as the appalling social consequences were gradually brought to their notice by the enlightened philanthropy of the age, a series of hesitating steps were taken to mitigate the evil. But it was not really checked until 1751, when spirits were highly taxed and their retail by distillers and shopkeepers was stopped (24 G. II, c. 40). [See § 36, 37.]

'The Act of 1751,' says the historian of Eighteenth Century London, 'really did reduce the excesses of spirit-drinking. It was a turning-point in the social history of London and was so considered when this time was still within living memory.' Even after that blessed date medical men still attributed an eighth of the deaths of London adults to excess in spirit-drinking; but the worst was over, and after the middle years of the Century tea became a formidable rival to alcohol with all classes, both in the capital and in the country at large.

At the height of the gin era, between 1740 and 1742, the burials in the London region had been twice as many as the baptisms! The capital had been supplied with inhabitants by the unfailing stream of immigrants from the healthier and more sober countryside. The change for the better after the middle of the Century was very great. In 1750 the London death-rate had been 1 in 20; by 1821 it had fallen to 1 in 40. The population of greater London doubled between 1700 and 1820 (674,000 rose to 1,274,000), but the annual number of registered burials was unaltered. In other words, although the target that London exposed to the darts of Death was twice as large in 1820 as it had been a century before, the number of hits he scored showed no increase. (See Mrs. George, *London Life in the Eighteenth Century*, pp. 24–38.)

While the period of cheap gin lasted (1720–1750) it had done much to reduce the population of the capital. In the country at large, its ravages had been severe, but ale had held its own better in the village than in the town. Social historians have indeed sometimes exaggerated the effect of gin-drinking on vital statistics outside the London area. For example, gin cannot account for the rapid increase in the death-rate between 1700 and 1720, for in those years the great consumption of cheap spirits had scarcely begun. And whereas the death-rate in all England, as distinct from the London area, fell rapidly from 1730 to 1750, those were precisely the years when gin-drinking was at its worst.

We must therefore look for other causes, besides the decline of the consumption of spirits, to account for the remarkable fall in the death-rate that marked the middle period of the Century, and still more its last twenty years. The two reasons why death began to take a smaller toll of English infants, children and adults, were improved conditions of life and improved medical treatment. The great advance in agriculture during the Eighteenth Century gave more abundant food to many, though not to all. The advance in locomotion and the changes in industrial method gave more employment and higher wages and brought more numerous and more varied articles of purchase within the cottager's reach. It is true that the industrial and agricultural revolutions had some most unhappy effects on society and on the amenities of life in village and town. It did not always make for content, possibly not on the average for happiness. But it certainly provided more food and clothing and other articles per head of the population, though their distribution was scandalously unequal. And this greater abundance, by lengthening human life, was one cause why the population continued to rise.

But an even greater check upon the death-rate was the advance in medicine. Throughout the Eighteenth Century the medical profession was moving out of the dark ages of sciolism and traditional superstition into the light of science. The Physician, the Surgeon, the Apothecary and the unlicensed practitioner were all going forward apace in knowledge and in devoted service, especially to the poor, who had hitherto been horribly neglected. Science and philanthropy were the best part of the spirit of the 'age of enlightenment' and this spirit inspired the better medical training and practice of individuals.

At the beginning of the Century, smallpox had been the scourge most dreaded, as destructive of beauty and still more destructive of life. The woman traveller, Lady Mary Wortley Montagu, introduced inoculation from Turkey, and an Inoculation Hospital was set up in London. Although the remedy was suspected as unnatural and even impious, it made some headway and reduced the ravages of the disease. But smallpox still carried off a thirteenth of each generation until, at the close of the Century, Jenner discovered vaccination.

Scotland was beginning to make her great intellectual contribution to life south of the Border. The union of brains was following the Union of Parliaments and of commerce. It was the age of Hume, Smollett, Adam Smith and Boswell. And in this same period Sir John Pringle, the Hunter brothers and William Smellie came from Scotland to London; the Hunters, by their teaching, converted British surgery from the trade of the 'barber-surgeon' into the science of the specialist; Smellie similarly revolutionized the practice of midwifery; while Pringle reformed military hygiene, on scientific principles which had also a great influence on the habits and the treatment of the civilian population.

The great improvement in professional skill was supported by the foundation of Hospitals, in which the age of Philanthropy gave sober expression to its feelings, just as the age of Faith had sung its soul in the stones of cloisters and Cathedral aisles. Lying-in hospitals were founded in the principal towns. County hospitals for all sorts of patients were set up. In the capital, between 1720 and 1745, Guy's, Westminster, St. George's, London and Middlesex Hospitals were all founded; the mediaeval St. Thomas's had been rebuilt in the reign of Anne, and at Bart's teaching and practice were improving apace. In the course of 125 years after 1700, no less than 154 new hospitals and dispensaries were established in Britain. These were not municipal undertakings—municipal life was then at its lowest ebb; they were the outcome of individual initiative and of co-ordinated voluntary effort and subscription. [See § 26, 27.]

At the same time the growing benevolence of the age was moved to cope with the appalling infant mortality among the poor and especially among deserted bastard children. Jonas Hanway, who did much to reduce these evils, had declared that 'few parish children live to be apprenticed.' And thousands of infants did not even live to be parish children, but died abandoned in empty rooms or exposed in streets by mothers to whom they would only mean expense and shame. Captain Coram, with his kind sailor's heart, could not endure the sight of babes lying deserted by the roadside, while respectable citizens passed by with the shrug of the Pharisee. For years Coram agitated the project of a Foundling Hospital; at length he obtained a charter from George II; Handel gave an organ; Hogarth painted a picture; subscriptions poured in, and in 1745 the Hospital was completed and opened. Many infant lives were saved, and many deserted children were brought up and apprenticed to trades. [See § 25.]

A few years after the good Captain had died, a bad moment occurred in the history of the institution he had founded. In 1756 Parliament made a grant to its funds, on condition that all children brought to the Hospital should be admitted. Fifteen thousand were brought, and the not unnatural consequence was that of this unmanageable multitude only 4400 lived to be apprenticed. After that disastrous experiment, the Foundling Hospital again became a private institution with a limited entry—and a reduced death-rate. It long continued to do good work, till in the happier social conditions of the early Twentieth Century it was moved out of town, and the 'Foundling site' was secured as a playground for all kinds of children, and rechristened 'Coram's Fields.'

Early in the reign of George III, Hanway's persistent efforts were crowned by an Act of Parliament which compelled the parishes of the London area to keep their 'parish infants' no longer in the workhouses where they died apace, but in country cottages where they lived and throve.[1]

In the same spirit, General Oglethorpe had drawn attention to the scandal of debtors' prisons. In 1729 he induced Parliament to inquire into the horrors of the Fleet and Marshalsea, where the gaolers tortured debtors to death in the endeavour to extract fees from men who in the nature of the case had no money. [See § 32.] English prisons remained for the rest of the Century a national disgrace, being still farmed out to wretches of this kind by the local authorities who would not be at the trouble and expense to maintain them by properly paid public officials.[2] But Oglethorpe had at least called attention to the state of things and mitigated some of its very worst abuses. Previous generations had seldom inquired what went on inside these houses of woe.

---

[1] Hanway (1712–1786) is also famous for introducing the umbrella into England. For many years he carried one, in spite of the jeers of the populace and the interested anger of sedan chairmen and hackney coachmen, until in the last years of his life his example was generally imitated. But it would be more true to say that he reintroduced the custom, for in 1710, two years before Hanway was born, Swift had written in his *City Shower*:

> The tuck'd up sempstress walks with hasty strides
> While streams run down her oil'd umbrella's sides.

It is therefore probable that Hanway had seen umbrellas in use in London when he was a small boy. [See § 2.]

[2] John Howard, in 1773, began his life's work on prisons by a vain attempt to induce the justices of Bedfordshire and the neighbouring Counties to pay regular salaries to the gaolers in lieu of fees extorted from the prisoners.

The gallant General also became the founder and first governor of the new colony of Georgia, whither he transplanted many debtors and impoverished persons. He well deserved Pope's eulogium—

> One, driven by strong benevolence of soul,
> Shall fly, like Oglethrope, from pole to pole.

'Strong benevolence of soul' was characteristic of many in that age. It dictated the extraordinary domestic arrangements of Oglethorpe's formidable friend Dr. Johnson. From beginning to end of the Century, the new Puritanism of the ardently religious, such as Robert Nelson, Lady Elizabeth Hastings, the Wesleys, Cowper and finally Wilberforce, strove to practise the charity of the New Testament in place of the harsher precepts of the Old with which Cromwell's troopers had marched to battle. It was no accident that Uncle Toby, the Vicar of Wakefield, Mr. Allworthy and Parson Adams were leading characters in English fiction during its first great period. A keener sensitiveness to the needs and sufferings of others, particularly of the poor, was not only reflected in literature but was seen in the lives of philanthropists and in the successive activities of the age—the foundation first of Charity Schools; then of Hospitals; and, in the last years of the Century, of Sunday Schools. It overleapt the boundaries of race and colour. It melted the hard prudence of statesmen. 'Stormy pity' inspired much of the eloquence and some of the errors of Burke and of Fox on India and on France; and at length stirred the great rebellion of the English conscience against the slave-trade.

Yet while the new humanitarian spirit inspired private initiative, it had as yet little effect on executive, municipal or legislative action. Private employers treated their servants better than the Government treated its soldiers and sailors. The fleet had to be maintained by the haphazard and iniquitous compulsion of the press-gang, because voluntary recruiting was inadequate owing to the notorious conditions on board the royal ships. [See § 46.] The life of the fisherman and the merchant sailor was hard enough, but it was better than life on a man-of-war, where the food was foul and scanty, the pay inadequate and irregular, the attention to health nil, and the discipline of iron. The good Admiral Vernon, suffered in the reign of George II for being the sailors' outspoken friend, declared that 'our fleets are defrauded by injustice, manned by violence and maintained by cruelty.' [See § 47.]

The private of the army was no better treated. At home he had no barracks, but was billeted in ale-houses on a population that hated the red-coats and treated them accordingly. They were the more unpopular because they acted as the only efficient police force against rioting and smuggling. As to discipline, one soldier of George II had received 30,000 lashes in sixteen years—'yet the man is hearty and well and in no ways concerned.' While such was their lot at home, garrison duty in the West Indies was tanta- mount to a sentence of death. These were the men who by sea and land won England her empire and defended her trade and secured her wealth and happiness at home, and such was their reward. [See § 48.]

Throughout the Century, Parliament went on adding statute after statute to the 'bloody code' of English law, enlarging per- petually the long list of offences punishable by death: finally they numbered two hundred. Not only were horse and sheep stealing and coining capital crimes, but stealing in a shop to the value of five shillings, and stealing anything privily from the person, were it only a handkerchief. But such was the illogical chaos of the law, that attempted murder was still very lightly punished, though to slit a man's nose was capital. The effect of increased legal severity in an age that was becoming more humane, was that juries often refused to convict men for minor offences that would lead them to the scaffold. Moreover it was easy for a criminal by the help of a clever lawyer, to escape on purely technical grounds from the meshes of an antiquated and over-elaborate procedure. Out of six thieves brought to trial, five might in one way or another get off, while the unlucky one was hanged. It would have been more deterrent if they had all six been sure of a term of imprisonment.

To make matters worse, the chances of arrest were small, for there was no effective police in the island, except the 'runners' of the office which the Fielding brothers, about the middle of the Century, set up in their house in Bow Street.[1] Until the soldiers

[1] The novelist Henry Fielding and his remarkable half-brother Sir John, who was blind from birth, were the best magistrates London had in the Century. Actually they were Stipendiary Justices of Westminster. In a ballad of the period, the Highwayman sings:

I went to London one fine day
With my sweet love to see the play,
Where Fielding's gang did me pursue
And I was ta'en by that cursed crew.

were actually called out, there was no force capable of dispersing a disorderly crowd. Hence the disgraceful incident of the Gordon Riots (1780), when seventy houses and four gaols were burnt by the London mob. Indeed, the wonder is that our ancestors preserved public order and private property as well as they did. They must have been, on the average, at least as moral and law-abiding a folk as our own generation. For what would be the effect in our great cities to-day of abolishing the police?

Yet, until the Code Napoleon was received on the Continent, it is possible that English justice, bad as it was, may have been the best in the world, as Blackstone boasted. It had at least two advantages over the European codes of the *ancien régime*. It gave the prisoner in political cases a real chance to defend himself against the Government, an improvement made by the Treason Law of 1695, and by the general tendency of political and judicial practice since the Revolution. And in no cases, political or other, was torture permitted to extort evidence or confession. But it cannot be said that English justice eschewed torture as a means of punishment, for although breaking on the wheel was unknown in our island, the floggings, particularly in the army and navy, often amounted to torture.

The English were still fond of witnessing the punishment of those whose actions they disapproved. Two passages may be cited from the *Diaries* of Parson Woodforde, a benevolent soul unusually kind to men and animals:

1777. July 22. Robert Biggen, for stealing potatoes, was this afternoon whipped thro' the streets of Cary [Somerset] by the Hangman at the end of a cart. He was whipped from the George Inn to the Angel, from thence back through the street to the Royal Oak in South Cary and so back to the George Inn. He being an old offender there was a collection of 0.17.6 given to the Hangman to do him justice. But it was not much for all that—the Hangman was an old Man and a most villainous looking Fellow indeed. For my Part I would not contribute one Farthing to it.

1781. April 7. Gave my servant Will leave to go to Norwich ten miles by road this morning to see the three Highwaymen hung there today. Will returned about seven o'clock in the evening. They were all three hung and appeared penitent.

Whether or not English justice was on the whole less bad than the continental practice of the day, the philosophers of Europe and of England now began their famous attack on the existing systems of law and punishment. This greater sensitiveness to evils which all previous ages had accepted as matters of course, was part of the general humanitarian movement, connected on the Continent with Voltaire and the 'philosophers,' and in England connected equally with 'philosophy' and with religion. The Italian reformer, Beccaria, in his attack on the penal codes of Europe was followed by Howard's exposure of the still scandalous state of prisons at home and abroad, and by Bentham's analysis of the useless and complicated absurdities of English law, a vested interest dear to the heart of the most conservative of professions.

The excellent idea of the rule of law, as something superior to the will of the rulers, was strong among the Eighteenth Century English. It had been secured by the events of the Revolution and by the consequent irremovability of Judges, who were no longer jackals of government, but independent umpires between the Crown and the subject.

This high conception of the supremacy of law was popularized by Blackstone's *Commentaries on the Laws of England* (1765), a book widely read by educated people in England and America, for it was a legally-minded age. The fault was that the law thus idealized was regarded too much as static, as a thing given once for all, whereas, if law is indeed to be the permanent rule of life to a nation, it must be apt to change with the changing needs and circumstances of society. In the Eighteenth Century, Parliament showed little legislative activity, except in private acts for enclosure of land, for turnpike roads, or other economic measures. In administrative matters there was a lag in legislation, at a time when great industrial developments were every year changing social conditions, and adding to the needs of a growing population.

Therefore Jeremy Bentham, the father of English law reform, regarded Blackstone as the arch-enemy, who stood in the way of change by teaching people to make a fetish of the laws of England in the form which they actually bore at the moment, a form dictated by the needs not of the present age but of ages long past.[1]

[1] Professor Holdsworth thinks that Bentham somewhat exaggerated the conservative optimism of Blackstone, who was not in all ways as blind as his critic made out.

The first blast against Blackstone was blown by young Bentham in his *Fragment on Government* in 1776, that seminal year which saw the publication of Adam Smith's *Wealth of Nations*, the first part of Gibbon's *History*, and the American Declaration of Independence. When the octogenarian Bentham died in 1832, the laws of England had only just begun to be altered from what they had been when he first denounced them in Blackstone's day. Yet his prolonged efforts had not been in vain, for he had converted the rising generation. Onwards from that time our laws were rapidly changed in accordance with the common-sense, utilitarian principles that Bentham had laid down.

Reform was to be the specific work of the Nineteenth Century. The specific work of the earlier Hanoverian epoch was the establishment of the rule of law; and that law, with all its grave faults, was at least a law of freedom. On that solid foundation all our subsequent reforms were built. If the Eighteenth Century had not established the law of freedom, the Nineteenth Century in England would have proceeded by Revolutionary violence, instead of by Parliamentary modification of the law.

The abuses of the poor-law, of which so much was heard in Eighteenth Century England, were due to want of modern organs of government, and above all to an entire lack of central organization and control. The problem of the poor and of unemployment was in its essence national—or at least regional—yet every petty parish dealt with it separately, in a state of hostility to every other. Rural ignorance and parochial jealousy were left to cope with the terrible problem according to their own devices, and the chief anxiety felt was to drive out of the parish anyone who might conceivably become a burden on the poor-rate, a policy which checked the fluidity of labour and severely aggravated unemployment. But the problem of the poor in England had this advantage over the problem of police and prisons, that it was legally obligatory to raise a poor-rate in every parish to deal with its poor, whereas the ratepayers regarded it as an unusual hardship if the magistrate raised any rate to pay for roads, prisons, sanitation or police. [See § 49, 50, 51, 52.]

Rural England was governed by the patriarchal sway of the Justices of the Peace. It lay with them to decide if a local rate should be raised for any purpose, and how it should be spent.

The Justices, nominally appointed by the Crown, were really appointed by the Lord Lieutenant influenced by the opinion of the gentry of the shire. Nominally State officials, the J.P.s really represented local territorial power. The Privy Council no longer, as in Tudor and early Stuart days, kept them in awe and guided their action on national principles. The Revolution of 1688, in one of its aspects, had been a revolt of these unpaid local magistrates against the Central Government which had overstrained their loyalty in religion and politics. Owing to the infatuation of James II, the privileges of Parliament and the liberties of Englishmen were reasserted at the price of an excessive lack of central control over local authorities even in matters that were not political but social. The Privy Council by aiming at absolute power in all things, had lost powers which it had formerly exercised for the general good. In the Eighteenth Century the Justices of Peace might rather have been said to control the Central Government through the grand national Quarter Sessions of Parliament, than to be under any central control themselves. No local authority had then to consider 'Whitehall.' [See § 30.]

The powers and functions of the J.P.s covered all sides of country life. They administered justice in Quarter or Petty Sessions, or in the private house of a single magistrate. They were supposed to keep up the roads and bridges, the prisons and workhouses. They licensed the public houses. They levied a county rate when a rate was levied at all. These and a hundred other aspects of county business lay in their control. Yet they had not any proper staff, or any effective bureaucracy to carry out local administration. For that would have meant a big county rate which men were unwilling to pay; they preferred inefficient local government provided only it was cheap. Modern English practice is so different in this respect that it is difficult to realize how great has been the change.[1]

In the middle years of the Century, Fielding, Smollett and other observers of the injustices of life, bitterly satirized the irresponsible power of the J.P.s and its frequent misuse in acts of tyranny and favouritism. There was a corrupt type of J.P. known as 'trading justices,' men of a lower order of society who got themselves made

---

[1] The annual cost of poor relief between 1782 and 1793 was two millions a year; *all other kinds of expenditure met out of local rates did not exceed £200,000 a year!* (Halévy, *Hist. of Eng. People*, II, p. 233 (Pelican ed.).)

magistrates in order to turn their position to financial profit. But generally speaking, the Justices who did most of the work in rural districts were substantial squires, too rich to be corrupt or mean, proud to do hard public work for no pay, anxious to stand well with their neighbours, but often ignorant and prejudiced without meaning to be unjust, and far too much a law unto themselves.

It is a common error to regard the Eighteenth Century in England as irreligious. An ethical code based on Christian doctrine was a rule of life to a much larger proportion of the community than it had been in the late mediaeval and Tudor periods. Indeed, the age of Wesley, Cowper and Dr. Johnson was perhaps as 'religious' as the Seventeenth Century itself, though it had ceased to fight with the sword about rival doctrines of Christianity, and was therefore somewhat more tolerant of still wider differences of opinion.

Locke's argument that Toleration was not merely politically expedient but positively just and right, became generally accepted as the Eighteenth Century went on. It is arguable that this does not make that much abused era any less Christian. Human experience had so long associated religion with intolerance, that when intolerance cooled, people thought that religion had decayed. The deduction may be challenged.

Writing in the reigns of James II and William, even Locke had maintained that neither Atheist nor Romanist had an absolute claim on society for toleration, because the one undermined morality and the other the State. But in effect both were to benefit by the more liberal and latitudinarian philosophy which his influence helped to impose on the succeeding age.

Locke's *Reasonableness of Christianity* (the very title marks a new brand of thought and religion) was the starting-point of two movements, the Latitudinarianism that became for a while the prevalent tone of the Established Church, though not of Methodism; and the English Deistic movement which all respectable people regarded askance.

In the first thirty years of the Century the 'Deists,' such as Toland, Tindal and Collins, were allowed to print their cautiously expressed views without being prosecuted; while they were answered not only by the satire of Swift but by the arguments of men who outmatched them in intellect—Bishop Butler, Bishop

Berkeley, Bentley and William Law. Voltaire, the bolder and more formidable disciple of these English Deists, found no such antagonists in France, but had more to fear from active persecution by Church and State. Partly for that reason continental Deism became more uncompromising and more anti-Christian than English. Indeed, the most recent historian of Eighteenth Century thought speaks of 'that peculiarly English phenomenon, the holy alliance of science and religion, which persisted (in spite of Hume) till near the close of the Century.' (Basil Willey, *The Eighteenth Century Background*, p. 136.) [See § 43.] David Hartley, after whom Coleridge named his son, proclaimed this 'holy alliance.' In the words of Pope's comfortable epigram:

> Nature and Nature's laws lay hid in night;
> God said, *Let Newton be!* and all was light!

The Harmony of science and religion was nobly symbolized by the erection in 1755 of Roubillac's statue of Newton in the ante-chapel at Trinity College, Cambridge.

It is true that, in the early years of George III's reign, there were Britons of the intellectual calibre of Hume and Gibbon who were avowed sceptics. Yet even Gibbon thought well to veil his real thought in the decent obscurity of the ironical. And as every reader of Boswell's *Johnson* is aware, these great sceptics and their lesser followers were ill spoken of in society, while the batteries opened upon them by orthodox writers were overwhelming in quantity, though no longer in quality. In 1776, a date usually regarded in retrospect as belonging to the period most marked by infidelity and laxity of doctrine, Hume wrote to Gibbon about the reception of the first part of his Roman history, 'the prevalence of superstition in England prognosticates the fall of philosophy and the decay of taste.' Hume was too pessimistic, but he was speaking from real experience. [See § 44.]

In any case, the scholarly scepticism of the English Eighteenth Century was addressed only to a highly educated audience. Its optimistic philosophy was the outcome of upper-class conditions of life. When, in the period of the French Revolution, Tom Paine appealed to the multitude on behalf of Deism as the proper creed of democracy, a new age had arrived. In the lifetime of the fastidious and conservative Gibbon, it has been said that infidelity, like hair-powder, could only be worn by the aristocracy. The mass of the nation was either actively or passively Christian, accepting the religion that it was taught. [See § 53, 54.] The lowest strata of society had indeed been taught nothing at all, but these also the Charity Schools and the Wesleyan mission were striving to raise out of ignorance to the mental level of understanding Christians.

English Eighteenth Century religion both within the Establishment and among the Dissenting bodies, was of two schools, which we may call for brevity the Latitudinarian and the Methodist. If either is left out of the foreground, the social landscape of that age is wrongly delineated. Each of these two complementary systems had its own function; each had the defects of its qualities, which the other made good. The Latitudinarian stood for the spirit of Tolerance, for lack of which Christianity had for centuries past wrought cruel havoc in the world it set out to save; the Latitudinarian stood also for Reasonableness in the interpretation of religious doctrines, without which they were unlikely to be received by the more scientific modern mind. Methodism, on the other hand, renewed the self-discipline and the active zeal without which religion loses its power and forgets its purpose; and this new evangelism was allied to an active philanthropy. Both the Latitudinarianism and the Methodism of that era have suffered change with the changing times. But the principles which they respectively rescued and embodied have flourished in new forms and combinations, which preserved religion as a powerful force in English life through many changing generations.

Ever since the Revolution, political circumstances had favoured the Latitudinarians. And after the accession of George I the Whig statesmen, who held the keys of higher Church patronage, felt specially bound to protect the Hanoverian dynasty by encouraging the broader churchmanship of scholar statesmen like Gibson and Wake and even of the questionable Hoadly, and discouraging 'enthusiasm,' which in Walpole's day meant the High Church and Jacobite fanaticism of Atterbury and Sacheverell. As the Century wore on, 'enthusiasm' of all sorts, including Wesley's, was regarded as bad form by the clergy of the Establishment and by the upper class.

By the time that George III ascended the throne, the Church was fully reconciled to the House of Hanover, and the political

motive for Latitudinarianism ceased to operate. But the movement continued, driven forward by its own momentum and by
forces deeper than political. Locke and Newton ruled from their
graves. The increasingly scientific spirit of the age demanded that
'the reasonableness of Christianity' should be proved and empha-
sized. The miraculous seemed less actual, and to some less
credible. 'Unalterable law' in the Universe, such as the law of
gravitation which preserved the stars from wrong, was now
regarded as an attribute of God's glory.

> The spacious firmament on high,
> With all the blue Ethereal sky,
> And spangled Heavens, a shining frame
> Their great Original proclaim.
> Th' unwearied Sun, from day to day,
> Does his Creator's Power display
> And publishes to every land
> The work of an Almighty hand.

That hymn of Addison's had appeared in the *Spectator* in 1712,
but it echoed down the Century, till young Coleridge and
Wordsworth 'took up the wondrous tale.'[1]

It was easy for such a religion to slide into Unitarianism or
Deism. Indeed, the English Presbyterian body largely became
Unitarian, with the philosopher and scientist Priestley as its leading
man. In previous centuries religion had been, first and foremost,
dogma. Now, it was fashionable to preach it as morality, with a
little dogma apologetically attached. The religion of the Established Church has been thus described by Canon Charles Smyth:

In the Anglican Church of the Eighteenth Century, the dominant
influence was that of Archbishop Tillotson (1630–1694). His legacy
was partly good and partly evil. On the one hand, he established as the
idiom of the English pulpit, in an age in which our churches, like the
great churches of the friars in the later Middle Ages, were designedly
'fitted for auditories,' a plain, practical and perspicuous prose. The
triumph of the Tillotsonian style marked a decisive break with the
traditional forms of pulpit oratory, deriving from the mediaeval Church.
Latimer, Andrewes, Donne and Taylor were all, in their different ways,
essentially mediaeval. It is possible to see how Tillotson saved Anglican
homiletics from degenerating into a morass of pedantry and affectation.

---

[1] *Cf.* Coleridge's *Hymn before Sun-rise, in the Vale of Chamouni.* For Wordsworth's
relation to Locke, etc., see Mr. Basil Willey's *Seventeenth Century Background,* chap.
XII, and his later and equally valuable work *The Eighteenth Century Background.*

On the other hand, the content of his preaching was little more than a prudential morality, based rather on reason than on revelation, and appealing deliberately to sober common sense. The Gospel of Moral Rectitude rendered to the English character a service which only bigotry would ignore; for 'if, as is the case, the Englishman wherever he is placed, carried with him a sense of duty, this is due to Tillotsonianism.' (Baring Gould.) Yet it falls far short of the Christian gospel; although it still sits enthroned, as our true National Religion, if not in the pulpits of the Church of England, at least in the consciences of English men and English women. (*The Priest as Student*, S.P.C.K., 1939, pp. 263–264.)

In the early years of George III, the parson was rising in the social and cultural scale, living on equal terms with the gentry as never before. But he was not for that any more in touch with the bulk of his parishioners. His sermons, carefully composed, were read from the pulpit as literary exercises, meant to flatter the taste of the elegant young people who sat in the high pew around the slumbering squire, but too abstract and impersonal to move the patient rustic audience in the body of the church. And in the new industrial and mining districts the neglected inhabitants altogether escaped the ministrations of the Establishment, whose antiquated geography was seldom brought up to date by the creation of new parishes. That mission field was left to Wesley.

It was natural that an aristocratic, unreforming, individualistic, 'classical' age should be served by a Church with the same qualities and defects as the other chartered institutions of the country. There was perfect liberty for the individual parson to act according to his own lights, however eccentric. He might have as many twists in his mind as Laurence Sterne; he might even, if he were so ill bred, be a 'methodist' like Cowper's dangerous friend, John Newton, or Berridge of Everton whose preaching threw the people of his own and other men's parishes into the physical agonies of conversion. More often the parson was a 'typical Englishman,' kindly, sensible, mildly pious. [See § 55.] It was a Church renowned for scholarship, culture and freedom. But little pressure was exerted either by episcopal authority or by public opinion to compel the clergy to exert themselves more than they wished.[1]

---

[1] To understand the English Eighteenth Century Church, and the country life of which it was an essential part, read the *Diaries* of the Rev. James Woodforde,

§44 Edward Gibbon

§45 Edmund Burke

§46 The Press Gang (1779)

§47 Sailors going aboard men o' war at Portsmouth (1749)

§48 The soldier's return (1770)

§49 Distribution of charity at Durham (*c.* 1778)

§50 Birmingham Workhouse in 1781 (the central block dates from 1733)

§51 A beggar woman

§52 The disabled cobbler

§53
Church attendance
(c. 1747)

§54
Divine service in
Bath Abbey (c. 1788)

§55 Wayside prayers (*c.* 1788)

§§56 & 57 The old and new meeting-houses at Birmingham (1781)

§58
George Whitefield preaching

§59 John Wesley

§60 The first silk mill at Derby (built in 1718)

§61 Birmingham in 1781—"a town of small industries"

§62 Colliers' houses on the road to Newcastle (*c.* 1788)

§63 Colliers loading coal trucks (*c.* 1788)

§64 Cotton twist mill in Flintshire (built 1783)

§65 Copper and brassworks in Flintshire (built about 1786)

§66 Welsh cattle drovers

§67 A country road in Wales

§68 Welsh farming (*c.* 1780)

§69 A Welsh coal mine in 1785

A living was regarded, like a seat in Parliament or a College Fellowship, as 'a piece of patronage' awarded as a favour and enjoyed as a privilege. An amusing illustration of this way of thought is found in the following epitaph, recorded in Nichols' *Literary Anecdotes* (III, p. 52) :

Here rests all that was mortal of Mrs Elizabeth Bate,
Relict of the Reverend Richard Bate,
A woman of unaffected piety
And exemplary virtue.

She was honourably descended
And by means of her Alliance to
The illustrious family of Stanhope
She had the merit to obtain
For her husband and children
Twelve several employments
In Church and State.
She died June 7, 1751, in the 75th year of her age.

It was characteristic of the age that Gibbon in his Autobiography records a passing regret that he 'had not embraced the lucrative pursuits of the law or of trade, the chances of civil office or India (sic) adventure, *or even the fat slumbers of the Church.*' Ecclesiastical history written by Archdeacon Gibbon would have been as scholarly and as voluminous, but would perforce have been even more decorous and subtly ironical than the actual masterpiece of Edward Gibbon, Esquire.

The social gulf between rich and poor clergy was still almost as wide as in mediaeval times. But the proportion of the well-to-do was greater, for they now included not only prelates and pluralists, but a number of resident parish clergy of good family and connections, living in the parsonage and attending to its duties. The rise in the value of tithes and glebe farms, with the improvement of agriculture, helped this development. In Queen Anne's reign, out of some 10,000 livings, as many as 5597 had been worth less

beginning with Mr. John Beresford's introduction. The receipt of his tithe and the working of his own glebe farm kept parson Woodforde in touch with agricultural life.

'1776, Sep. 14. Very busy all day with my barley, did not dine till 5 in the after noon, my harvest men dined here today, gave them some beef and some plumb Pudding and as much liquor as they would drink. This evening finished my harvest, and all carried into the Barn—8 acres. Dec. 3. My frolic for my people to pay tithe to me this day. I gave them a good dinner, surloin of beef roasted, a leg of mutton boiled and plumb puddings in plenty.'

than £50 a year; a hundred years later only 4000 were below £150. Throughout the Eighteenth Century, country gentlemen came more and more to regard livings in their gift as worth the acceptance of their younger sons. The ideal arrangement, well established by the time of Jane Austen, as her readers know, was a good Rectory, with a bow window, built in a pleasant spot a mile from the manor-house, and inhabited by a son or son-in-law of the squire. The family group was kept together in that way, and the religious needs of the village were served by a gentleman of education and refinement though perhaps of no great zeal— for it was only after the beginning of the Nineteenth Century that the gentleman-parson was likely to be 'serious,' that is to say, evangelical.

But half the livings of England were not so endowed as to support a squire's son. There was still a large class of poor parsons, though not so numerous as in the days of Chaucer, or the days of Charles II when Eachard had written his *Grounds and Occasions of the Contempt of the Clergy*, of which the chief were their poverty and their lowly birth. But even in the reign of George III there were still thousands of impoverished and despised 'blackcoats,' occupying livings of fifty to a hundred pounds a year, or drawing salaries of fifty pounds as curates to absentee pluralists. Pluralism was not, however, always an abuse, for often the best arrangement possible was that a single clergyman should serve two neighbouring parishes, neither of which could by itself support a parson.

The Bishops, almost without exception were either relations of noblemen, or former chaplains to noblemen or tutors to their sons. Some of them, like Joseph Butler, Berkeley and Warburton, were great philosophers or scholars. But none had been raised to the Episcopate for services rendered to the Church, but for services rendered to learning, to lay patrons or to political parties. Church promotion, like many other good things, had been swept into the net of Whig and Tory party patronage, which had succeeded the royal patronage of times gone by. In the Middle Ages the Bishops had been the King's civil servants; now their secular duties had been cut down to regular attendance at the sessions of Parliament, to vote for the Minister who had appointed them and who might yet promote them—for some Bishoprics were worth ten times as much a year as others.

But the Eighteenth Century prelate, having discharged his Parliamentary duties, had more leisure to devote to his ecclesiastical functions than those mediaeval Bishops could afford who had been whole-time servants of the Crown. Some, though by no means all, of the Hanoverian Bishops laboured arduously in their dioceses, especially on journeys over long, bad roads to confirm the faithful. Between 1768 and 1771 the Archbishop of York laid his hands on the heads of 41,600 candidates for confirmation, and the Bishop of Exeter in 1764–1765 confirmed 41,642 in Cornwall and Devon alone. It is impossible in face of such figures, to say that the Bishops were entirely neglectful of their ecclesiastical duties, or that the religious zeal of the population ran wholly into the Wesleyan mission. There is much evidence that Church life, in many districts at least, was strong and vigorous. Nevertheless, there was elsewhere much laxity and neglect. At any rate, the aristocratic clergy we have described were more often examples of the Latitudinarian merits than of the Methodist virtues.

The way of life which came to be called 'Methodism' was older than its name and older than the mission of the Wesley brothers. [See § 56, 57.] As boys, they had been brought up in its atmosphere in the Epworth rectory of their High Church father. It was a way of life devoted not only to religious observance but to self-discipline and work for others. It was seen to perfection in the lay non-juror Robert Nelson, and it inspired those Churchmen and Dissenters who collaborated with him during the reigns of William and Anne in founding the Society for Promoting Christian Knowledge and the Charity Schools. It was seen to advantage in the strict, beneficent life of the charming Lady Elizabeth Hastings (1682–1739), immortalized by Steele's epigram 'to love her was a liberal education'; she devoted her great wealth to charity, in particular to well-devised schemes for the schooling and the University education of poor scholars. 'Methodism' in one form or another inspired much of the philanthropic work of the century that ended with Wilberforce.

This 'method' of religious life was widely spread among the trading and professional classes, whether Church or Dissent. It was at once Puritan and Middle Class in character; it was even stronger among the laity than the clergy; its devotees were not withdrawn from the business of life but strove to dedicate it to

God. 'Conduct, not dogma, stamped the Puritan of the Eighteenth Century. . . . He was irresistibly drawn towards the service of man, who through misery or ignorance, or debauchery, deprived God of the glory that was His due. To men of such a mould charity was obligatory.'[1] The citadel of this way of life was the middle-class home, with its family worship, whence it went out to convert the souls, educate the minds and care for the bodies of the neglected poor.

The greatest and most justly famous of the manifestations of 'methodism' was the revivalist preaching of the Wesleys and Whitefield, which deeply moved a vast mass of human beings hitherto neglected by Church and State. [See § 58, 59.] And fortunately John Wesley's genius lay not only in his power as a revivalist preacher but in his gifts as an organizer. By forming his converts into permanent congregations he began a new chapter in the religious, social and educational history of the working class. The coincidence in time of Wesley and the Industrial Revolution had profound effects upon England for generations to come.

The 'steady laicisation of religion' was the logical outcome of the Protestant atmosphere of the England of that day. The active part taken by the laity, individually and collectively, in religious organization and philanthropic work related thereto had been marked in the days of Robert Nelson under Queen Anne, and was yet more in evidence a hundred years later, particularly among the Wesleyan congregations.

Another important contribution made to modern English religion by the Eighteenth Century was the hymn-book. Isaac Watts (1674–1748), John Wesley's brother Charles and others of less note, produced a body of hymns which, alike in Church and Chapel, gradually displaced the metrical version of the psalms in popularity with congregations who loved to make a joyful noise before the Lord.

Among other ways of dedicating life to God and man was the quiet work of the Quakers. They left to Wesley the task of popular revivalism, wherein they themselves had laboured so fervently in the days of their founder. They had now settled down

---

[1] Miss Jones' *The Charity School Movement* (Cambridge Press, 1938), pp. 6–7 and *passim*. That remarkable book and Professor Norman Sykes' chapter in *Johnson's England* (Oxford Press, 1933), and his *Birkbeck Lectures* for 1931–33 and *Life of Gibson* throw new light on Eighteenth Century religion.

into bourgeois respectability, redeemed by the spirit of love that permeated with its pure influence the exclusive but philanthropic society of Friends. Early in the reign of George II they were already famous for their knack of prospering in honestly conducted business; the poet Matthew Green, who died in 1737, had written of the Quakers and their unorthodox doctrines:

> They, who have lands, and safe bank stock,
> With faith so founded on a rock,
> May give a rich invention ease
> And construe scripture how they please.

The Friends had ceased to be a scandal to Mr. Worldly Wiseman, and had become an accepted national institution.

The humanitarian spirit of the Eighteenth Century with the care it bestowed on the bodies and minds of the poor and unfortunate, made a real advance towards better things. But even so it had its faults. The foundation of hospitals and the improvement of medical service and infant welfare were pure gain. But the educational work done, valuable as it was, is more open to retrospective criticism. The Charity Schools, followed by the Sunday School movement that took on such large proportions after 1780, were indeed the first systematic attempt to give any education to the bulk of the working people, as distinct from selected clever boys to whom the old Grammar Schools had given opportunity to rise out of their class. The new Charity Schools and Sunday Schools had the merit of trying to do something for all, but they had the demerit of too great an anxiety to keep the young scholars in their appointed sphere of life and train up a submissive generation. Modern education may in our time have gone too far in an opposite direction, creating an unwanted intellectual proletariat. But the Eighteenth Century fault, carried over into the education of the early years of the Nineteenth, was excessive emphasis on the difference of classes and the need for 'due subordination in the lower orders.'

The historian of the Charity Schools has well written:

The Eighteenth Century was marked by a very real sense of pity and responsibility for the children whose physical and spiritual interests were lamentably neglected, coupled with a determination to reform them by application of what Defoe aptly called 'the great law of subordination.' The political and religious unrest of the Seventeenth Century contributed in no small degree to the desire of the upper and middle classes to establish social discipline among the poor, who in contemporary opinion were peculiarly susceptible to the poison of rebellion and infidelity. . . . But it would be a misreading of the age of benevolence to see in the prominence enjoyed by the principle of subordination a harsh and unsympathetic attitude of the superior to the lower classes. Far from it. The Eighteenth Century was the age of well defined social distinctions, and it used a language in accordance with its social structure.[1]

But in the early Nineteenth Century, the age of Hannah More, too much of the education and charity bestowed on the poor continued to be class-conscious and patronizing, when an equalitarian spirit unknown in the Eighteenth Century was beginning to render such anxious condescension unpalatable and out of touch with the needs and problems of a different age.

> God bless the squire and his relations
> And keep us in our proper stations

was a sentiment that scarcely aroused comment in the days of Sir Roger de Coverley, but this Sunday School attitude became a cause of scoffing and offence after the Industrial Revolution had put an end to the unconscious simplicity of traditional feudalism.

While the Eighteenth Century made a beginning of mass instruction by starting the Charity and Sunday Schools, it lost ground in Secondary Education by permitting many of the old Grammar and endowed schools to decay. It was indeed a general feature of the age that, while private enterprise and philanthropic zeal opened new paths, chartered institutions grew lazy and corrupt. The resounding defeat of James II's attack on law and chartered rights gave to the hundred years that followed a legal and conservative character that was carried even to excess. To show a charter was to be above criticism. There was no talk of Reform, either of Parliamentary Constituencies, Town Corporations, Universities or Charitable Institutions, until near the end of the Century, and then, alas, 'the unhappy example of France' made Reform anathema. Just as the co-optive municipal oligarchies spent their corporate revenues on gluttonous feasts and

[1] Miss M. G. Jones, *The Charity School Movement*, p. 4. And see Prof. Tawney's review of it in the *Economic History Review* for May 1939.

neglected the duties of town government, in the same spirit the headmasters of endowed schools often neglected and in some cases closed their schools and lived on the endowment as if it was their private property.

But the loss thus incurred by Secondary Education was made good by private schools, financed by fees only, which made much progress in the Eighteenth Century. Such schools, including the Dissenters' Academies, supplied at moderate cost a good education, in which living languages and science held a place besides classics. The old endowed schools had no more use than the Universities for such newfangled subjects.

The Dissenting Academies, that contained men of the calibre of Priestley, also to some extent made good the deficiencies of Oxford and Cambridge. The only two Universities in England excluded all who were not churchmen, and gave so bad and so expensive an education to those whom they deigned to admit, that their numbers shrank to miserable proportions, not half what they had been in the days of Laud and Milton.

Indeed, the spirit of chartered monopoly was seen at its worst on the banks of Isis and Cam. The College Don could hold his Fellowship for life, unless he took a Church benefice; he was not compelled to do any academic work, he was not permitted to marry, and in most Colleges he was forced to take Holy Orders. In their lazy, self-indulgent, celibate clericalism the Dons of the Eighteenth Century resembled the monks of the Fifteenth, and were about as much use. Gibbon, who as a Gentleman Commoner was admitted to the Fellows' table at Magdalen, Oxford, in 1752, thus described their habits:

From the toil of reading or thinking or writing they had absolved their conscience. Their conversation stagnated in a round of college business, Tory politics, personal stories and private scandal; their dull and deep potations excused the brisk intemperance of youth.

At both Universities the undergraduates were entirely neglected by the great majority of the Fellows, though here and there a College Tutor zealously performed duties that ought to have been shared by the whole Society. Noblemen's sons and rich Fellow Commoners, who were much in evidence, and for whom large allowance was made in matters of discipline, were often accompanied by private tutors of their own. The Professors of the

University seldom performed any of their supposed functions. No lecture was delivered by any Regius Professor of Modern History at Cambridge between 1725 and 1773; 'the third and most scandalous' of the holders of that Chair died in 1768 from a fall while riding home drunk from his Vicarage at Over.

At Oxford, by 1770, no serious examination at all was held for a degree. At Cambridge the Mathematical Tripos offered a real test for the rival merits of the more ambitious candidates for honours. Gibbon indeed declared 'Cambridge appears to have been less deeply infected than her sister with the vices of the Cloyster: her loyalty to the House of Hanover is of a more early date, and the name and philosophy of her immortal Newton were first honoured in his native Academy.'

The movement of internal reform, by which the two Universities put themselves upon the road of self-improvement, only began in the very last years of the Century. It may be dated in Trinity, Cambridge, from the crisis of 1787, when it was decided after a severe struggle which carried the disputants before the judgment seat of the Lord Chancellor, that its Fellowships must be justly awarded according to the results of a careful examination. After that change, the College at length drew ahead of its rival St. John's in numbers and academic pre-eminence, though the College of Wordsworth and Wilberforce continued to produce men of great distinction.

The notorious Jacobitism of Oxford under the first two Georges had been highly significant of the limitation of the power of government, and the immunity secured to the subject by charter and the rule of law. Church patronage was in the hands of the Whig Ministers, who would sooner have made a Mohammedan than a Jacobite Bishop. But the Oxford and Cambridge Colleges were outside their jurisdiction, and the failure of James II's attack on the Universities was a red-light warning which preserved academic liberty in England from interference by future governments. If Oxford Dons, after securing their emoluments by taking Hanoverian oaths, chose to get fuddled on Jacobite toasts, King George's Ministers could do nothing about it. In this manner the essential liberty of the Universities, which had been infringed in various degrees by Tudors, Stuarts and Cromwellians, was established by Eighteenth Century practice. In some respects this immunity was abused, but we may thank

God that it was preserved, when we consider the state of slavery into which academic life has fallen in countries which had no such venerable tradition of the rule of law and the liberty of the subject.[1]

Yet in spite of the decadence of the only two Universities that then existed in England, in spite of the decay of the endowed schools specially charged with secondary education, the intellectual life of the country was never more brilliant, and the proportion of men of genius per head of population in the irregularly educated England of George III was immensely greater than in our own day. It would seem that the very highest products of the human mind are the outcome of chance and freedom and variety rather than of uniform organization—of the balance of town and country rather than the dead weight of life in great cities, of literature rather than of journalism, of arts and crafts rather than of the machine. But even if the future can never again produce giants like Burke, Gibbon and Johnson, let alone Milton, Newton and Wren, the number of educated people capable of enjoying an intellectual life of some kind may yet be greater than in the past. [See § 94.]

In the Eighteenth Century the Welsh people recovered, through the instrumentality of religion and education, the consciousness of a spiritual and intellectual life of their own, separate from that of England. The story is singular as well as important.

The Welsh-Englishman, Henry VIII, intended by his political union of the two countries to make the Welsh a part of the English people on free and equal terms. To a large extent he succeeded, because there was no English exploitation of the land and its inhabitants as in Ireland, nor did religion divide the two races. The Welsh gentry in Tudor times adopted the English language, outlook and literature, and ceased to patronize the native Bards. The peasants, having no other leadership, acquiesced; but they continued to speak their own tongue, and to sing its songs to the harp.

In Elizabeth's reign the Church, by translating the Bible and Prayer Book into Welsh, began unconsciously to counteract the

---

[1] For the Universities at this period see A. D. Godley's *Oxford in the 18th Century*; C. E. Mallet, *History of the University of Oxford*, vol. III; D. Winstanley, *Unreformed Cambridge*; Gunning's *Reminiscences of Cambridge from the year 1780*. For Oxford in 1774-5 an intimate and delightful picture will be found in Parson Woodforde's *Diaries*.

Anglicizing policy of the State. That was the seed of much that followed, but it was long ere the full harvest came up. English Puritanism of the Cromwellian type did not attract the Welsh, who remained Cavalier so far as they took any side at all. King Charles's regiments of foot who perished at Naseby came for the most part from the hills of Wales.

When the Eighteenth Century opened, the smaller Welsh squires, like their counterparts in England, were being bought out by the larger landlords. Wales was becoming, legally, a land of great estates; but in its fundamental social structure it was a land of small peasant farms; they averaged thirty to a hundred acres each, they were held on short or annual leases, and were devoted to the old-fashioned subsistence agriculture, feeding the families who cultivated them, rather than serving the market. [See § 68.] There were few big farmers, and few middle-class people of any sort. Under the cloak of the great estate system, Wales was in reality an equalitarian democracy of peasant farmers; and in South Wales there were miners as well. [See § 69.]

Wales was a land of old enclosure, like other Western and Celtic parts of the island. The open-field system had never existed there, except in those parts of Pembrokeshire where the English had settled; and there too enclosure was now taking place. The ordinary Welsh farms were fenced with stone walls or sod banks.

The traditional ways of these remote and rustic folk were not in Stuart times disturbed by the impact of any emotional movement—social, national, political or religious. They were devoted to their traditional music of harp and song, and their religion consisted largely in the singing of hymns. But they were too illiterate to be in the full current of the Bible-reading Protestantism of the day. Economically, and intellectually, Wales was shut off from English penetration by the geographic difficulties of approach. As late as 1768 Arthur Young described Welsh mountain roads as 'mere rocky lanes, full of hugeous stones as big as one's horse.' [See § 66, 67.]

If, then, the Welsh were to have a religious or educational revival of any sort they must make it for themselves; and they did. Beginning in the reigns of William and Anne and going on throughout the Eighteenth Century, Welsh philanthropists promoted an educational and religious mission among their countrymen. The Methodist Churches eventually became the most important part of Welsh evangelicalism, but it had started before John Wesley was born.

To teach the peasant to read, and to put the Welsh Bible into his hands were the motives of those who established popular education throughout the length and breadth of Wales. In England, too, no doubt, the Charity and Sunday Schools were founded for religious reasons, but they were associated with the more mundane objects of defending the State Church either against Dissenters or against Jacobites, and of training up the children of the poor to be industrious and amenable members of a carefully graded social economy. In the simpler, equalitarian peasant society of Wales no such problems presented themselves, and 'middle-class' ideas of utility were unknown; those who founded the Schools desired only to save the souls of men and women, that is to say, to bring them up as Bible-reading, evangelical Christians. This object was achieved, and at the same time the Welsh people, by becoming literate, had new vistas of intellectual and national culture opened to them, coloured always by religion but spreading out into other spheres.

The historian of the Charity Schools, herself a Welsh woman, has written:[1]

It would be difficult to exaggerate the importance and effect of the Charity School movement upon the history and character of the Welsh people. The steady concentration upon piety as the aim and end of all instruction changed a gay and simple people, indifferent in religion and lacking in political consciousness, into a people whose dominant interests were religious and political. The Bible had become the Welshman's manual. Its language was his language, its teaching dominated his social and political life. In it, and in the hymns of Williams of Pantycelyn, the emotional and intellectual interests of the peasantry found satisfaction.

The political influence of the Charity School movement was no less important. Modern Welsh nationalism is the child of the literary and linguistic renaissance of the Eighteenth Century, and in this, as in the religious revival, the charity school movement played a part of chief importance. Before the schools began their work, Welsh, once 'the language of princes and poets,' was in danger of destruction. By the end of the Eighteenth Century it was again the medium of poetry and prose, no longer princely, but bearing upon it the marks of its peasant origin and pious inspiration.

[1] *The Charity School Movement, A Study of Eighteenth Century Puritanism in Action.* M. G. Jones, Fellow of Girton College, 1938, p. 321.

Chapter Three

DR. JOHNSON'S ENGLAND

2. *The Agricultural and Industrial Revolutions begin—Improved communications—Overseas Trade—The City.*

ALTHOUGH 'the Industrial Revolution' is by far the most important movement in social history since the Saxon conquest, it is as difficult to say when it began as to decide when 'the Middle Ages' came to an end. Capitalism, coal, transoceanic commerce, factories, machinery, and trade unions had all, as we have seen, had their part in English life long before the Hanoverian epoch. But the last half of the Eighteenth Century is regarded as the time when industrial change, stimulated by scientific invention and a rising population, entered decisively on that headlong career that shows no sign of slackened pace to-day.

With similar qualifications we may ascribe 'the Agricultural Revolution' to the Eighteenth Century. The immense increase then brought about in the agrarian productiveness of the island was rendered necessary by the rapid growth of its population, which in those days could not have been fed from overseas. This pressing national need was successfully met and exploited, owing to the peculiar social and economic conditions of the time. In the Eighteenth Century the landlords as a class were able and willing to devote their personal attention and their accumulated wealth to the improvement of the land and the methods of cultivation. The capital created by the incipient industrial revolution was much of it conducted by the channel of the great-estate system to fertilize agriculture with money derived from cloth, cotton, coal and commerce. But capital also flowed in the opposite direction, from land into industry: many of the new industrialists who set up factories, mills and businesses in the Eighteenth Century, derived the money they so employed from their own or their fathers' success as cultivators of the land. The County Banks, now growing up in great numbers, assisted this

76

double flow of capital from industry into agriculture and from agriculture into industry.

Indeed, the connection of the agricultural with the industrial revolution was more than a coincidence in time. Each helped on the other. They may indeed be regarded as a single effort by which society was so reconstructed as to be able to feed and employ a population that was rising in numbers with unexampled rapidity, owing to improved medical conditions.[1]

The changes effected in a hundred years may be summarized by contrasting the situation in the reigns of George II and George IV.

When George II (1727–1760) began to reign, manufacture was a function of country life. The 'manufacturers'— a term then used to describe not the capitalist employers but the hand-workers themselves—inhabited ordinary villages each of which supplied its own clothes, implements, and buildings of the commoner kind, as well as its own bread, meat and beer. [See § 65.] Only the 'gentleman's seat,' in the park near at hand, sent to the county capital or to London for its best furniture, its books, china and other amenities in an age of taste and expense, and its more refined wants for the table, though its ordinary food still came off the estate.

Moreover, many rustic villages manufactured not only cheap goods for their own use, but some special line of luxury goods for the market. To take one example out of very many: I possess an Eighteenth Century grandfather clock, still keeping good time, which was made in the small Warwickshire village of Prior's Marston. The woollen cloth, which still constituted the chief item in home and foreign trade, was still manufactured, as regards the main processes in the countryside, and the rapidly growing cotton industry was conducted in the cottage. The towns took some part in the manufacture, but were chiefly distributing centres: Bristol and Norwich disposed of cloth made in Cotswold and East Anglian villages; Leeds and Halifax sold goods

---

[1] In Eighteenth Century Ireland the population rose even faster, from about one and a half millions to four millions. But social conditions and racial characteristics in that island were not favourable to economic change, and instead of industrial or agricultural revolution, there was chronic starvation and frequent famine among the potato-fed population, culminating in the disaster of 1847.

In a well-known passage of the *Wealth of Nations* (Bk. I, ch. xi), Adam Smith connected the physical strength and beauty of the Irish in London with the potato diet of their own land! Whether he was right about that or not, potatoes were an easy but dangerous way of feeding a vast population.

woven in the stone farms or cottages each with its field and cow, scattered along the steep sides of the Yorkshire clothing dales. [See § 60, 61.]

The towns of early Hanoverian England subsisted, not so much by the goods they themselves manufactured, as by their markets, their shops and their commerce. London indeed was industrial as well as commercial, and already displayed many characteristics of modern 'great city' life. Birmingham had always been a town of small industries. And the ports had a sea-life of their own, from great Bristol and its growing rival Liverpool, to little Fowey and Aldeburgh, whose best days already lay in the past. But most other towns were appanages of the countryside which each served. They had forgotten the jealous civic patriotism of the walled mediaeval burgh, and had lost the manufacturing monopoly of its gilds. They were markets for farmers, and meeting-places to which the gentry and their families resorted to shop, to dance and to conduct the affairs of the County. Many squires of the middling sort, especially those who lived more than a hundred miles from the capital, not being able to afford a 'London season,' built themselves good houses in or around the county town, whither their families, on matrimonial hopes intent, migrated from their rural homes for a part of every year. Cathedral cities flourished deferentially in the venerable shadow of clerical patronage. But larger county towns such as Newcastle-on-Tyne and Norwich were, in addition, entrepôts of national trade.

The England over which George IV reigned (1820–1830) was already very different. By that time there had grown up, especially in the West Midlands and the North, a new portent—a number of 'manufacturing towns' and urban districts, given over to factories and machine industry, quite dissociated from the rural life of the country around. The harmonious fabric of old English society suffered a perpendicular cleavage between town and country, as well as expanding the old lateral cleavage between rich and poor. It is true that at that date the harsh distinction between rural and urban life was still confined to certain regions; but during the reign of Victoria it became universal.

A corresponding change in country life itself was already far advanced in the reign of George IV. The manufacture of specialized goods, including many processes of cloth and cotton

III   London from the Terrace of Richmond House (c.1746)

manufacture, had left the country cottages for the factory regions. The improvement of roads had abolished the need for a self-sufficing village, and dwellers in the country now bought in the town articles which their fathers and mothers had made for themselves. Many a village tailor, carpenter, brewer, miller and harness-maker found his occupation gone. The huswife's spindle seldom now twirled on the cottage floor: the term 'spinster' was becoming an anachronism. And the modern farmer produced corn and meat primarily for the town market, only secondarily for home consumption.

By 1820 the 'agricultural revolution' had enclosed the open fields into rectangular hedged fields, where scientific rotation of crops and of pasture could be conducted, and fat stock fed up to a size and weight undreamed of in earlier times. Hundreds of thousands of acres of waste and old woodland had also been enclosed for arable.[1] Even the familiar figure of the highwayman had gone from the macadamized roads, since the heaths and thickets where he lurked had been ploughed up. The orderly new 'plantations' were guarded by gamekeepers, man-traps and spring guns. [See § 72, 73.]

The changes so effected have been called in retrospect 'the agricultural revolution,' because they worked not by expansion of an old economic and social system but by the creation of a new one. Great compact estates cultivated in large farms by leasehold tenants employing landless labourers covered more and more of the acreage of England, at the expense of various forms of petty cultivation and ownership. Small squires, and peasants with diminutive rights in the soil were bought out to make room for the new order. The open fields of the great midland corn area were enclosed into the chess-board pattern of fenced fields which has ever since been the hall-mark of the English landscape. And even in the half of England where enclosed fields had always been the rule, analogous social changes were taking place. For everywhere the larger owners were consolidating their estates by purchase; everywhere squires and farmers were busy with new methods. And everywhere better roads, canals and machines were diverting industry from cottage and village to factory and

---

[1] If Gregory King's estimate (1696) and the Board of Agriculture return of 1795 are approximately correct, two million acres had been added to the agricultural land of England and Wales in a hundred years.

town, thereby cutting off the peasant family from spinning and other small manufacturing activities by which its meagre budget had been eked out.

Taking into account the great variety of local conditions, it is true to say of England as a whole that enclosure was only one, but possibly the most important, of the many changes that combined to reduce the numbers of the independent peasantry, while increasing the aggregate wealth of the countryside.[1]

These changes were still going forward apace in the era of Trafalgar and Waterloo, but they had set in on a great scale between 1740 and 1789, and the whole process may therefore be considered in this chapter. When completed it had changed the immemorial manner of life in rural England.

In the reigns of the later Stuarts and George I the enclosure of open fields, commons and waste was proceeding rapidly, by agreement between the parties concerned or by purchase; but enclosure was still a local expedient rather than a national policy. But after the third decade of the Eighteenth Century the work began to be carried on by a new and more wholesale procedure: private Acts of Parliament were passed which overrode the resistance of individual proprietors to enclosure; each had to be content with the land or the money compensation awarded to him by Parliamentary Commissioners whose decisions had the force of law. Batches of these revolutionary Acts were hurried through every Parliament of George III (1760–1820), assemblies not otherwise famous for radical legislation. But this was the radicalism of the rich, often at the expense of the poor.

The pace of the enclosure of land grew more rapid every decade from 1740 onwards, and was fastest of all at the turn of

[1] In the Lake District, Wordsworth observed that between 1770 and 1820 the number of the freehold 'statesmen' was halved and the size of their holdings doubled: the little farms were amalgamated, because they proved insufficient to support families when the invention of the 'spinning jenny' concentrated spinning in factories and so took away profitable work from the peasant's wife and children. Thus the change was not in that district due to enclosure, for the dales had long before been covered by a network of stone walls which the small freeholders themselves had erected round their own fields.

In the Midland shires, on the other hand, enclosure of the open fields was a determining cause of the disappearance of many small peasants with rights in the land. On the other hand, even in Midland and Eastern counties, enclosure did not by any means always reduce the number of owner cultivators of the yeoman type; see Clapham, I, pp. 103–105, and J. D. Chambers' article in *Ec. Hist. Rev.*, Nov. 1940.

the century. By the time Victoria came to the throne the work of enclosing the open cornfields was nearly complete, though the enclosure of commons continued for the first thirty years of her reign. The area seriously affected by the enclosure Acts comprised about half the English Counties, running south from the East Riding of Yorkshire through Lincoln and Norfolk and the Midland Shires to Wilts and Berks. More than half the total acreage of Northamptonshire was enclosed by Act of Parliament, and over forty per cent. of Hunts, Beds, Oxford, and the East Riding; Leicester and Cambridge Shires were not far behind.

But Kent, Essex, Sussex, the Northern and Western Counties and Wales were little affected by the Enclosure Acts, because so much of their acreage consisted either of fields enclosed many ages ago, or else of moorland pastures so extensive that no one could afford to enclose them until the age of wire fencing. Thus not two per cent. of the area of Northumberland came under the Enclosure Acts, although precisely at this period its landlords were investing great sums of Tyneside capital in agricultural improvement.

For the age of enclosure was also the age of new methods of draining, drilling, sowing, manuring, breeding and feeding cattle, making of roads, rebuilding of farm premises and a hundred other changes, all of them requiring capital. Ever since the Restoration there had been a rapidly increasing movement to accumulate land in large compact estates; the magnates of the realm, the great political Peers, owned a much larger, and the lesser rustic squires a much smaller acreage of England in 1760 than in 1660. The landlord class had therefore more capital and more credit to devote to the now fashionable cause of agricultural improvement.

Owners of large compact estates took the lead—men like 'turnip Townshend,' the retired statesman early in George II's reign; and forty years later 'Coke of Norfolk,' the friend of Fox and enemy of George III. Both Townshend and Coke introduced into Norfolk new crops and new methods—above all, root crops and the marling of light land. Their example put their backward county at the head of English agriculture. Between 1776 and 1816 Coke so improved his land as to raise the rental of his Holkham estates from £2200 to £20,000 a year, and yet make the fortunes of the tenants who paid these higher rents; he granted them the security of long leases on strict terms as to cultivation. And according to radical Cobbett, they spoke of their landlord as affectionate children speak of their parents. His 'sheepshearings' at Holkham became famous all over Europe, and were attended by agricultural experts who gathered, sometimes six hundred together, in that remote corner of Norfolk, to see how land should be farmed and sheep fed. Eighty of the visitors at a time could be taken under the roof of their princely host, and the rest were billeted in the neighbouring farms.

Townshend and Coke had imitators among their brother landlords in every shire. And the farmers of the new type, like Robert Bakewell of Leicestershire, breeder of improved sheep and cattle, were themselves active innovators. The net result was a great increase in the amount of corn produced for the national consumption as bread and beer, and an even greater increase in the numbers and size of the animals. For much of the best land in England, hitherto cultivated in vast open cornfields where the cattle strayed among the stubble in search of food, was now enclosed in moderate-sized fields divided by hawthorn hedges, wherein beasts could be pastured on good grass. And at the same time much more of the arable land was used for raising crops such as artificial grass and roots, to feed the cattle and sheep through the winter. [See § 76, 77.]

And so, for the first time since mankind took to farming, the wholesale slaughter of stock at the end of autumn ceased. Salted meat was replaced by fresh beef and mutton. The immediate result was that scurvy and other skin diseases, which had afflicted even the noblest households like the Russells and Verneys in the Seventeenth Century, grew rare even among the poor. The new facilities for feeding animals all the year round encouraged landlords and farmers to purchase pedigree stock and to study scientific breeding. The average weight of cattle and sheep sold at Smithfield doubled between 1710 and 1795.[1]

Nor was this astonishing increase in the production of beef and mutton made at the price of any diminution of arable. On the

---

[1] Equally remarkable was the improvement in all kinds of horses in Eighteenth Century England. In the Stuart era the English had gone to Arabia and Barbary for sires to their race-horses and hunters. In the reign of George III all the world came to England for horses, from the race-horse to the hardly less noble cart-horse. The horse was then essential to sport, travel and agriculture, and to all these the English gentlemen of the age were devoted. [See § 117, 118, 119.]

contrary, the output of wheat and barley was for a long while able to supply bread and beer for a home population that nearly doubled itself in the course of the Century, while the corn bounties kept up English exports; it was only in the last half of the Century that, as the population rose even more rapidly, the imports of grain from abroad gradually equalled and then passed the quantity exported.

The improvement of land was carried to such a point that wheat was grown where only rye, oats or barley could be grown before. The soil and climate of England is only in a few regions, chiefly in East Anglia, suited to the cultivation of wheat. Yet such was now the artificial improvement of the land by capital supplied by the great estates, that in the course of the Eighteenth Century, Englishmen of all classes became so dainty as to insist on refined wheat bread that had previously been regarded as a luxury of the rich. This new demand began in the town but spread to the country, even to paupers. The abandonment of the coarser wholemeal breadstuffs was bad for the purity of the loaves actually provided by dishonest bakers, bad for the health and bad for the teeth of the English race. But it was a proof of the efficacy of capitalist high-farming.[1]

The social price paid for economic gain was a decline in the number of independent cultivators and a rise in the number of landless labourers. To a large extent this was a necessary evil, and there would have been less harm in it if the increased dividend of the agricultural world had been fairly distributed. But while the landlord's rent, the parson's tithe, and the profits of farmer and middleman all rose apace, the field-labourer, deprived of his little rights in land and his family's by-employments in industry, received no proper compensation in high wages, and in the Southern Counties too often sank into a position of dependence and pauperism. [See § 70, 71.]

The rapid rise in the numbers of the population kept down the market price of labour, at the very time when the labourer was losing his independent sources of livelihood. The wage-earner of George III's reign could therefore make no such bargain for a living wage as his forbears in the reign of Edward III had been able to make, when the Black Death had rendered labour scarce.

---

[1] *The Englishman's Food*, J. C. Drummond and A. Wilbraham (1939), pp. 157, 195, 222–226; *The Bread of our Fathers*, Sir William Ashley, 1928.

Moreover, the poor were now unarmed and untrained to war. 'Bows and bills' no longer rendered the commonalty formidable as in the period of the rising of 1381: in those days they had not been afraid, in spite of Parliamentary Statutes, to come out again and again, with old archers at their head, on strike for the wages and the rights they claimed.

Nor could the hard case of the peasant any longer win such ready hearing from statesmen and publicists as during the far less extensive enclosures of Tudor times. Enclosure had then been regarded as a public crime; now it was regarded as a public duty. Without sympathy from the classes that were framing the Enclosure Acts, the peasant was unable to state his own case with effect. If he lost his strip in the open cornfield, or the pasture for his cow upon the common, the few guineas given him in exchange were soon dissipated in the public house. Even if the Parliamentary Commissioner awarded him some distant acre of land in lieu of his common rights, how could he afford to enclose and drain it? He could only sell it again cheap to the big men, engaged in sharing out the new compact farms that were taking the place of the common and the open field. For they alone could afford to fence and drain at their own charges, as an investment of capital that might some day bring large returns.[1]

In future, to farm the land of England one must either have capital of one's own or have behind one the capital of others. The tenant farmer benefited by his landlord's capital and both had resort to loans from the Bank. The English banking system grew with the enclosure of land, for even the wealthy did much of their fencing and other improvements on borrowed money. Under such a system the poorest class, who had no credit, had little chance of farming with success, and that chance was further diminished by the too frequent disregard of their interests in the new distribution of the village lands. The enclosure of commons, though very desirable from the point of view of national

---

[1] The great expense and difficulty of enclosing and draining the land of a village is illustrated in detail in the case of Bourn, described in Gunning's *Reminiscences of Cambridge*, II, pp. 244–250. In addition to the fencing, an entirely new system of draining had to accompany enclosure, when the furrows between the old strips (that had acted as drains as well as boundaries) were filled up. This ridge-and-furrow draining had in the long run been bad for the soil and the enclosers spent much money in levelling the surface and putting drains underground. The ridge was sometimes five feet above the furrow!

production, meant depriving the poor man of his cow and geese and often of many other small rights of fuel-cutting and so forth, by which he had eked out an independent livelihood. (Ernle, *English Farming*, pp. 305–307.)

It is, indeed, by no means certain that under the new system the rural poor were worse off materially than they had been in the past (Clapham, *Ec. Hist. Mod. Britain*, Bk. I, chap. IV). [See § 79, 80, 81.] But they had less economic independence of squire and farmer. In an aristocratic age that did not seem to signify. But when, in the following era, democracy, armed with new strength in the cities, turned a hard, sharp eye on the 'agricultural interest,' it felt an instinctive dislike for an aristocratic preserve. There was no longer in England, as there still was in other European countries, a peasantry to plead for protection. And so, at the end of Victoria's reign, when the pinch of foreign competition came at last, the urban electorate would listen to no proposal to save British agriculture from ruin.

In the Eighteenth Century, many of those who were divorced from the land by the change of system, went off not unwillingly and made good elsewhere. Of the mercantile, industrial and professional families who grew up and flourished in the new and wealthier England, a large proportion were descended from small squires, yeomen and peasants who had migrated to the towns, with the price of their land in their pockets. The biographies of eminent Victorians often begin with the 'yeoman ancestor.' The Colonies too profited by that sturdy type. Many also of the freehold yeomen retained their own farms and rented other farms besides, rising to greater prosperity through the agricultural changes. The Englishman's instinct to 'better himself' gave the impulse to the rapid growth of wealth, power and intelligence in the country, the towns and oversea. It is only in certain directions that the English are 'a conservative nation.' In the industrial and agricultural 'revolutions' they blazed the trail for the whole world. And because they were the first to tread the new ground, they made some terrible mistakes.[1]

[1] On the agricultural revolution of the Eighteenth Century see Mr. Orwin's chap. X of *Johnson's England* (1933); Mr. East's chap. XIII of Dr. Darby's *Historical Geography of England* (1936); Gilbert Slater's *The English Peasantry and the Enclosures of Common Fields* (1907); Hammond's *Village Labourer* (1911); Lord Ernle, *English Farming*, chaps. vii–xi. For the early Nineteenth Century see Clapham, vol. I, chap. v.

The movement from country to town, alike of men and of manufactures, was conditioned by the improvement of roads and of water carriage. Arthur Young, with the interests of the countryside always at heart, rejoiced to note that when a good turnpike road was made, opening out new markets and enabling new ideas to circulate by the come-and-go of more frequent travel, rents in the district soon rose with the improvement of agriculture. On the other hand, he saw and deplored the beginning of that 'rural exodus' which has been going on ever since. And that also he ascribed to the better roads. In his *Farmer's Letters* (ed. 1771, p. 353), he wrote:

To find fault with good roads would have the appearance of paradox and absurdity; but it is nevertheless a fact that giving the power of expeditious travelling depopulates the Kingdom. Young men and women in the country villages fix their eyes on London as the last stage of their hope. They enter into service in the country for little else but to raise money enough to go to London, which was no such easy matter when a stage coach was four or five days in creeping an hundred miles. The fare and the expenses ran high. *But now!* a country fellow, one hundred miles from London, jumps on a coach box in the morning, and for eight or ten shillings gets to town by night, which makes a material difference; besides rendering the going up and down so easy, the numbers *who have seen London* are increased tenfold, and of course ten times the boasts are sounded in the ears of country fools to induce them to quit their healthy clean fields for a region of dirt, stink and noise.

Without improving communications neither the industrial nor the agricultural revolution could have taken place. The subjects of Queen Anne had great ships in which they sent heavy goods with ease to America and to India, but inside their own island they were still dispatching sacks of coal and hardware strapped to the sides of pack-horses, because wheeled traffic would have stuck in the mud and broken in the ruts of English roads wherever their route crossed a pocket of clay. This state of things had to be changed before much more could be done in the way of economic progress.

There was no effective highway authority, either local or central. Not the county but the parish was charged, most absurdly, with the upkeep of highroads used for the most part by travellers from a distance. The parish naturally scamped the work or left it undone. As it appeared impossible in the Eighteenth Century to reform or readjust local government, recourse was had to private initiative, in which the improving spirit of that age resided. Turnpike companies were granted Parliamentary powers to erect gates and toll bars, and mulct the actual users of the roads, in return for remaking and maintaining some particular stretch of highway. Between 1700 and 1750 as many as four hundred Road Acts were passed; between 1751 and 1790 sixteen hundred! This was the principal machinery by which land communications were steadily improved throughout the Hanoverian epoch. There were many stages in the improvement of roads, and as many in the corresponding improvement of vehicles. In the days of Queen Anne, the 'glass coach' had been tugged along at a walking pace by a team of six horses. By 1750 the stage-coach, drawn by two or four horses, was lighter and more rapid; but it still had no springs, had heavy wheels like a wagon, carried six inside but had no seats for passengers outside, though the humble were sometimes allowed to cling to the luggage on the roof. [See § 74.] Stoppages and overturns were frequent; and the red-coated guard with his blunderbuss was much in requisition, for the highwayman, still at the height of his glory, could easily ride down any attempt to escape. In 1775 the Norwich coach was waylaid in Epping Forest by seven highwaymen, of whom the guard shot three dead before he was himself killed at his post.

Private carriages, also, gradually became more light and elegant as the roads improved. To drive a lady in a phaeton built for two, with its high wheels and smart pair of horses, was a fashionable diversion in the last part of the Century. [See Plate IV.] For long journeys a usual practice was to hire post-chaises with postilions, especially on main thoroughfares where a regular change of horses could be obtained at the posting inn. The roads were thronged as they had never been in any past age, for while the number of vehicles increased the number of riders had not yet diminished. The degree of social, commercial and intellectual intercourse in the days of Dr. Johnson, due largely to improved traffic, was a cause and a characteristic of the high civilization of the period.[1]

---

[1] In 1774 Parson Woodforde paid £4 8s. for a post-chaise from Oxford to Castle Cary in Somerset, a distance of a hundred miles which he performed in a day. This shows the speed but also the expense of 'post-shaying.'

Indeed, a rage for travel seized on Englishmen of all classes, each according to his means. The wealthiest made the grand tour of France and Italy; after six months or two years spent partly in inns and partly as guests in the houses of the foreign nobility, they returned to their country homes with a rich spoil of pictures and statues, selected by their good taste or foisted on their ignorance. [See § 95, 96, 97.] The walls of English manors were crowded with genuine and spurious Old Masters from oversea, side by side with the home products that Reynolds, Romney and Gainsborough were supplying in such profusion. The English 'milords' (and all English gentlemen were 'milords' to the foreign innkeeper) had almost the monopoly of tourist travel in Europe, and their requirements became the standard of posting inns from Calais to Naples. In 1785 Gibbon was told that 40,000 English, counting masters and servants, were touring or resident on the Continent.

At home the improved roads carried visitors so far afield that in 1788, according to Wilberforce, 'the banks of the Thames are scarcely more public than those of Windermere,' though as yet no one but the shepherds went up the neighbouring mountains. Owing to better roads and vehicles, Bath in the days of Beau Nash was so crowded with visitors that it was thought worth while to rebuild its streets in a style befitting the solid splendour and comfort of that age. And at the first census of 1801 this fashionable resort was found to contain 30,000 inhabitants and to stand ninth in the list of English cities in order of population. [See § 85, 86, 87.]

But the condition of the roads still varied greatly according to the nature of local soils. As late as 1789 the highways in Herefordshire, after the autumnal rains set in, were impassable to wagons and carts, and for half the year the county families could only visit one another on horseback, the young ladies riding pillion behind their brothers; towards the end of April the surface was levelled by means of 'ploughs,' each drawn by eight or ten horses. (Gunning's *Reminiscences*, I, p. 100.) In most counties, however, such primitive conditions no longer applied to the main highways but only to the by-roads.

By constant experiment in new engineering methods and new road surfaces, Turnpike Trustees finally reached the perfection of Macadam's roads, along which the Tantivy coaches, with relays of horses at the coaching inns, cantered at anything up to ten miles an hour, in the brief interval of highway glory between Waterloo and the Railways. By 1840 there were 22,000 miles of good turnpike roads in England, with nearly 8000 toll gates and side bars.

As the highways improved, the transport of goods progressed at the same steady pace as the traffic of passengers. The wagon first supplemented and at length superseded the pack-horse. One of the commonest sounds upon the road was the chime of bells announcing the approach of a wagon drawn by four great horses, from whose collars the music was suspended. By an unwritten law of the road, the wagon team had precedence, and all other traffic must draw aside to let it pass.

The improvement of 'inland navigation' was hardly less important than the improvement of roads in opening the way to industrial change. The first half of the Eighteenth Century had been a period of much activity in deepening the navigable rivers and supplying them with locks; the second half saw the construction of new artificial waterways. The Duke of Bridgewater is known as 'the father of inland navigation,' but he could be more accurately described as the father of English canals, for there had always been 'inland navigation' on the natural course of rivers: York, Norwich and many other centres of up-country commerce had always depended on their water traffic. His Grace of Bridgewater, like many other Peers, was a coal owner, and took his duties and opportunities as such very seriously. To link up his Worsley collieries with Manchester by canal, this great nobleman in 1759 allied his Parliamentary influence and his capital to the genius of his half-illiterate engineer Brindley. [See § 82, 83.] That famous partnership, so characteristic of the English as contrasted with the continental nobility, set going the movement that in the next fifty years netted all England with waterways. Improved engineering technique pierced tunnels through the Pennines and Cotswolds, and carried aqueducts high across river valleys.

The canal movement began in the rapidly developing industrial region of South Lancashire and the West Midlands, and soon spread over the whole country. In the 'sixties, Brindley, supported by his Duke, carried through the remarkable engineering feat of the Manchester-Liverpool Canal. In the following decade they linked the Mersey to the Trent by the Grand Junction Canal: its effect on those parts of the countryside which it served was thus described by Thomas Pennant in 1782:

The cottage, instead of being half covered with miserable thatch, is now covered with a substantial covering of tiles or slates, brought from the distant hills of Wales or Cumberland. The fields, which before were barren, are now drained, and by the assistance of manure, conveyed on the canal toll-free, are clothed with a beautiful verdure. Places which rarely knew the use of coal are plentifully supplied with that essential article upon reasonable terms; and, what is of still greater public utility, the monopolizers of corn are prevented from exercising their infamous trade; for, communication being opened between Liverpool, Bristol and Hull, and the line of Canal being through countries abundant in grain, it affords a conveyance of corn unknown in past ages.

The canal system and the turnpike roads did more than stimulate the exchange of goods inside the island; they hastened the growth of overseas trade. Goods from Europe, America, Asia, and Africa could now be distributed in much greater quantities throughout the length and breadth of England; and they could be more readily purchased abroad by the increased export of coal and manufactured goods. For the heaviest mineral and textile products of the Black country and the Pennines, and the fragile ware of the Staffordshire Potteries could now be easily carried by water to the ports of London, Liverpool, Bristol or Hull for shipment oversea.

In this way the whole character and scope of British commerce began to assume its modern form of supplying necessaries for all, instead of merely luxuries for the rich. In the Middle Ages, England's overseas trade had been a quest for wine, spices, silks and other fashions for nobles, knights and merchants, little affecting the peasant population. In Stuart times this was still true in the main, although the greater tonnage of ships meant a bigger bulk of imports and exports, and the use of articles of luxury was spreading among the larger and wealthier middle classes of that era. But it was only in the Eighteenth Century that articles of general consumption were brought from oversea to clothe the bodies and quench the thirst of the King's humbler subjects.

To give one example out of many; in Charles II's reign thousands of well-to-do Londoners frequented the 'coffee-houses,' to enjoy the fashionable new drinks brought over by the East India Company. But early in the reign of George III all classes in town and country were drinking tea in their own homes. In his *Farmer's Letters* for 1767 Arthur Young complained that 'as much superfluous money is expended on tea and sugar as would maintain four millions more subjects on bread.' Tea drinking had become a national habit, a rival to the consumption of spirits and beer; 'the cups that cheer but not inebriate' were already as well known and as highly valued in the labourer's cottage as in the poet Cowper's parlour. In 1797 Sir Frederick Eden wrote:

Any person who will give himself the trouble of stepping into the cottages of Middlesex and Surrey at meal-times, will find that in poor families tea is not only the usual beverage in the morning and evening, but is generally drank in large quantities at dinner.

The poor sweetened the bitter herb with large quantities of sugar. Sugar from the British West Indian Islands was now on every table, whereas in Shakespeare's day, a very limited luxury supply had come from Mediterranean ports.[1]

Until the younger Pitt reduced the high duties, the scale on which smuggling was carried on was prodigious. In 1784 Pitt calculated that thirteen million pounds of tea were consumed in the Kingdom, of which only five and a half millions had paid duty. (Lecky's *England*, ed. 1902, V, p. 296.) Smuggling added to the interest of people's lives almost as much as poaching, and was regarded as equally innocent. Parson Woodforde, a truly good as well as 'respectable' man, wrote on March 29, 1777. 'Andrews the smuggler brought me this night about 11 o'clock a bagg of Hyson Tea 6 pound weight. He frightened us a little by whistling under the parlour window just as we were going to bed. I gave him some Geneva and paid him for the tea at 10/6 per pound.' The inhabitants of this inland rectory thought and spoke of 'Andrews the smuggler' just as one might speak of 'Andrews the grocer'!

With tea, sugar and tobacco finding their way into all homes (whether through the custom house or the smuggler's cave) and

[1] As late as 1700 England consumed only 10,000 tons of sugar, though she had by that time 'sugar colonies' of her own. But by 1800 she consumed 150,000 tons. That is to say, allowing that the population had doubled, the average use of sugar by each Englishman had risen seven and a half times in the Eighteenth Century. For the tea-habits of the working class, see J. C. Drummond, *The Englishman's Food*, pp. 242–244.

with timber mainly supplied from abroad,[1] we are approaching the historical confines of modern England, a community that subsists as the centre of a great overseas Empire and a greater overseas trade providing articles of common consumption for all classes. And already, when George III came to the throne, some of England's chief home industries, particularly the rapidly expanding cotton manufacture of Lancashire, depended absolutely on raw material brought from distant lands. It was left to the Victorian era to add bread and meat to the list of goods supplied mainly from oversea. That removed the last limit assignable to the expansion of the little island in wealth and population, but gave a dangerous pledge to fortune in time of war.

To return to the mid-Eighteenth Century. The port of London received ships from every quarter of the globe; but it monopolized the East Indian trade of England. Not only saltpetre, spices and silks continued to pour into the Thames from China and India, but tea, porcelain and woven cotton goods were now being imported from those distant parts in such quantities that they came within the reach of the mass of the population. They created new wants and the popular demand was so good that home-manufacturers took to making cotton goods and china ware. [See Plate III.]

The American trade was shared by London with Bristol and Liverpool. Liverpool in the Middle Ages had been subsidiary to the port of Chester but, as the estuary of the Dee silted up, the old Roman city gradually lost its sea trade, and the upstart town at the mouth of the Mersey took its place. In the census of 1801 Liverpool showed 78,000 inhabitants, more than any provincial city except its neighbour Manchester-Salford with 84,000.

The branch of American trade specially belonging to Liverpool was the slave-trade, which was closely connected with the cotton manufacture of Lancashire. More than half the slaves carried across the Atlantic made the 'middle passage' in the holds of English ships, though the horrible commerce was shared by French, Dutch and Portuguese competitors. In 1771 as many as fifty-eight 'slavers' sailed from London, twenty-three from Bristol and one hundred and seven from Liverpool. They transported 50,000 slaves that year.

[1] Between 1788 and 1802 Britain imported nearly 200,000 loads of fir timber every year from Northern Europe (Clapham, I, p. 237).

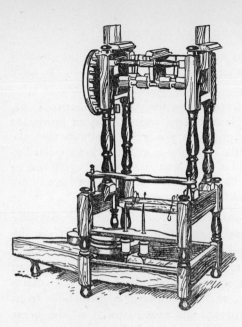

Arkwright's original
spinning machine (1769)

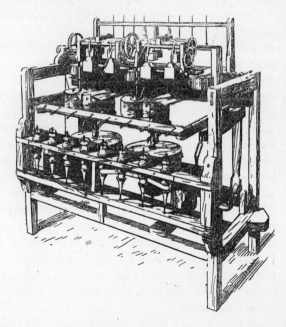

Arkwright's
improved spinning
machine (1775)

One of the first to object to the slave-trade on moral grounds was Dr. Johnson, and another was Horace Walpole, who as early as 1750 wrote to Mann—

We have been sitting this fortnight on the African Company: we, the British Senate, that temple of liberty, and bulwark of Protestant Christianity, have this fortnight been pondering methods to make more effectual that horrid traffic of selling negroes. It has appeared to us that six-and-forty thousand of these wretches are sold every year to our plantations alone! It chills one's blood. I would not have to say that I voted in it, for the Continent of America!

The Liverpool 'slavers' carried cargoes of finished Lancashire cotton goods to Africa, exchanged them for negroes, took the slaves across the Atlantic and returned with cargoes of raw cotton, besides tobacco and sugar. The planters of the West Indian Islands and the American mainland bought Lancashire cotton goods to clothe their slaves, and the supply of negro labour from Africa enabled them to provide the raw material of the great Lancashire industry. The guilty trade and the innocent manufacture were mutually assistant in more ways than one.

Cotton goods were also used by all classes in England, and were already a formidable rival to 'good English cloth.' In a pamphlet of 1782 we read: 'As for the ladies, they wear scarcely anything now but cotton, calicoes, muslin, or silks, and think no more of woollen stuffs than we think of an old almanac. We have scarcely any woollens now about our beds but blankets, and they would most likely be thrown aside, could we keep our bodies warm without them.' In the middle of the Century the great increase of the raw material of cotton gave employment to many thousands of men, women and children in their own homes. The cotton worker's cottage was a miniature factory; the women and children were engaged in picking the cotton, the men in weaving it. This domestic system was a source of independence and livelihood to many families and to many single women who would otherwise have been paupers. But it was not an ideal mode of life. For when the home was a workshop for cotton, it could be neither clean nor comfortable, and the huswife who was in fact a manufacturer could only give odds and ends of her time to cooking and household duties.[1]

As the Century went on, inventions like Arkwright's gradually

[1] Ivy Pinchbeck, *Women Workers and the Industrial Revolution*, chap. VI.

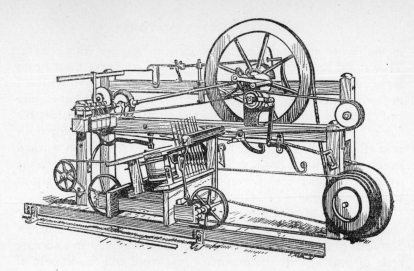

Crompton's 'mule' (1774–79)

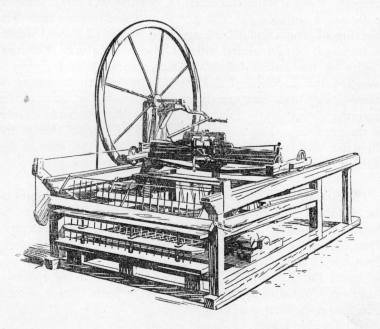

Hargreaves' spinning jenny (designed 1764–67; patented 1770)

95

moved more and more of the work into regular cotton mills. They stood beside running water in the hill country; until steam replaced water-power, the cotton industry was not concentrated in towns. [See § 64.] The Census of 1801 showed that Lancashire had risen in a hundred years from a County of some 160,000 to a County of 695,000 inhabitants, the richest and most populous next after Middlesex. This change was due to the cotton worked in cottage homes or in the mills beside the Pennine streams, to the overseas commerce of Liverpool, and to the trade and various textile manufactures of Manchester.

Cotton was already great, but woollens were still the greatest and by far the most widely diffused national industry, still the favourite of Parliament, protected and encouraged by an elaborate code of laws against the export of raw wool and the import of made cloth. After the invention of Hargreaves' 'spinning jenny' (1767) and Crompton's 'mule' (1775) wool spinning gradually moved from the cottage to the factory, from the country to the town, though the process was not complete till the Nineteenth Century. But the more skilled art of weaving was still conducted in farms or cottages containing one or more looms each. The weaving of woollen cloth was still a source of additional wealth to hundreds of agricultural villages all over England. The merchants of the cities—Leeds, Halifax, Norwich and Exeter— collected and disposed of the goods. Only with the coming of steam-power in a later age did the weavers follow the spinners from the cottage to the factory, from the village and small town to the great city. For several generations of gradual change the domestic and the factory systems existed side by side in the textile industries.

The British West Indian islands and the Southern Colonies of the mainland sent to the mother country not only cotton but sugar and tobacco. It was the age of the long churchwarden pipe. Then, rather suddenly, in the early years of George III, smoking went out of fashion among the upper classes. '*Smoking has gone out*,' said Dr. Johnson in 1773 (Boswell's *Tour to the Hebrides*, Aug. 19). And it remained 'out' for eighty years. Army officers were still to be seen,

Like Mars
A smoking their pipes and cigars,

§§70 & 71
Agricultural labourers

§72 The turnpike road

§73 Footpads attacking a traveller in 1773

§74 Stage-coach on the Dover road in 1775

§75 The ale-bench

§76 Cowherd and milkmaid

§77 Rabbiting

§78 Roasting a baron of beef in Durham

§79 A Northumberland farm kitchen

§80 Burning kelp

§81 Bamburgh fishwives

§82 The Worsley–Manchester Canal: Barton Aqueduct

§83 Canal tunnel at the Worsley coalfield

§84 The first cast-iron bridge. Ironbridge, Shropshire

§85 The Pump Room of the King's Bath at Bath (1789)

§§86 & 87 Bath in 1788–90

§88 Drinking posset (*c.* 1775)

§89 Country dancing in the servants' hall (*c.* 1775)

§90 & 91 Highnam Court,
Gloucestershire
(Interior decoration, *c.* 1760)

§90 The music-room
Copyright "Country Life"

§91 The dining-room
Copyright "Country Life"

§92 Cricket in 1750 on the Artillery Ground

§93 Cricket in 1793 at Marylebone

§94 The Encaenia at the Sheldonian, Oxford (c. 1780)

as a symbol of their dare-devil attitude to life! But for other gentlemen to take tobacco was regarded as 'low' or 'fast,' until the Crimean War brought back into fashion smoking and wearing beards, both in imitation of 'our Crimean heroes.'

But the mass of the people were not bound by the vagaries of fashion, and the national consumption of tobacco increased as the reign of George III went on. So did the wearing of cotton and the use of sugar. The West Indian Islands were therefore regarded as the richest jewels of the English Crown. The nearest approach to 'American millionaires' known in the England of that day were Creoles, British owners of West Indian slave plantations, in which much English capital was invested. The other wealthy class from overseas of whom there was talk and criticism, were the 'nabobs.' The nickname was given to those returned Anglo-Indians who had exploited the new conquests of Clive with an unscrupulous greed, to which the next generation of the English rulers of India put a check. The 'nabobs' raised the price of Parliamentary seats and made themselves otherwise objectionable to the old-established aristocratic society into which they intruded with their outlandish ways.

The northern colonies of the American mainland took English cloth and other manufactured goods, and sent back timber and pig-iron. Timber, iron and naval stores had also to be sought in Scandinavia and the Baltic, for Eighteenth Century England, having exhausted its natural forests, was short of wood for ship-building, house-building and fuel. Coal largely made good the fuel deficiency for domestic purposes and for many manufactures, but it was only now beginning to be applied on a large scale to the smelting of iron. And so, in spite of England's potential wealth in iron-ore, much iron was imported from lands which still had virgin forests to burn.

The manufacturing progress of Eighteenth Century England, rapid as it was, did little to harm the amenities of the island in that fortunate era. London was still the only 'great city,' and Wordsworth in 1802 thought that 'earth has not anything to show more fair' than the sight of it from Westminster Bridge. For buildings still added to the beauty of the land, and ships to the beauty of the sea. The 'coal and iron age' was yet to come.

Josiah Wedgwood (1730–1795) is a characteristic figure of this time, when industry, already beginning to move towards mass production, was not yet divorced from taste and art. He is typical of the fine bourgeois life of Eighteenth Century England. Middle-class employers, even while developing their business on a great scale, were still in close personal touch with their employees, and many of them took an active part in the best cultural and artistic life of the period. 'Captains of industry' were not necessarily 'Philistines.'

The importations of the English and Dutch East India Companies had already inspired Europe to rival Asia in the beautiful art of porcelain. Nor was England behind in the race. The 'china' of Chelsea, Bow, Derby and Worcester vied with the exquisite products of Sèvres and Meissen. These, indeed, were all luxury articles, above the reach of ordinary purses. But Wedgwood, in his Staffordshire works, catered for all classes with his pottery and jasper ware, creating a big market both at home and abroad. He was equally successful in the 'Useful' and the 'Ornamental' Branch of his productions. He laboured with equal zeal at finding new types of beauty, some drawn from the classical models of newly discovered Pompeii, and at extending and cheapening his business. He experimented ceaselessly with new scientific methods, new moulds and new designs. He was indefatigable in promoting canals and turnpikes to reduce his costs of transport and percentage of breakages, and connect his remote Staffordshire potteries, built far inland, with his raw material of china clay in Cornwall and with the overseas markets he hoped to exploit. Between 1760 and 1790 he succeeded in filling not only England but Europe and America with his goods. During this period pewter went out of general use, and was succeeded by earthenware plates and vessels, so that eating and drinking became more hygienic and more delicate. In the next generation, men no longer spoke of 'common pewter' but of 'common Wedgwood.' Thus a Radical paper writes satirically of 'lords and ladies' as the 'china trinkets of the nation, very superior to the common wedgewood pottery of the mass of the people.' (*The Black Dwarf*, Sept. 17, 1817.) [See § 121.]

The most potent and characteristic phase of the whole Industrial Revolution, the connection of iron with coal, was only now beginning. From the reign of Queen Anne onwards, successive generations of the Darby family had been evolving by practical business experiment the application of coal-coke to the smelting of iron, in place of wood-charcoal. In 1779 the third of the Abraham Darbys completed the world's first iron bridge, spanning the Severn at 'Ironbridge,' near the family works at Coalbrookdale, Shropshire. [See § 84.] The great development of the iron trade that followed, with increasing momentum especially in the early Nineteenth Century, took place chiefly in South Wales, South Yorkshire and Tyneside, regions where coal and iron were found together, either near the sea or with easy access to it by river or canal. [See § 62, 63.] But the 'coal and iron age' cannot be dated earlier than the Napoleonic wars.

'In 1769 Arkwright patented the water frame, and James Watt his steam engine: 1769 therefore was the birth year of mechanical power in cotton and engineering. Both Watt and Arkwright had their atmosphere, the atmosphere of mechanical speculation in the bustling north.' The patents issued in the quarter of a century following 1760 were more numerous than those issued in the previous century and a half. (C. R. Fay, *Great Britain from Adam Smith to the Present Day*, 1928, p. 303.)

The Industrial Revolution was well under way. Of the nine millions to which the population of England and Wales had risen at the end of the Century, about one-third were engaged in agriculture but 78 per cent. still lived in the country.

The constant growth of England's home industry and overseas trade throughout the Eighteenth Century depended on the finding of money for those purposes. And it was not then so readily available as in later times; government was a strong competitor in borrowing. But the technique of the money market was being perfected in London. After the decline of Holland, the City 'became the centre of the world's finance, where capital was more easily to be had than anywhere else on the globe.'

Joint-stock methods had suffered a set-back with the bursting of the South Sea Bubble in 1720, but they lived down that discredit, and men learnt to be a little wiser in the future. The Joint-Stock Company was indeed admirably suited to the social structure of that aristocratic but commercially minded Century, for the landed magnate could, without becoming that abhorred thing 'a tradesman,' meet on the board the City man and act with him, so that the political influence of the one could be joined to the business brains of the other. But even more than the Joint-Stock Company, the growth of provincial Banks all over the island financed both the industrial and the agricultural revolutions. These Banks were family or one man concerns, therefore not always secure, but on the whole able to supply the needs of expanding business with the necessary funds.

Then, too, there were the Jew and the Quaker, both rising into the front rank in the City and the Banking World of England, each bringing certain qualities of value.

Between the time when the Jews were expelled by Edward I and the time when they were readmitted by Cromwell, the English had learnt to manage their own financial and business affairs. There was therefore no danger of Hebrew domination and of the answering reaction of anti-semitism. By Hanoverian times, England was strong enough to digest a moderate influx of Jews and, as the prosperity of Holland declined, many of them moved from Amsterdam to London and became prominent there in stock-broking. The Jew helped the development of 'the City.' 'He was ubiquitous and enterprising, persistent but not pugnacious; he ran after customers without regard to his dignity, and made a profit out of articles and transactions which other people rejected or despised. For international finance the Jews had a special bent, overcoming by their tribal bonds the boundaries of nations, and yet as individuals retaining that mental detachment which is so necessary to financial analysis.'[1] During the Seven Years' War, Sampson Gideon was important in the City as a banker; in the next generation the Goldsmids came to the front; and in 1805 Nathan Rothschild founded the most famous of all Jewish houses in London, usefully linked with the family's establishments in other European lands. But besides the great City Jews, there was also a low type of Hebrew moneylender now prominent, abhorred not without reason by his victims, the impecunious and unthrifty of all classes.

The Quakers, too, were becoming a power in finance. They took to Banking, like the Gurneys of Norwich, and had much to do with the establishment of the best English tradition therein; honest, quiet, liberal and peace-loving, they had a steadying effect on the excitable violences and Jingoisms of the financial world.

[1] C. R. Fay, *Great Britain from Adam Smith to the Present Day*, p. 128.

Chapter Four

DR. JOHNSON'S ENGLAND.

*3. Social conditions favourable to art and culture—Love of natural landscape—
Country house life—Sport—Food—Drama and music—Newspapers—
Printing and publishing—Libraries—Domestic servants.*

IF the England of the Eighteenth Century, under aristocratic
leadership, was a land of art and elegance, its social and economic structure was assistant thereto. As yet there was no great
development of factories, producing goods wholesale, ruining
craftsmanship and taste, and rigidly dividing employers from
employed. A large proportion of wage-earners were fine handi-
craftsmen, often as well-educated, as well-to-do and socially as
well considered as the small employer and shopkeeper.

Under these happy conditions, the skilled hands produced, for
the ordinary market, goods of such beautiful design and execution
that they are valued by connoisseurs and collectors to-day: china,
glass and other ware, silver plate, books beautifully printed and
bound, Chippendale chairs and cabinets, all sorts of articles for
ornament and use. Even the commonest type of grandfather
clocks that told the time in farmhouse kitchens were simple and
effective in design, the outcome of a tradition followed with
individual variations by innumerable small firms.

Architecture was safe in the plain English style now known as
'Georgian.' In those days all buildings erected in town or
country, from town halls and rural mansions to farms, cottages
and garden tool-houses, were a pleasure to the eye, because the
rules of proportion, in setting doors and windows in relation to
the whole, were understood by common builders. [See § 13, 14.]
Those simple folk, by observing the rules of proportion laid down
for their guidance in Gibbs' handbooks, kept hold of a secret
afterwards lost by the pretentious architects of the Victorian
era, who deserted the plain English Georgian style to follow a
hundred exotic fancies, Greek, mediaeval or what not, and were
book-wise in everything concerning their work, except the
essential. [See § 6.]

In the Eighteenth Century, art was a part of ordinary life and trade. The pictures of Hogarth, Gainsborough, Reynolds, Romney and Zoffany; the school of miniature portraits that culminated in Cosway; the engravings of Vertue and Woollett; the busts and statues of Roubillac; the furniture and decorations of the Adam brothers [See § 100, 101, 102, 103.]—these were not outbreaks of genius in protest against its surroundings, but the natural outcome of the ethos of the age, parts of a process of supply and demand. [See § 90, 91.] And the same may be said of the literary world of Gray, Goldsmith, Cowper, Johnson, Boswell and Burke. [See § 45.] In its quiet, settled unity of aim and thought it was a classical age, unlike the vexed Victorian, when most of the great men—Carlyle, Ruskin, Matthew Arnold, the Preraphaelites, William Morris, Whistler, Browning and Meredith—were in a state of revolt against the debased ideals of their time, or were fighting berserk each to impose his own strange genius upon the public. Yet the Eighteenth Century, it is true, produced the greatest rebel of all: William Blake was born in 1757.

The spirit bloweth where it listeth: the social historian cannot pretend to explain why art or literature flourished at a particular period or followed a particular course. But he can point out certain general conditions favourable to a high level of taste and production in Dr. Johnson's England.

Wealth and leisure were on the increase, widely diffused among large classes; civil peace and personal liberty were more secure than in any previous age; the limited liability of the wars we waged oversea with small professional armies gave very little disturbance to the peaceful avocations of the inhabitants of the fortunate island. Never was an Empire won at smaller cost than was ours in Canada and India. As to Australia, Captain Cook had merely to pick it up out of the sea (1770). Even the disastrous war in which we threw away the affections of the old American Colonies, though it caused a considerable disturbance in trade, otherwise affected but little the even tenor of life in the defeated country, because our hold on the sea, though challenged, was maintained; even when the French fleet for a while sailed the Channel (1779) it was not starvation but invasion that we had to fear, and the danger soon passed. And so it was again in the Napoleonic Wars. The fact that our island grew most of its own food and also commanded the paths of the ocean, was the dual basis

> Of Britain's calm felicity and power.

which Wordsworth viewed with a just complacency, as he surveyed sea and land together from the summit of Black Comb, in the twentieth year of the War with Revolutionary France. One year of modern totalitarian war is more dislocating to society and more destructive of the higher branches of civilization in England, than a cycle of warfare in the days of the elder or the younger Pitt.

But wealth and security cannot alone account for a great age of taste and art. The Victorian age was even more wealthy and even more secure; yet the houses it built and the things it put into them (except the books) were of no high order. In the Eighteenth Century, taste had not yet been vitiated by too much machine production. Both the maker and the purchaser of goods still thought in terms of handicraft. The artist and the manufacturer were not yet divided poles asunder. They were both men of a trade supplying a limited public, whose taste was still unspoiled because it had not yet seen much that was really bad. Life and art were still human, not mechanical, and quality still counted far more than quantity.

Another circumstance favourable to the arts in the Hanoverian epoch was the aristocratic influence which coloured many aspects of life besides politics. The social aristocracy of that day included not only the great nobles but the squires, the wealthier clergy, and the cultivated middle class who consorted with them on familiar terms, as we read in Boswell's Johnsonian dialogues, and in the life-history of the most princely of professional men, Sir Joshua Reynolds. That great society, broad-based on adequate numbers, and undisputed in its social privilege, could afford to look for quality in everything. The higher ranks of this aristocracy set the tone to the bourgeoisie and professional class, and they in return supplied the nobles with brains and ideas—as, for instance, Burke supplied Lord Rockingham. The leaders of the Eighteenth Century were not harassed by the perpetual itch to make money and yet more money, to produce more and yet more goods no matter of what sort, as were those mighty children of Mammon who in the Nineteenth Century set the tone to England, America and all the world. The aristocratic atmosphere was more favourable to art and taste than either the bourgeois or the democratic have since proved in England, or the totalitarian in Europe.

Indeed, aristocracy functioned better as a patron of art and letters than even the old-fashioned form of Kingship. Monarchy may sometimes have taste, as in the France of Louis XIV and XV, but it concentrates everything at Court as the one acknowledged centre of light and leading. But the English aristocracy had not one centre but hundreds, scattered all over the country in 'gentlemen's seats' and provincial towns, each of them a focus of learning and taste that more than made up for the decay of learning at the official Universities and of taste at the Hanoverian Court. George II patronized Handel's music but nothing else. It did not matter, because patronage had passed into thousands of other hands—though not yet into the hands of millions. Oxford University did nothing for Gibbon, and Royalty had nothing to say to him except, 'Hey, what Mr. Gibbon, scribble, scribble, scribble!' But the reading public of the day was just of the size and quality to give proper recognition to his greatness the moment his first volume appeared (1776).

Eighteenth Century taste was not perfect. The limits of its sympathy in literature are notorious. Even in art, too much, perhaps, was thought of Reynolds and not enough of Hogarth and Gainsborough. By the foundation of the Royal Academy in 1768 Sir Joshua made the purchase of pictures fashionable among the rising middle class seeking a hall-mark of gentility. No doubt he thereby conferred a material benefit on his brother artists by creating a yet wider demand for their wares. But did that most noble knight unwittingly prepare the way for the vulgarization of art? And did his Royal Academy serve to stereotype overmuch particular kinds of painting and sculpture? [See § 104, 106.]

The romantic circumstance of the discovery of the buried cities of Herculaneum and Pompeii excited an immense curiosity, which had better consequences, perhaps, for archaeology than for art. [See § 95.] Graeco-Roman statuary of the second order was taken as the standard of judgment, and the next generation of Academy sculptors, Nollekens and Flaxman, insisted that all statues, even of contemporary British statesmen, must be moulded on that fashion, must be draped in the toga of the ancients (like the statue of Fox in Bloomsbury Square) and in other respects must cease to follow the true Renaissance tradition of Roubillac (died 1762). Oddly enough, at the very same time Benjamin West reversed this law of clothes as regards historical *painting*; in spite of the grave but friendly remonstrances of Sir Joshua himself, West insisted that his picture of the death of Wolfe (exhibited in the Academy of 1771) should show the general and his men in contemporary British uniform and not in ancient armour, as modern heroes in battle were wont to be painted for their greater renown. By his obstinacy in favour of this bold innovation, West won a charter of liberty for the school of historical painting which he founded, and which he made exceedingly popular especially through the medium of engravings.

But in spite of the vagaries of fashion in art and much variety in the powers of its leading practitioners, the tone of the Eighteenth Century was favourable to high quality in the arts and crafts. England was filled full of beautiful things of all kinds, old and new, native and foreign. Houses in town and country were as rich as museums and art galleries, but the books, the engravings, the china, the furniture, the pictures were not flaunted or crowded for exhibition, but were set in their natural places for domestic use in hospitable homes. [See § 90, 91.]

Indoors and out it was a lovely land. Man's work still added more than it took away from the beauty of nature. Farm buildings and cottages of local style and material sank into the soft landscape, and harmonioulsy diversified and adorned it. The fields, enclosed by hedges of bramble and hawthorn set with tall elms, and the new 'plantations' of oak and beech, were a fair exchange for the bare open fields, the heaths and thickets of an earlier day. Nor indeed had all these disappeared. And near to almost every village was a manor-house park, with clumps of great trees under which the deer still browsed. [See § 75, 76, 77.]

In the last decade of the Century arose the great school of landscape painters, chiefly in water-colour—Girtin and the youthful Turner, soon to be followed by many more, including Crome and Cotman of the Norwich school, and Constable himself. They depicted England at her best, at the perfect moment before the outrages on her beauty began. In earlier years the fashionable demand had been for portraits and subject pictures rather than for landscapes, in spite of the power in that line shown by Gainsborough and Richard Wilson. But all through the period there had been growing up a conscious admiration of scenery, of landscape in its broader outlines. It was reflected and stimulated by literature from the first appearance of Thomson's *Seasons* in 1726, onwards through Cowper, till Wordsworth finally transformed and sublimated the theme. But no written word could express the unique glory of our island, which the painters alone could show, the shifting lights and shades of sky, earth and foliage in our water-laden atmosphere. Thus the joy of the English in their land received its expression in letters and in art, at the hands of Wordsworth and the landscape painters, just as the Eighteenth Century closed and the new era began.

As far back as the reign of George II, this novel delight and interest felt in the wilder and larger features of landscape had altered the fashion of laying out the 'grounds' of a country house. The formal garden, the walks decorated by leaden statuettes in the Dutch style prevalent under William and Anne, and the yew hedges clipped into fantastic shapes, were swept away in order to bring the grass and trees of the park up to the walls of the manorhouse. The fruit and vegetable garden within its high brick walls, now regarded as an essential appendage of a country house, was placed at a little distance, out of sight of the front windows. These changes were conducted under the influence of William Kent and his successor 'Capability Brown,' so called from his habit of saying, when called in to consult on the new laying out of a gentleman's grounds,

'I see great *capability* of improvement here.' [See § 110, 111.]

No doubt there was loss as well as gain. It was sad that hundreds of those charming lead figures were cast away, to be melted down to shoot Americans and French. But the abolition of Dutch gardens to make room for grass slopes and trees visible from the windows, testified to the growing delight in natural scenery, which soon led Englishmen to take pleasure even in mountain forms, to flock to the Lake District, and in the following century to the Scottish Highlands and the Alps, hitherto abhorrent to civilized men. [See § 112, 114, 115.]

This instinctive craving for the larger features of untamed nature was an inevitable reaction on the part of a society growing over-civilized. In older times forests and thickets were everywhere close at hand, and man was constantly at war with the

V "To drive a lady in a phaeton . . .

was a fashionable diversion in the last part of the century"

wilderness; in those days he sought relief from the struggle in formal gardens. Now he had conquered. The countryside, though still beautiful, was tamed down to an affair of hedgerows and 'plantations.' So nature in her shaggy reality must be deliberately sought out further afield, in accordance with Rousseau's mystic doctrines.

The taste for mountains which began in the latter part of the Eighteenth Century, was accompanied by a corresponding love for the 'seaside,' hitherto neglected. It is true that in the first half of the Century the new custom of resort to 'seaside watering-places' had been medicinal in purpose. At the doctor's orders people went to inhale the sea air at the village of Brighthelmstone (Brighton), or drink the well-water at Scarborough, and even to dip in the waves. A picture of Scarborough beach in 1735 shows male visitors swimming [See § 116]; and at Margate by 1750 'Beale's bathing machines,' dragged by horses took either sex into the water, which they could enter down a ladder under cover of a hood, and thence if they wished swim out.

But those who went for the medicine of the body, found also a medicine of the soul. The contemplation of the sea and of coast scenery added an attraction which drew ever larger crowds to the cliffs and sands, primarily for health, but also for a mental pleasure that was a part of health. It is significant that in the latter part of George III's reign the waves of the sea were, for the first time, being truly and lovingly delineated by Turner. Ships had been well painted before, but not the real waters on which they sailed. Poets had often before described the terrors of the ocean; now they also described its beauty and exhorted it to roll on!

In the Eighteenth Century, for the first time, the sites of new country houses were chosen for aesthetic, not merely for practical reasons. They were often placed on rising ground to 'command the prospect.' This was rendered possible by the increasing control of the wealthy over artificial supplies of water. Cowper, who disapproved of 'the great magician Brown,' complained that the houses he induced people to build on exposed hill tops were very cold until trees had grown up to protect them, and that his landscape gardening cost so much as to ruin many of his more enthusiastic patrons (*The Task*, Book III). Certainly people tended to 'overbuild' themselves, and mortgaged their estates in their zeal for 'improvement,' like the last Earl Verney of Claydon.

Fashion has many odd vagaries. A taste for artificial ruins preceded by many years the 'Gothic revival' in literature, religion and architecture. Before Pugin or Sir Walter Scott were born, and half a century before their influence was felt, ruined mediaeval castles were being erected as part of the 'landscape,' and fanciful 'Gothic' ornament was fastened on to some houses.[1] [See § 107, 108, 109, 113.] But fortunately the mansions which the Eighteenth Century folk built for their own habitation were for the most part sound Georgian, sometimes with touches of the classical, such as porticos and pediments, which could, however, be made to blend not unnaturally with the Georgian style, itself of renaissance origin. The more pretentious were in the Palladian or some other style that the owner had observed on his Italian tour. [See § 98, 99.]

In these country houses, great and small, life was lived at its fullest. The zeal for estate management and agricultural improvement took the squire out on his horse at all hours of the day, and the ladies at home were as usefully employed, organizing and providing for their large households, and themselves busy with the needle or in the preserving room. For weeks and months together large parties of visitors were entertained with much eating and drinking, with field sports, with music and literature, with cards and dice which sometimes brought ruin to host or guest. [See § 88, 89.] It was usual now for a country house to have a library proportioned to its size, filled with leather-bound volumes stamped with the family arms or crest—the English, Latin and Italian classics, and many large tomes of splendidly illustrated travels, local histories or books of engravings and prints. Twentieth Century civilization has nothing analogous to show to these private libraries.

In many respects it was a free-and-easy society. Charles Fox set the fashion of dressing carelessly. The House of Commons—the central point of the English aristocracy—produced the impression of *déshabillé* on a foreign visitor in 1782:

[1] Even before the building of the Gothic parts of Strawberry Hill begun by Horace Walpole in 1750, Gothic ornament in external and interior decoration of houses, of a very meretricious kind, was not unknown; it was followed by a taste for 'Chinese' motifs. But these fancies were exceptional. See Ketton-Cremer, *Horace Walpole*, pp. 151–154. [See § 105.]

The members have nothing particular in their dress; they even come into the House in their great coats and with boots and spurs. It is not at all uncommon to see a member lying stretched out on one of the benches, while others are debating. Some crack nuts, others eat oranges. There is no end to their going in and out; and as often as anyone wishes to go out, he places himself before the Speaker and makes him his bow, as if, like a schoolboy he asked his tutor's permission. (Moritz, *Travels*, H. Milford, 1924, p. 53.)

Perhaps no set of men and women since the world began enjoyed so many different sides of life, with so much zest, as the English upper class at this period. The literary, the sporting, the fashionable and the political 'sets' were one and the same. When the most unsuccessful of all great politicians, Charles Fox, said on his deathbed that he had lived 'happy,' he spoke the truth. Oratory at its highest, politics at its keenest, long days of tramping after partridges, village cricket, endless talk as good as ever was talked, and a passion for Greek, Latin, Italian and English poetry and history—all these, and alas also the madness of the gambler, Fox had enjoyed and had shared with innumerable friends who loved him. Nor had he been less happy during the long wet day at Holkham which he spent sitting under a hedge, regardless of the rain, making friends with a ploughman who explained to him the mystery of the culture of turnips.

In versatility of action and enjoyment Fox represented the society in which he was so long the leading figure. All the activities of town and country, of public and private life, were pursued and relished by those liberal minded, open-hearted aristocrats, whom their countrymen felt not the slightest wish to guillotine. The more fashionable among them had grave faults. In spite of the saying 'as drunk as a lord,' there is indeed ample evidence that excessive drinking was a habit among all classes of Englishmen, low as well as high. But heavy gambling and connubial infidelity were perhaps most observable in the highest grade of society at that time, before the evangelical influence, having dealt first with the common people, returned to lay a restraining hand on the upper class, fitting them for the ordeal of the Nineteenth Century, when their conduct would be canvassed and their privileges challenged. Meanwhile the hour was theirs and it was golden. [See § 120.]

This classical age, when Dr. Johnson's Dictionary (1755) did much to fix the words recognized as good English, saw also the settlement of spelling by rules now insisted on among all educated people. In the age of Marlborough, even queens and great generals spelt very much as they liked. But in 1750 Lord Chesterfield wrote to his son:

I must tell you that orthography, in the true sense of the word is so absolutely necessary for a man of letters, or a gentleman, that one false spelling may fix a ridicule upon him for the rest of his life. And I know a man of quality who never recovered the ridicule of having spelled *wholesome* without the w.

At the same time he advises the young man to read Plato, Aristotle, Demosthenes and Thucydides, whom none but adepts know, though many quote Homer. It is Greek, adds Chesterfield, that must distinguish a man; Latin alone will not. It is significant that the high-priest of fashion at that period when fashion meant so much, regarded classical scholarship of a very real kind as proper to the character of a gentleman.

Older forms of the chase were yielding to the pursuit of the fox. The hunting of deer, the King of sports in all past ages, became a memory, except on Exmoor and in a few other regions. As early as 1728 some Hunts had already come down to the ignominious 'carting' of deer, the beginning of the end. The reason is evident: the destruction of forests, the enclosure of wastes and the encroachments of agriculture caused the continual decrease of the herds of wild deer that used to roam the countryside at large. In the reign of George III, stags browsing under the oaks were an ornament to a gentleman's park, safely enclosed within its pales, but were no longer beasts of the chase. The owner or his gamekeeper would shoot them in season, for the table.

Hare-hunting, beloved of Shakespeare and of Sir Roger de Coverley, went out more slowly. Although fox-hunting was gaining ground throughout the Eighteenth Century, as late as 1835 a sporting magazine enumerated 138 packs of harriers as against 101 packs of foxhounds. The harriers had this advantage, that the countryman on foot could keep within view of the shorter circles of the hunted hare, more easily than he could follow the longer and straighter run of the fox. But although the democratic and pedestrian element formed a smaller part of the field in fox-hunting, 'the hunt,' with its red or blue coats, its hounds and horn, caught the imagination of all classes in the countryside; spirited fox-hunting songs were shouted as loudly and as joyously on the ale bench as round the dining table of the manor.

In the reign of George III fox-hunting had become in its essential features what it has been ever since, except that very few then joined a Hunt who were not resident in the County. But it had ceased to be an affair of one or two neighbours riding over their own lands. The hounds now ran over a whole district, and great Hunts like the Badminton, the Pytchley and the Quorn carried the science to the point where it has remained ever since. The runs became longer as the Century advanced, and the Enclosure Acts, by cutting up the open fields with hedges in the hunting shires of the Midlands, made a greater call on the quali- ties of the horse and its rider. But even as early as 1736, Somerville, the squire-poet of *The Chase*, describes jumping as an important part of the game:

> with emulation fired
> They strain to lead the field, top the barred gate,
> O'er the deep ditch exulting bound, and brush
> The thorny-twining hedge. [See § 117.]

Shooting in the Eighteenth Century was rapidly taking the place of the hawking, netting and liming of wild-fowl. Its pro- cedure was moving towards present-day practice, but more slowly than that of hunting. 'Driving' the birds had not yet come in. The long, hand-cut stubble still made it easy for sportsmen to get near partidges, walking up to them behind the faithful setter. Pheasants were not driven out of covers high over the heads of the 'guns,' but were flushed out of the hedgerows and coppices by packs of yelping spaniels and shot as they rose. In northern moorlands, grouse were less numerous than to-day, but less wild. Blackgame and duck were very numerous on suitable land, and everywhere troops of hares did much injury to the farmer; rabbits were not quite such a pest as they are now (1939), because the proportion of grass land to arable was smaller. Ruffs and reeves, bittern, plovers, wheatears, landrails and other wild birds were shot as freely as more regular game.

The muzzle-loading flint-and-steel gun of slow ignition was very different from the modern ejector; its action being slower, it was necessary to shoot much further in front of the bird, a feat reflecting all the more credit on the performance of Coke of Norfolk, who on more than one occasion killed 80 partidges in less than a hundred shots. Reloading was a matter of time, and, if carelessly done, of danger; therefore after each shot the sportsman had to halt and the dog was bidden 'down charge' while the 'charging' of the gun took place. In the middle of the Eighteenth Century, gamekeepers, like Black George in *Tom Jones*, were not so generally respectable a class of men as their successors of a later day. They were often 'the worst of poachers, taking one brace for the master, and two for themselves.' But neither the gentry nor their keepers were the only people who took game; there was never a truce to the poaching war in old England.

In Stuart times cricket had grown up obscurely and locally, in Hampshire and Kent, as a game of the common people. The original method of scoring, by 'notches' on a stick, argues illiteracy. But in the early Eighteenth Century cricket enlarged both its geographic and its social boundaries. In 1743 it was observed that 'noblemen, gentlemen and clergy' were 'making butchers, cobblers or tinkers their companions' in the game. Three years later, when Kent scored 111 notches against All England's 110, Lord John Sackville was a member of the winning team of which the gardener at Knole was captain. Village cricket spread fast through the land. In those days, before it became scientific, cricket was the best game in the world to watch, with its rapid sequence of amusing incidents, each ball a potential crisis! Squire, farmer, blacksmith and labourer, with their women and children came to see the fun, were at ease together and happy all the summer afternoon. If the French *noblesse* had been capable of playing cricket with their peasants, their chateaux would never have been burnt.

Until the later years of the Century the two wickets each consisted of two stumps, only one foot high, about twenty-four inches apart, with a third stump or bail laid across them. The space between the stumps was known as the 'popping hole,' into which the batsman had to thrust the end of his bat, before the wicketkeeper could 'pop' the ball into it at the risk of a nasty knock for his fingers. The bowler trundled the ball fast along the ground against the low wicket; when, as often happened, the balls passed between the stumps without hitting them, the batsman was not out. The bat curved at the end like a hockey-stick. Towards

§95 Sir William Hamilton—antiquary and diplomat

§96 The Uffizi Gallery at
Florence (in the 1770's).
Most followers of the
Grand Tour would visit
this

§97 The sculpture gallery
at Newby Hall, Yorkshire

§98 Hatchlands, Surrey (1759)

§99 West Wycombe Park, Buckinghamshire (1735–65)

§100 Robert Adam

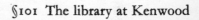

§101 The library at Kenwood

§102 Syon House—the anteroom

§103 Adelphi Terrace in 1792

§104 Self-portrait of Sir Joshua Reynolds as a young man

§103 Horace Walpole

§106 The life school at the Royal Academy (1772)

§107

Arthur Young (the agriculturist) thought in 1770 that these farm-buildings (§109) combined "much beauty and utility". The waterfall (§108) is his own sketch of a scene than which (he says) "nothing can be fancied more grand, more beautiful or romantic"

§108

§109

§110 William Kent

§111 "Capability" Brown

§112 An eighteenth-century landscape garden. Stourhead, Wiltshire

§113 Mow Cop Folly, Cheshire (built 1750)

¶114 An eighteenth-century picnic in the Farne Islands

§115 The servants' picnic

§116 Bathing at Scarborough in 1745

the end of the Century the game was radically altered by abolishing the 'popping hole,' adding a third stump, and raising the height of the wicket to 22 inches. The straight bat was soon adopted as a result of these changes. [See § 92, 93.]

Eighteenth Century Englishmen were much addicted to the pleasures of the table, and our island cooking had already taken on certain characteristic merits and defects. [See § 78.] Foreigners were astonished at the vast quantity and excellent quality of the fish and of the red and white meat consumed, but did not appreciate the English policy about vegetables, which only came in as trimmings to meat. English cooks seemed as incapable of turning out a vegetable dish as of producing anything better than 'brown water' by way of coffee. But, however served, vegetables from the kitchen gardens of rich and poor were now abundant and various: potatoes, cabbages, carrots and turnips, sprouts, cucumbers and salad were eaten with the meat as plentifully as they are to-day. And already sweet dishes and puddings— especially 'plumb pudding' as Parson Woodforde ominously spelt it—held pride of place on the English table.

Woodforde's flour bill for the year 1790, indicating the very limited amount of bread baked and eaten at the Rectory, was £5.7.6. For the same period his bill for meat was £46.5.0. The English middle-class household of this period was essentially carnivorous and well 'above the bread level' in its diet. For the same year his bill for malt for his home brewing was £22.18.6. The worthy parson recorded his meals in his diary: a good, ordinary dinner for a fair-sized company (1776) was a 'leg of mutton boiled, a batter pudding, and a couple of ducks.' Another (1777) consisted of 'a couple of rabbits smothered with onions, a neck of mutton boiled, and a goose roasted, with a currant pudding and a plain one, followed by the drinking of tea.' 'A very elegant dinner,' which he enjoyed at Christ Church, Oxford (1774), comes nearer to our conception of those corporate feasts in which the more privileged among our ancestors so much delighted:

The first course was, part of a large cod, a chine of mutton, some soup, a chicken pye, pudding and roots etc. Second course, pidgeons and asparagus, a fillet of veal with mushrooms and high sauce with it, rosted sweetbreads, hot lobster, apricot tart and in the middle a pyramid of syllabubs and jellies. We had a desert of fruit after dinner, and Madeira, white Port and red to drink as wine. We were all very cheerful and merry.

In the country parts, riding home on a dark night 'when merry' was a frequent cause of accidents and death.

The young German, Moritz, who resided in England in 1782 with a meagre purse, fared less well than Parson Woodforde, for he was at the mercy of English landladies, who treated him as too many of them still treat their unlucky guests,

An English dinner [he wrote] for such lodgers as I am, generally consists of a piece of half-boiled or half-roasted meat; and a few cabbage leaves boiled in plain water; on which they pour a sauce made of flour and butter.

(This fluid, I suspect, was in Voltaire's memory when he said the English had a hundred religions and only one sauce!)

But, adds Moritz:

The fine wheaten bread which I find here, besides excellent butter and Cheshire cheese, makes up for my scanty dinners. The slices of bread and butter, which they give you with your tea, are as thin as poppy leaves. But there is another kind of bread and butter usually eaten with tea, which is toasted by the fire, and is incomparably good. You take one slice after the other and hold it to the fire on a fork till the butter is melted so that it penetrates a number of slices all at once : this is called *toast*.

Economic circumstances made the first half of the Eighteenth Century an age of relative plenty for the working class. Many of them, at least, breakfasted on beer, bread and butter, quantities of cheese, sometimes meat. At midday many made a plentiful if coarse meat meal. Smollett, in *Roderick Random* (1748), describes his entry into

a cook's shop, almost suffocated with the steams of boiled beef, and surrounded by a company of hackney coachmen, chairmen, draymen and a few footmen out of place or on board wages, who sat eating shin of beef, tripe, cowheel and sausages at separate boards, covered with cloths which almost turned my stomach.

But the innumerable local varieties of wages and conditions of life make generalizations about working-class diet exceedingly unsafe. Many lived mainly on bread and cheese, some vegetables, beer and tea.

The theatre had a vigorous popular life in Eighteenth Century England. In the early years of its resuscitation under Charles II it had been confined to London and to Court patronage. It now spread far and wide. Companies were established in the larger provincial towns, and strolling players were always moving round the countryside, acting in barns and town halls before rustic audiences. Parson Woodforde records their periodic appearance in the Court House of Castle Cary, a Somersetshire village of 1200 inhabitants, where from time to time they acted *Hamlet*, the *Beggar's Opera* and other good pieces. Farquhar's *Beaux' Stratagem* remained a favourite long after the untimely death of its author in 1707, but there was a shortage of good new plays, until more than sixty years later Goldsmith and Sheridan again supplied a few first-rate comedies.

On the other hand, as we should expect in the country that so effectually patronized Handel's Oratorios, the musical side of the theatre was excellent. Thomas Arne (1710–1778) set Shakespeare's songs and wrote the incidental music of many plays. And the English light opera (which had a continuous life from the *Beggar's Opera* to Gilbert and Sullivan) flourished exceedingly in the days of Dibdin (1745–1814). As a very young man he wrote the music of *Lionel and Clarissa*; and he long continued to supply his countrymen with the sentimental, patriotic and nautical songs they loved to sing, such as 'Poor Jack' and 'Tom Bowling.' To the people of England, music was not then an affair only of listening. They were not ashamed to try their own voices, for they rode and walked and worked out of doors, not always in a hurry and not always in a crowd; and indoors they had much leisure, and if they wanted music must make it for themselves. [See § 8.]

The dramatic genius of Garrick in the middle of the Century, and of Mrs. Siddons after him, made the London theatre famous. The garbled versions of Shakespeare that they acted—*Lear* with a 'happy ending'—arouse our horror. But we must recognize the service done by the actors and the literary critics of that age, who between them persuaded the English that Shakespeare was the greatest glory of our nation. He was read, quoted, known far more generally than to-day, for poetry and great literature had not then to meet any serious competition from printed matter of a more ephemeral kind. The reading world was just the size to give great literature its best chance. Milton was then known and honoured only less than Shakespeare.

The printed newspaper had by the middle of the century quite displaced the written 'news letter.' Early in George III's reign, its price was twopence or threepence owing to the tax, and in size it had grown to the 'folio of four pages' that Cowper expected every evening in his country retreat, and read aloud over the teacups to the ladies,

> Fast bound in chains of silence, which the Fair,
> Though eloquent themselves, yet fear to break.

Each of the four folio pages had four columns. After 1771, when the right to publish debates was silently conceded by the two Houses of Parliament, that task became an important function of the newspaper. Since the limited public that bought it was intensely and intelligently political, more than half the news space was in session time given up to these reports. One or more of the four folio pages were devoted to paying advertisements, telling of books, concerts, theatres, dresses and various kinds of people in want of domestic employment. The rest of the paper was occupied by poetry, articles serious and comic, letters to the paper signed with the correspondent's name or pseudonym, snippets of information and gossip theatrical or social, interspersed with *Gazette* announcements and long official reports of foreign affairs. The modern newspaper was in the making. But as yet its circulation was limited: 2000 was regarded as a good circulation; in 1795 the *Morning Post* fell to 350, while the *Times* rose to 4800. Great fortunes could not yet be made or lost in journalism: the prize was influence, particularly in politics. There were a number of good provincial papers, like the *Northampton Mercury*, the *Gloucester Journal*, the *Norwich Mercury* and the *Newcastle Courant*.

Just as the theatre and the newspaper had, since the reign of Charles II, spread from the capital to the provinces, so had the printing and publishing of books. The lapse of the Censorship and the Licensing Act in the reign of William III had removed the legal restriction on the number of printing presses, with the result that not only were the printing and publishing firms in London greatly increased in number, but provincial presses were set up in many other towns. The business of publishing and bookselling were then conducted by one and the same firm.[1] Between 1726 and 1775 there were about 150 of these firms in England outside London, and about as many in the Capital.

The vigorous literary and scientific life of many provincial towns in Dr. Johnson's day was stimulated by the local newspapers and the local publishing firms, which often attained to a high standard. Before the end of the Century such first-rate work as Bewick's *British Birds* with his famous woodcuts was being printed and published in Newcastle-on-Tyne. Eighteenth Century printing, though less fanciful than the Elizabethan, and less mechanically correct than the Victorian, was superior to both as a beautiful art.

Much publishing, especially of the large and expensive volumes in which that aristocratic century delighted was done by subscription, for which the author touted among his friends and patrons. The fine private libraries accounted for much of the trade. But Circulating Libraries, of which the first was started in 1740, were to be found both in London and the provinces, particularly in the health resorts. Bath and Southampton had very fine Circulating Libraries. Book clubs among neighbours and private friends were also common.

Poetry, travels, history and novels all had a place in popular reading. The German Moritz, after his residence in England, bore remarkable testimony to our literary civilization at that period (1782):

Certain it is, that the English classical authors are read more generally, beyond all comparison, than the German; which in general are read only by the learned, or at most by the middle class of people. The English national authors are in all hands, and read by all people, of which the innumerable editions they have gone through are a sufficient proof. My landlady, who is only a taylor's widow, reads her Milton; and tells me that her late husband first fell in love with her on this very account; because she read Milton with such proper emphasis. This single instance would prove but little; but I have conversed with several people of the lower class, who all knew their national authors, and who all have read many, if not all of them.

In the course of the Eighteenth Century the accumulation of great consolidated estates by the nobility and wealthier gentry, and the developments of capitalist agriculture, led to the general

---

[1] The most long-lived of these was Longmans. In 1724 Thomas Longman bought the business. It is still a family concern and was conducted on the old site in Paternoster Row till its destruction by enemy action in 1940. Only the business is of course now confined to publishing only, bookselling having become a separate trade.

disappearance of the small squire of £100 to £300 a year, who worked his own land or let a couple of farms. This particular type of man, once so important in the life and government of the countryside, was now much less in evidence. But his place was in some respects taken by an increased number of gentry and professional men living on various kinds of small incomes in the country, but less rooted in the soil than the old rustic squire. There was gain as well as loss in the change. It made for a higher level of culture: Mr. Bennet in *Pride and Prejudice* is an example of the new type, more attached to his library than to the land. Parson Woodforde, the diarist, had only £400 a year, but on that he was able to keep five or six servants indoors and out, to look well after his relations, to travel freely, and to exercise a generous hospitality to rich and poor. His habit of noting in his diary every sixpence he spent or gave, may indicate that he knew he had to be careful and therefore succeeded in living in such good style within a modest income.

The best type of domestic or outdoor employee cost only £10 a year and his keep: many were content with much less. On these conditions, armies of servants, male and female, filled the households of the gentry. [See § 89.] Not a few became 'old servants,' privileged and intimate, whom their masters and mistresses never dreamt of turning off; it was an important and humanizing element in old English life. The floating population of maids, who soon went away to be married, learnt during their term of domestic service many arts of cooking and housekeeping, that afterwards served them well as wives and mothers. Villages and cottages had also their own immemorial traditions in these matters. In those days, when it was not yet possible to buy everything, including tinned meals, in the shop round the corner, the feckless and untrained housewife was more utterly disastrous and therefore less common than in the city life of to-day.

BOOKS FOR FURTHER READING

In the notes and text of this and the previous chapters I have mentioned a number of works of value on special aspects of the subject. I particularly commend the student to the social parts of Lecky's *History of England in the Eighteenth Century* and to a recent work of great value, *Johnson's England*, edited by Professor Turberville for the Oxford Press in 1933, with articles by many different authorities on special aspects of life in that period. This book has now come down to a time in our annals when contemporary memoirs, novels, diaries and biographies and letters like those of Horace Walpole make the study of social history more real and very delightful. A very remarkable short essay on Eighteenth Century England is pp. 72–91 of the first volume of W. P. Ker's *Collected Essays* (1925).

Chapter Five

SCOTLAND AT THE BEGINNING AND AT THE END OF THE EIGHTEENTH CENTURY.

The Union, 1707—Culloden and the Conquest of the Highlands, 1746.

SINCE the scope of this work is confined to the social history of England, nothing has yet been said about the neighbouring kingdom of Scotland. For more than two centuries after the wars of Edward I and Wallace, English and Scots had few dealings with one another save at the point of the spear. In the reign of Elizabeth they ceased to be active enemies, because they had an interest in common, to defend the island against the powers of the Catholic reaction; but they adopted radically different forms of ecclesiastical polity, which further differentiated the character of social and intellectual life on the two sides of the Border.

By the accession of James VI of Scotland to the English throne (1603) his two kingdoms were linked by the uneasy bond of a Dual Monarchy. James himself understood Scotland better than England; but under his son and grandsons the smaller of the two kingdoms was governed in accordance with plans concocted in London by Bishops, courtiers or parliament-men, who knew nothing of Scotland's needs and habits, and only sought to make her serve some English partisan policy of the hour. The Edinburgh Privy Council took its orders from Whitehall. The Scots deeply resented this vassalage to England, whether the absent overlord was named Charles, Oliver or James. They wrapped the plaid of their own prejudices more tightly round them, and were more suspicious than ever of influences emanating from their over-great neighbour.

Under these political conditions, social life in the two countries continued to flow in separate channels. There were also economic and physical obstacles in the way of more international intercourse. Communications were hindered not only by tariffs but by the state of the Great North Road. London was nearly a week's journey from Edinburgh, and the English counties that lay nearest the Border were the most primitive and the most hostile to the Scots. In religion, in law, in education, in agricultural methods, in the mutual relation of classes, Scotland showed no tendency to approximate to English example, still less to give any lead to England.

Indeed, so repugnant to one another were the two neighbour nations over which King William uneasily reigned, that before his death in 1702 it had become clear to the wiser heads in both his Kingdoms that either there must be a closer political and commercial union, or else the crowns would again become separate and war would almost certainly ensue. For after the Revolution of 1688 the Edinburgh Parliament assumed a new attitude of independence, that rendered it impossible for the English any longer to control the affairs of Scotland through the instrumentality of her tame Privy Council. The system of Dual Monarchy was breaking down. The choice before the two countries lay between a closer union negotiated on equal terms, or the severance of the existing connection.

The right choice was made, though with deep misgivings on the part of the Scots. Under Queen Anne as first sovereign of the new State of 'Great Britain,' the Union took place of the Parliaments and commercial systems of the two nations made one, while their Churches and laws remained distinct. The Union of 1707 meant, in effect, that Scotland lost her Parliamentary life (which had never meant very much to her though it had meant rather more in recent years), while she gained in return full partnership in England's markets and colonies. That privilege opened to her the opportunity of getting rid at last of her grinding and perennial poverty.

For a generation or more the benefits of the Union seemed to hang fire. But after the liquidation of the Jacobite and Highland questions in 1745–1746, Scotland sprang forward along the path towards happier days. Her agriculture, which had been to the last degree antiquated and miserable, could, before the Century closed, give lessons to the improving landlords of England. Scottish farmers, gardeners, engineers and doctors came south and taught the English many things. Englishmen began to travel in Scotland and to admire both her mountains and her men. Scots took a large share in the commerce and colonization of the

British Empire, in the wars of Britain, in the government of India. Released from the prison of poverty where she had languished for ages, Scotland burst into sudden splendour. Her religion lost much of its gloom and fanaticism, while remaining vital and democratic. The genius of her sons gave a lead to the thought of the world: Hume, Adam Smith, Robertson, Dugald Stewart, extended their influence not only over all Britain but into the salons of continental philosophers, while Smollett, Boswell and Burns made their native country famous in letters, and Raeburn in art. Thus the latter part of the Eighteenth Century saw the golden age of Scotland, which was prolonged for a second generation of glory when Sir Walter, with his Lays and romances, imposed the Scottish idea upon all Europe.

To bring out clearly the extent and character of the changes that took place in Scotland during the Hanoverian epoch, I shall in this chapter describe her first as she was at the time of the Union in the reign of Queen Anne,[1] and then as she had become in the middle years of George III.

[1] For this purpose I have availed myself of my account of Scotland in the second volume of my *England under Queen Anne*.

I

SCOTLAND AT THE TIME OF THE UNION OF 1707

King William, 1689–1702—*Queen Anne*, 1702–1714.

EVER since the days of Burns and Sir Walter Scott the English have delighted in Scottish tradition and story, highland and lowland alike, sometimes to the point of sentimentality. They go to Scotland to admire her scenery, and in their own country and throughout their world-wide Empire they have acknowledged, not without envy, the sterling qualities of her sons. But in the reign of Anne, ignorance was still the fruitful parent of hostility and contempt. Contact between the two peoples was slight, and for the most part unfortunate. Scots still sought their fortunes less often in England than on the continent of Europe. Jacobite exiles lived in Italy and France. Presbyterian clergy and lawyers went to Dutch universities to finish their education at the fountain-heads of Calvinist theology and Roman law. Scottish overseas merchants dealt with Holland and Scandinavia, but were excluded from the Colonies of England. Englishmen who crossed the Cheviots on business were few, except the Borderers who nursed a traditional hostility to everything Scottish; the jealous Northumbrians used to warn travellers from the South that Scotland was 'the most barbarous country in the world.' Scottish drovers sold their cattle in the fairs of north England, but otherwise the business done between the two lands was so slight that the London mail bag sometimes brought only one letter to Edinburgh.

Perhaps not more than a dozen people in the year visited Scotland for pleasure. And of these few the weaker sort were speedily driven back across the Border by the badness of accommodation in the slovenly inns, where good French wine and fresh salmon could not alone compensate for the want of other palatable victuals, and for the utter filth of the lodging. And while the English traveller complained of his own treatment, he was no less bitter on the stabling of his horse in a place 'hardly fit for a hoghouse,' where the poor beast was offered straw to eat in place of hay. If indeed these tourists had come provided with introductions and could have enjoyed Scottish hospitality in gentlemen's houses, as the native gentry did upon their journeys, they would have fared less ill.

Nor was there in Scotland anything specially to attract the seeker after the beautiful as it was understood in those days. No Southerner then admired wild moorland scenery; the Scots doubtless loved, in their innermost hearts, the

> land of brown heath and shaggy wood,

but they had not yet, through the medium of literature, expressed that still unconscious passion even to themselves, still less to their unfriendly neighbours. The Englishman who rode from Berwick to Edinburgh, despised the Lowland scenery as divided between melancholy wastes and ill-managed fields of oats. It was unenclosed; almost treeless; devoid, except in the immediate neighbourhood of Edinburgh, of the fine mansions and parks, well-built farms and stately parish churches which the traveller had left behind him in his own country. As to the Highland mountains, the very few Englishmen who ever penetrated into their recesses in the way of business or duty pronounced them 'horrid,' 'frightful' and 'most of all disagreeable when the heath is in bloom.'

The Scot was either a Jacobite or a Presbyterian, and in either capacity he alienated four-fifths of English sympathy. And the English of all religions or none were shocked or amused at the rigour of the social discipline of the Kirk. Cromwell's troopers, in their day of power in Scotland, used to seat themselves in derision on the 'stool of repentance' in the parish churches; and in Anne's time that instrument of moral reformation was as alien to the free spirit of the English Dissenting sects as it was to the mild authority of the village parson. Calamy, the leader of the English Nonconformists, in his tour of fraternization among the Scottish Presbyterians in 1709, gave offence by calling some proceedings of their Church Assembly 'the Inquisition revived.' And apart from all questions of politics and religion, the national and personal pride of the Scot appeared to the unimaginative Englishman ridiculous when associated with poverty. That a 'gentleman' should be proud though out-at-elbows seemed absurd to the English merchant in his broadcloth. And the Scot, when at every turn he encountered this vulgar scorn, only became more silent and more dour.

The Scots, indeed, regarded the English with sour aversion, as purse-proud and overbearing neighbours. Popular poetry, tradition, history—strong influences on an imaginative and emotional race—all pointed to England as the ancient enemy. Four centuries of intermittent warfare with the Southerner formed the subject of Scottish legend and ballad. Hardly a place in the Ancient Kingdom but its inhabitants could tell how the English had burnt it. And Flodden, still unavenged, was the lyric theme vibrating in every Scottish heart.

The Edinburgh Parliament, though it had become somewhat more important after the Revolution, had never stood for much in the social life and imagination of the people. It held its sessions in the great hall off the High Street, known as the Parliament House; after the Union it was assigned to the lawyers of the capital, and still remains the most famous room in Scotland. There, under its high, open-timbered roof, Nobles, Barons and Burgesses sat together; they were reckoned as three separate Estates, but they debated and voted in a single Chamber.

The Barons, or County members, unlike the corresponding class in the English House of Commons, were not elected on a popular franchise of forty-shilling freeholders, but were each chosen by a few score gentlemen who happened to be, in the eye of the old Scottish law, tenants-in-Chief of the Crown. The Burghs, too, were all of them as 'rotten' as the rottener part of the English Boroughs. The representative element was therefore weaker in the Scottish than in the English Parliament; such representation of the people as there actually was, could only be called 'virtual.' Partly for this reason, partly because the social structure of Scotland was still essentially feudal and aristocratic, the Nobles were the most powerful element in the Chamber. It was chiefly they who led its debates, headed its factions and formulated its acts and policies.

The predominance of the aristocracy was not confined to Parliament. In each district of the countryside the common people were attached by custom, pride, awe and hope of protection to some great House that represented their region in the eyes of Scotland. The lairds, as the Lowland gentry were called, were trained to use the arms with which they commonly rode abroad; the local nobleman entertained them royally at banquets in his mansion, espoused their quarrels, pushed their interests, and confidently expected them in return to follow his standard, if he raised it for the Government that had given him office, or against the Government that had neglected his claims.

If Whig and Jacobite came to blows, as they nearly did on several occasions under Anne, and as they actually did in 1715, it would be to the banners of Argyle, Atholl, Mar or some other grandee that each region would rally, in the Lowlands only to a less degree than in the Highlands. If all the nobility had been united against the Government, the little Scottish army would not long have availed to hold them down. But like other classes they were divided. And nearly all who engaged in politics were greedy of office, for nearly all were embarrassed by the need of keeping up feudal state on the meagre rentals and payments in kind of a countryside desperately poor; and they had all been taught to regard office as the natural remedy of a great nobleman's finances. But many, both in the Jacobite and in the Whig camp, were patriots as well as self-seekers, and some were, besides, shrewd and politic statesmen, who knew how to pursue their country's true interest, and whose aristocratic position and upbringing set them above the necessity of courting popularity with the mob. Such were the men who passed the Union.

After the Nobles came the lairds or country gentlemen. Their tall, stone mansions, each with its corbel-stepped gable roof, stood up gaunt and fortresslike in the treeless and hedgeless landscape. Architecture did not flourish as in England. Many of these country houses had grown up by clumsy additions to the war-towers of former days. [See § 127.] There was seldom any window on the exposed north side, even when it commanded the best or the only view of the landscape. The day of lawns, avenues and walled gardens was yet to come. The farm buildings, with their homely smells and litter, abutted on the mansion; the cornfields came up to its walls on one side, and on another was an ill-kept garden of kale, physic-herbs and native flowers.

The interior was equally devoid of luxuries common in the south of the island. The furniture was of the simplest, the floors had no carpets, the walls were usually devoid of paper, panelling, arras or pictures. The bed-chambers had no fire-places, except in the envied 'fire-room.' The drawing-room held a closed bed ready for guests, since it was not always safe for a convivial laird to ride home o' nights, any more than for Tam o' Shanter from his humbler festival. Hospitality took the form of plentiful plain meats served in one course, washed down by Scottish ale and French brandy and claret—and, in the Highlands, by the local whisky. Tea was only known to the Scottish subjects of Queen Anne as an expensive medicine. Thrift was a dire necessity, but hospitality was a national instinct. Neighbours would arrive on horseback on surprise visits of half the day in length; they were heartily welcome, for the means of passing the time in a country house were fewer than in contemporary England.

Near Edinburgh and other towns golf was a time-honoured institution. [See § 122.] And all over Scotland hares, grouse, blackgame and partridges were pursued with dogs, hawks, and snares, and less often with the long gun. But the red deer, once common, were already withdrawing into the Highland glens. The extraordinary abundance of salmon and trout afforded not only good sport, but a cheap food for the people. In some parts the gentry despised salmon as a dish that cloyed, and farm-hands struck if they were fed upon it every day.

The gentry of the Lowlands were divided not unevenly into Presbyterian and Episcopalian, a division scarcely distinguishable from the political division of Whig and Jacobite. Tories there were none, in the English sense of the word, for the Tory was an Episcopalian who had accepted the Revolution Settlement because it left his Church established and privileged, whereas in Scotland the Revolution left the Episcopal Church disestablished, and not even tolerated according to law; Scottish Episcopalians, therefore, were necessarily Jacobites, looking to a counter-revolution for their relief. This was the essential difference between English and Scottish politics, and it deeply affected social life and relations in the Northern Kingdom.

Family and religious discipline tended to be more strict in Presbyterian than in Episcopalian families. There was usually more pleasure and freedom in a Jacobite household. But deep Presbyterian piety and a strict sense of public duty did not prevent Forbes of Culloden from indulgence in hard drinking, convivial hospitality, profound learning and liberal culture. And when

Anne came to the throne, the services of psalmody, preaching and extempore prayer were very much the same in the Episcopal Meeting House as in the Presbyterian Parish Church. The Prayer Book only began to find its way into some of the Meeting Houses in the last half of her reign. The doctrines professed by the rival denominations differed little except on Church government, and not much even on that, seeing that the Episcopalians too had their Presbyteries and Kirk Sessions with inquisition and discipline over morals.

The division therefore was deep only on its political side; it did not touch the basis of a common Scottish mentality and civilization. Free thought had not yet spread from the land of Shaftesbury and Bolingbroke to the land of Hume. In the reign of William an unfortunate Edinburgh student had been hanged for expressing doubts as to the Trinity and the authority of the Scriptures, in terms that would only have provoked a frowning rebuke in a London coffee-house.

Nearly all Scottish families, especially those of the gentry, regularly attended either the Parish Church or the Episcopal Meeting House, where they received much the same spiritual medicine, diluted with different quantities of water. Poverty and religious controversy combined to form a national character, overriding the acute political divisions, and uniting all Scots in a mental and moral antagonism to the wealthier, more libertine civilization on the south of the Cheviots. The popularity of Addison's and Steele's *Spectators* among Edinburgh ladies and gentlemen at the end of Anne's reign was one of the first instances of a real intellectual invasion of North by South Britain. As a consequence of the Union such influences began to multiply.

The intellectual unity of the nation and the good understanding of its component classes were all the greater because Scottish lairds in those days sent their own bairns to the village school. The idea of sending a Scottish gentleman's son to an English public school was rendered unthinkable alike by thrift and by patriotism. Education in the village school strengthened the young laird's love of his native land and landscape, and inclined him when he came to man's estate to sympathy with his tenants who had once been his schoolfellows. The broad Scots tongue, of which the highest were not ashamed, the traditions and ballads of the countryside, were the common heritage of all. That was why, two generations later, in the days of Burns and Scott, the poetry and traditions of Scotland went forth to conquer the imagination of men bred in less fortunate countries, where rich and poor had no culture in common. Scotland was at once more feudal and more equalitarian than England. An amazing freedom of speech, between classes that were yet perfectly distinct in a strict social hierarchy, characterized the relation of men who had sat on the same bench at school, and whose fathers had ridden shoulder to shoulder to fray and foray.

But in the age of Anne no literary or intellectual palms were won by Scotland in the world's arena. Her poverty was still too bitter and her religion was still too narrow. But the seeds of greatness were there; that very poverty and that very religion were forming the national mind and character. Already Swift, who hated the Scots as Presbyterians, confessed that their youth were better educated than the English; while Defoe wrote, though with some exaggeration:

You find very few gentry either ignorant or unlearned. Nay, you cannot ordinarily find a servant in Scotland but he can read or write.

When Forbes of Culloden, in 1705, went to finish his legal education at Leyden University, he was led to contrast the grave and studious habits of his own countrymen abroad with the 'riot and debauchery' of the young English spendthrifts making the grand tour, 'who repaid the forbearance and politeness of the inhabitants with contempt and ignorance.'

Scottish school education would, however, by modern standards, be judged miserably inadequate. At the Reformation the Nobles had stolen the Church endowments, which had been earmarked for education by the 'devout imagination' of John Knox. Since then, the Church had continued to strive for the cause of educating the people, but with all too little support from the gentry and the cheeseparing 'heritors' who controlled the money spent on the schools. The excellent laws of 1633 and 1696 had ordained that a well-appointed school should be set up in every parish and maintained by local rates. But the reality was very different. In Anne's reign many parishes had no school at all, and where a school was to be found it was too often a dark, draughty, dirty hovel, and the master or mistress usually lived on starvation wages. In Fife, at the end of the Queen's reign, only two men out

§117 An eighteenth-century hunt. Sir Robert Walpole and his hounds

§118

A country race-course

(c. 1786)

§119 The Prince of Wales at Newmarket in 1791

§120 London Clubs. St. James's Street, 1792

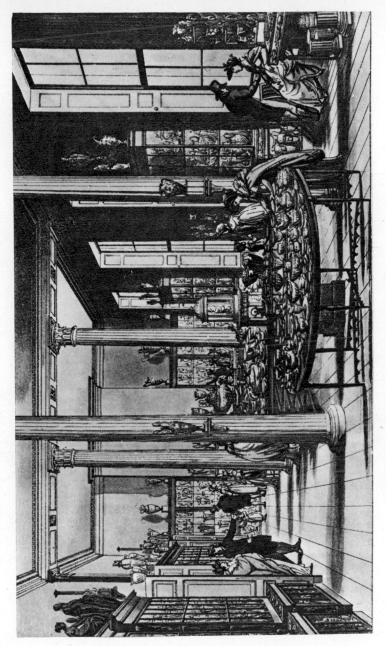

§121 Wedgwood's shop in St. James's Square (1809)

SCOTLAND

§122. Golf in 1746 below Edinburgh Castle

§123 High Street, Edinburgh (1750)

§124 A butcher's shop

§125 Wayside refreshment

§126 Edinburgh Castle (*c.* 1746)

§127 Many Scottish country houses had grown up "by additions to the wartowers of former days". Hawthornden Castle (contrast with §§130, 131)

§128 Scottish cottager spinning

§129 A Scottish interior

(Note the box-bed and the hens roosting in the rafters)

§130 The Drum, Midlothian (1724–34). (Contrast with §127)

§131 Interior (slightly later in date) of The Drum, Midlothian

§132 The Grassmarket

§133 The New Town

§134 The Tron Church, Edinburgh

§135 The General Assembly of the Kirk of Scotland
in the Tron Church, Edinburgh (1787)

of three could sign their names, and one woman out of twelve, while in Galloway few of the people could read.

On the other hand, though there were not enough schools, in those that there were Latin was very often taught; and it was usually well taught in the Burgh schools maintained by the towns. The village and the Burgh schools were not merely primary schools; some of the older and better scholars were being prepared for the University by masters who were themselves College men. Many, indeed, of the half-starved dominies, though they could not afford to buy books, had the root of the matter in them; and though they taught only a part of the population, that part was the pick of the Scottish democracy, lads taught to make sacrifices to obtain education, who used the slender equipment of learning available to them as no other nation in Europe could do, and so in the end raised themselves and their country to higher ranges of civilized life.

The Universities of Scotland were in a dull condition at sunrise of that century which was to set in the golden glow of Principal Robertson, Adam Smith and the Edinburgh philosophers. An age of violent civic commotion is seldom favourable to academic institutions controlled by the State. The Episcopal regime of Charles II had excluded half the Scottish men of learning from academic life, and the Revolution extruded most of the other half, replacing them by men who had learnt more fanaticism than scholarship in moorside conventicles subject to attack by dragoons.

The students were of all classes, sons of nobles, lairds, ministers, farmers and mechanics. The most part were seeking to be beneficed clergymen, but there were far too many candidates. The number of small bursaries and the Scottish peasant's zeal for knowledge overcrowded the sacred profession in days when there were few other openings for an educated man. The lot of the 'stickit minister,' the laird's tutor and the underpaid schoolmaster was hard. But those who were able to obtain charge of a parish were not so ill off by the modest standards of that day. Calamy, the English Nonconformist leader, wrote after his visit to the Presbyterians of North Britain in 1709:

As for the settled ministers of the Church of Scotland, though they are not so plentifully or profusely provided for as many of the Established Church in England, yet are there none but what have a competency, whereupon to live easily and conveniently and above contempt.

The Scottish lad, in his hard struggle to reach this harbour, supported life at the University from the sack of oatmeal leaning against the wall of the garret where he lodged in the town. On holidays fixed for the purpose, the rustic student tramped home with the empty sack, and returned with it refilled from the harvest of his father's 'infield.'

The peasants on a Scottish estate lived on terms of traditionally familiar intercourse with the laird, who on his daily ride across his lands had to listen to the sharp tongues of an outspoken race. None the less they were living under him in a position of servitude at once feudal and economic. This kind of relationship was remarked on by English travellers as something new in their experience. Private jurisdictions over tenants, civil in some cases, civil and criminal in others, were common all over Scotland, though such feudal courts had long ago ceased in England. Statesmen in London held that the Protestant Succession was in imminent danger from these *superiorities*, which removed the Scottish vassal from the protection of the royal courts and subjected his person and property to Jacobite overlords.

The peasantry held their farms on annually terminable leases which left them at the mercy of the laird or his factor, and fatally discouraged any attempt on their part at improving the land they tilled. And the laird on his side seldom put capital into the improvement of his tenants' farms. Had he wished so to do, he lacked the means. A rent-roll of £500 sterling was considered great wealth in Scotland, £50 was common, and many 'bonnet lairds' supported their families on £20 of rent and the produce of their own 'infield.' These figures could be multiplied by ten to represent the wealth of the corresponding grades of the English squirarchy. Moreover, Scottish rents were paid more than half in kind: sheep, poultry, oatmeal, barley and peat were brought to the door of the manor-house by the tenantry—not in carts, for they had none, but balanced on the backs of half-starved horses. Another source of supply for the laird's household was the cloud of pigeons from his dovecot, which preyed on the surrounding fields, transforming a large proportion of the tenants' meagre crops into flesh for the landlord's table. For the rest, the Scottish farmer, like the villein of mediaeval England, had to manure, sow and reap the 'infield' of the laird, often on days between two spells of bad weather, when he might otherwise have saved his own precarious harvest and secured his family against starvation during the coming year.

Under these conditions it is no wonder that in Queen Anne's reign nine-tenths of the fields of Scotland were unenclosed by wall or hedge. The cattle had to be tethered or watched all day and shut up all night. Only in the Lothians the wealthier landlords had begun the process of enclosing by stone walls. Quickset hedges were hardly anywhere to be seen, and the want of them was not regretted, for it was believed that they harboured birds which would eat the corn. A similar suspicion attached to trees. Saplings were not only eaten off by the cattle but deliberately broken by the peasants, in spite of proclaimed penalties. But there were few trees for them to injure except close round the manor-house and the kirk. The ancient forests where, according to the instructions of Robert Bruce's 'testament,' the population used to shelter in time of English invasion, had now almost everywhere disappeared. And the modern movement for plantations, to keep the wind off the land and supply the market with timber, was only in its infancy. The general aspect of Scotland was then more treeless than ever before or since. Here and there, particularly in Clydeside, could be seen woods of some size and pretension; and, in the distant and unvisited North, old forests still rustled their branches to the Highland winds. Even in the Lowlands the denes and steep banks of the burns sheltered in their dank recesses the sparse remains of the blanket of birch, alder and dwarf oak that had once been spread over the land.

The houses of the peasantry were in keeping with the starved aspect of the landscape and the want of any proper system of agricultural improvement. Rightly to imagine the home of a Scots farmer in Queen Anne's reign, we must forget the fine stone farms of a later date, and think of something more like the cabins of Western Ireland. It consisted almost always of one storey and often of one room. The style and material of building and the degree of poverty varied in different regions, but walls of turf or of unmortared stone, stopped with grass or straw, were very common; chimneys and glass windows were rare; the floor was the bare ground; in many places the cattle lived at one end of the room, the people at the other, with no partition between. The family often sat on stones or heaps of turf round the fire of peat, whence the smoke made partial escape through a hole in the thatch overhead. Since they worked on an ill-drained soil, only half reclaimed from marsh and rushes, and came back to a damp home in wet clothes for which they too seldom had any change, it followed that rheumatism and ague plagued and shortened their lives. [See § 128, 129.]

Men and women wore clothes made up in the immediate neighbourhood by local weavers and tailors; often spun and dyed in the wearer's own cottage. Children always and grown-ups often went bare-foot. The men wore the broad, flat, round, blue bonnets of wool, the distinctive headgear of Scotland in the eyes of the world. The laird and the minister alone sported a felt hat; but they too wore home-spun clothes made up by a country tailor. To the surprise of Dissenters from South Britain, the minister wore no black or clerical garments, either in or out of church, but made his rounds and preached his sermon in lay neck-cloth, and in coloured coat and waistcoat of homely wool.

In Scotland yet, as in the England of pre-Saxon times, much of the land that was potentially the best for agriculture was still uncultivated marsh cumbering the valley bottoms, while the peasants painfully drove their teams on the barren hillsides above. The enormous ploughs of primitive design were all of wood except the share and coulter, and were usually made by the farmers themselves; they were dragged along the slope by eight or ten small and meagre oxen, urged on by the blows and shrill cries of half a dozen excited farmers. The cortège, with the united efforts of beasts and men, scratched half an acre a day.

A group of farmers usually tilled their lands together, and shared the profits on the 'run-rig' system, each farmer claiming the produce of a 'rig' or 'ridge'—a different 'rig' being assigned to him each harvest. A single farm, paying £50 sterling rent or its equivalent in kind, might have half a dozen or more tenants, among whom the land was every year re-divided by lot. This system, and the precarious annual leases granted by the laird rendered agricultural improvement impossible. The quarrels inside the group of co-operating farmers—some of them of that dour type that bred Cameronians and Kirk seceders—too often held up the common cultivation for weeks at a time. Farmers had to wait every morning till the lazier or more sulky of their neighbours arrived to join the clumsy operations of the field.

The farm was further divided into an 'infield' and an 'outfield.' On the 'infield,' near the houses of the clachan, was lavished all the manure that could be locally collected, including sometimes the thatch covering the turf on the goodman's cottage roof. But the 'outfield,' perhaps three-quarters of the total acreage, was left unmanured, used as rough feed for cattle for eight or ten years on end, and then cropped for a year or two before relapsing into moorish pasture. This system was very inefficient compared to the three-field system usual in English open-field cultivation, but something like it was found in parts of West England, Wales, Cornwall and the East Riding.

Scottish crops consisted of oats for the staple food; and barley to make scones, or the Scots ale which was still the wholesome national drink of the Lowlander before the ill-omened invasion of whisky from the Highlands. Kale, pease and beans were grown for the cottage kitchen. But turnips and artificial grasses for cattle were unknown, and potatoes were grown only by a few gardeners to season the laird's dish of meat, not by farmers as part of the people's food.

The tyranny of these primitive customs of cultivation, approved by the people themselves, kept them always near the verge of famine. Their grain, but little multiplied by such methods of agriculture, went in the three shares celebrated in the old saying:

Ane to gnaw, and ane to saw, and ane to pay the laird witha'.

The lairds were bound fast by their own poverty, unable to help themselves or their tenants. Yet it was the lairds who, in the century now dawning, learnt so to make use of the commercial conditions introduced by the Union as to revolutionize the system of agriculture and create a new prosperity for all classes.

The last half-dozen years of William's reign had been the 'dear years' of Scottish memory, six consecutive seasons of disastrous weather when the harvests would not ripen. The country had not the means to buy food from abroad, so the people had laid themselves down and died. Many parishes had been reduced to a half or a third of their inhabitants. This sombre experience, from which the nation was slowly emerging during the years when the Treaty of Union was under debate, coloured the North Briton's outlook, deepened his superstitions and darkened his political passions, especially in relation to the hated English who had watched the kindly Scots die of hunger, and had moved no finger save to make their lot worse by opposition to the Darien scheme. Fortunately a cycle of fat years under Queen Anne followed the lean years under King William. Then in 1709, after the Union was safely passed, the failure of the harvest again produced famine—unpeopling farms and hamlets and filling the villages with beggars. Until the methods of agriculture had been completely changed, such might always be the result of a single season of bad weather.

In these circumstances, the principal source of agricultural wealth, as distinct from mere subsistence, was sheep and cattle. The sheep's wool supported the home cloth manufacture, and both sheep and cattle were sold into England in great numbers. Stock-breeding flourished most in Galloway, but even Galloway had hardly recovered from the depredations on her livestock made by the Highlanders and other emissaries of a paternal government in the 'killing times' of the persecution under Charles II. It was reckoned that in 1705 Scotland sold 30,000 cattle into England; the usual price was something between one and two pounds sterling a head. This marketing of 'black cattle' was one of the most important of a Scottish laird's few sources of wealth. The sheep and cattle were small, even as compared to the small English beasts of that period. Their pasture was for the most part unimproved moorland. The cattle were shut up all night for want of fences. Of the remnant that had not been sold south to the English pastures, many had to be slaughtered at Martinmas on the approach of winter, for there was little hay and no root-crop on which to feed them. During the next six months salted meat supplied the tables of the gentry; but meat seldom graced the peasant's board at any time of year. On the return of the tardy Scottish spring, the poor beasts, mere skeletons after their winter-long imprisonment in the dark on rations of straw or boiled chaff, were led back from the byre to the pasture, a pitiful procession, half supported, half carried by the farmers. This annual ceremony was only too well named the 'Lifting.'

The standard of life in Scotland was very low in almost every material respect, but hardships had not crushed the spirit of the people, not even after the 'dear years' of William. To avoid the receipt of alms was a passion with common folk more decidedly than in wealthier England. The poor law system was totally different in the two countries. In England the poor had been, ever since Elizabeth's reign, a charge on the community; they were maintained by compulsory parish rates that amounted at the end of Anne's reign to a million pounds a year, then regarded as a heavy national burden. In Scotland there was no compulsory rate, and poor-relief was an obligation not on the State but on the Church. Endowments of the poor were made by private persons, announced in the kirk, and sometimes commemorated on boards hung upon its walls. In the kirk also stood the poor's box, which the thrifty Scots constantly replenished with most of the bad copper of the neighbourhood, besides a useful minority of good coins. The deacon was a lay officer of the Church, found in many parishes, though not in all; it was the deacon's business to distribute these alms among the necessitous, who were for the most part creditably unwilling to receive it. The duty of keeping their relations independent of such relief was keenly felt and nobly undertaken by persons themselves desperately poor.

Licences to beg from door to door in a given area were also issued by the Kirk Session to privileged 'gaberlunzies,' or 'blue gowns.' Many of them, like Edie Ochiltree, acted as welcome carriers of news to lonely farms, repositories of regional lore and legend—popular, respectable figures with a place of their own in rural society.

But unhappily there was a much larger number of unlicensed and less desirable vagabonds. The 'sorners' of Queen Anne's Scotland answered to the 'sturdy beggars' of Tudor England. The 'dear years' under William had swelled this army of broken and masterless men, though there is no support to Fletcher of Saltoun's wild guess that they numbered 200,000, which would have made them between a fifth and sixth of the whole population. But the 'sorners' were numerous enough to terrorize a countryside of lonely farms and clachans of two or three houses apiece; a company of 'ill men' could rob in the face of day, taking the last crust from the cottage, the cow from the byre, and sometimes wresting the child from its unhappy parents. The number and power of the 'sorners' was the penalty paid by Scotland for the want of a regular poor-law like the English. And in neither country was there any attempt at a proper police.

Fletcher of Saltoun, the grim republican patriot who lent a flavour of his own to the Scottish politics of the age, proposed as a remedy that the 'sorners' should be put into compulsory servitude; his idea was only the extension of existing practice in Scotland. Coal-mines and salt-mines were worked very largely by 'bondsmen,' veritable serfs, who could be caught and punished for running away. Even in modern establishments based on free contract, like the New Mills cloth factory in Haddingtonshire, there was a 'prison att the manufactory,' and hands who ran away or broke their contracts could be dealt with by summary methods. But the conditions of the employees of the New Mills were not bad by the standard of those days, whereas the hereditary bondsmen in the mines were treated by their masters as chattels, and were spoken of by the rest of the population with a kind of pitying terror, as 'the brown yins' or 'the blackfolk.'[1]

If Scotland at the time of the Union lagged behind England in agricultural methods, her industry and commerce were in no better way. Almost all her articles of export were food or raw materials—cattle and salmon for England, coal and salmon for Holland, salt and lead for Norway, herrings for the Iberian Peninsula. The Scots themselves wore cloth woven by village websters for local consumption; but only a very little linen or woollen cloth was sold abroad. The Haddington New Mills were famous, but they were not flourishing. There were, besides, other woollen factories, as at Musselburgh and Aberdeen, all clamouring to the Scots Parliament to support them with money and monopolies, and being only in part satisfied. The wool-growing landlords, on their side, compelled the legislature to allow them to export raw wool to Sweden and Holland, to the detriment of the market for Scottish cloth in those countries, and of course clean contrary to the established policy of England. The herring trade was a chief source of the nation's wealth, but even so the Dutch fisherman took many more herrings off the Scottish coast

---

[1] This iniquitous system of serfage was abolished at the end of the Eighteenth Century. Till then the Scottish miner, together with his wife and children who carried up the coal he cut, were transferable with the pit on any change of proprietorship. They could not leave their employment during life.

than did the Scots themselves. A great part of the business of the Edinburgh Parliament consisted of regulations to encourage and direct the meagre manufacturing and trading efforts of the country.

Though Scottish officers and regiments were winning honour for the land of their birth—the Scots Greys were as famous in the armies of Marlborough as in those of Wellington—the war with France meant little to the Scots at home. It was England's war, not theirs. Four years before the Union, the Edinburgh Parliament passed a Wine Act, to legalize the most popular part of trade with the enemy. The English were scandalized at this bold defiance of propriety in war-time, when they themselves were content with illegal smuggling to the French ports. But they dared do nothing, for if one of their cruisers had seized a Scots ship freighted with brandy, claret and Jacobite agents, they might have woken up one morning to find themselves at war with Scotland.

Since the Restoration, Glasgow had been reckoned as the second city in the kingdom, and the first for trade and manufacture. Probably on account of the famine and distress in William's reign, the population had recently declined: when the Union of 1707 was passed, it numbered only 12,500 souls out of a total of a million or more for all Scotland. The Glasgow merchants owned between them fifteen trading ships, with an aggregate tonnage of 1182 tons, and even these small vessels had to unload more than a dozen miles below the town, as the Clyde was still unnavigable to anything larger than a boat. Since no Scottish firm was permitted to trade with an English dependency, their commerce was confined to Europe, until the Union Treaty opened the tobacco trade with the English colonies to Bailie Nicol Jarvie and his fellow-citizens. In Anne's reign Glasgow was still a pretty little country town, with colonnades at the cross roads in the centre, where the merchants met to transact their modest affairs. It was, moreover, one of the four University towns of Scotland: 'there are only forty scholars that lodge in the College,' an English traveller noted in the year of Blenheim, 'but there are two or three hundred that belong to it, and all wear red gowns, as do likewise those at Aberdeen and St. Andrews.'

The fourth university town was Edinburgh herself—the headquarters of Scotland's law and law courts, the meeting place of the Parliament of the three Estates, and of that other Parliament which proved more enduring—the General Assembly of the Church. [See § 134, 135.] There, too, was Holyrood Palace, the empty nest whence Scotland's Kings had flown. At the other end of the mile-long Canongate and High Street—'the stateliest street in the world,' as a traveller of the period called it—rose the Castle on its rock, where the absent Queen Anne was represented by the red coats of her small Scottish army. The idle soldiers looked down upon the reek and roofs of Edinburgh, in perpetual wonder as to what might be brewing in the turbulent town below, and what riot, religious, political or economic, it would be their next duty to quell. [See § 123, 124, 125, 126.]

Although the antique City Guard of Edinburgh, with their Lochaber axes, were the laughing-stock of Scotland, yet house-breaking and robbery were almost unknown in the chief city of the kingdom, where men left their house doors unlocked all night. The fact speaks well for the honesty of the Scots, and is a credit to the hard religious system under which they were bred. It ruled the town effectually, preventing, in Scotland's very capital and centre of fashion, all theatrical shows and all dances; and on the Sabbath all 'idle gazing from windows,' all loitering and all walking fast in the streets. No wonder Dr. Pitcairn wrote his witty rhymes lampooning the clergy, and no wonder 'Hell-fire Clubs' and 'Sulphur Clubs' met surreptitiously to flout the Church in ways more questionable than the drama and the dance.

But not even the Church attempted on week-days to stop horse-racing on Leith sands, golf, cock-fighting or heavy drinking. On six evenings of the week the taverns were filled with men of all classes at their ale and claret, till the ten o'clock drum, beaten at the order of the magistrates, warned every man that he must be off home. Then were the High Street and Canongate filled with parties of every description, hurrying unsteadily along, High Court Judges striving to walk straight as became their dignity, rough Highland porters swearing in Gaelic as they forced a passage for their sedan-chairs, while far overhead the windows opened, five, six, or ten storeys in the air, and the close stools of Edinburgh discharged the collected filth of the last twenty-four hours into the street. It was good manners for those above to cry 'Gardy-loo' (*gardez l'eau*) before throwing. The returning roysterer cried back 'Haud yer han','' and ran with humped shoulders, lucky if his vast and expensive full-bottomed wig was not put out of action by a cataract of filth. The ordure thus sent down lay in the broad High Street and in the deep, well-like closes and wynds around it making the night air horrible, until early in the morning it was perfunctorily cleared away by the City Guard. Only on Sabbath morn it might not be touched, but lay there all day long, filling Scotland's capital with the savour of a mistaken piety.

This famous sanitary system of Edinburgh aroused much comment among the English travellers and made the Scots 'traduced and taxed of other nations,' as being, in Defoe's words, 'unwilling to live sweet and clean.' But it is only fair to quote his defence of them in the matter:

Were any other people to live under the same unhappiness, I mean as well of a rocky and mountainous situation, thronged buildings from seven to ten or twelve story high, a scarcity of water, and that little they have difficult to be had, and to the uppermost lodgings far to fetch, we should have a London or Bristol as dirty as Edinburgh; for though many cities have more people in them, yet I believe that in no city in the world so many people live in so little room.

Edinburgh indeed was an extreme example of the French type of town, kept within its ancient limits for reasons of safety and defence, and therefore forced to find room for growth by pushing its tenement flats high in air—in contrast to the ground plan of the easy-going peaceful towns of England, that sprawled out in suburbs ever expanding, to give each family its own house and if possible its own garden. French influence and the disturbed condition of Scotland in the past had confined the capital within its walls and pushed its growth up aloft. It was not, indeed, so long since it had been a matter of great peril for a gentleman to pass the night in a house without walls, like Darnley in Kirk o' Fields. And so the Scottish grandees had no fine Edinburgh mansions like those of the English nobles in Bloomsbury and the Strand, but were fain, during the session of Parliament, to live each in a flat over the High Street.

In such a town, where every flat was accounted as a separate 'house,' and no houses were numbered, it may well be imagined that it was difficult for letters to reach their destination, or for strangers to find their way. Indeed, without the services of the self-disciplined regiment of keen-eyed, quick-witted, dependable 'caddies,' business could scarcely have been carried on in the mazy wynds and stairways of old Edinburgh.

Scottish literature was centred in the capital, but it gave no sign as yet of the great awakening that lay before it in the latter half of the new century. The material was there in the heart and mental habits of the nation, but the Promethean fire had not yet descended. The mind of the people throve on the ballads sung, the stories told, the doctrines debated round the peat-fire in the peasant's cottage. Printed books, other than the Bible, consisted chiefly of theology or political pamphlets.

There was no native journalism. The two papers, issued three times a week at Edinburgh, were the old-established *Gazette* and its rival the *Courant*, started in 1705; both existed by special permission of the Privy Council; they were tame organs of officialdom, in form mere imitations of the London papers, full of continental and English news but telling the Scots nothing about their own affairs. With the disappearance of the Scottish Privy Council soon after the Union, the Edinburgh press acquired a certain freedom, and in the last years of Anne's reign began to have a life of its own, with a somewhat larger variety of newspapers.

The Scottish peasant, cramped in feudal bonds and mediaeval poverty, had one method of escape from his material lot—religion. Other intellectual food was not offered him. Bible on knee, in harsh, delightful argument with his minister or his cronies, he inhabited a realm of thought and imagination, deep, narrow, intense, for good and for evil utterly unlike the merry-go-round of disconnected information and ideas in which the popular mind of our own day gyrates. Never consulted by his betters about politics, and without representation in the Estates of Parliament, he took all the keener interest in the proceedings of the assemblies where his influence was felt, the hierarchy of Church courts— the Kirk Session of the Parish, the Presbytery of a dozen parishes, the Provincial Synod, and the national General Assembly annually held at Edinburgh. In all of these the laity were represented, as they were not in the purely clerical convocations of York and Canterbury. It has often been said that the Church Assembly was Scotland's Parliament more truly than the three Estates. And in the absence of any representative local government, the Kirk Session, where the lay elders kept the minister in awe, was the nearest approach to a parish council.

The parish church, with its roof of turf or thatch, was a small and tumble-down building; it had no mediaeval splendours or amenities, and would in England have been deemed more fitted for a barn. In the country churches there were seldom pews, except for the elders and a few privileged families. Most men and women stood during the service, or else sat on 'creepies,' stools such as that with which Jennie Geddes had marked her disapproval of the Prayer Book service. Yet the hard, ill-furnished room was crowded every Sabbath for two services of three hours each by a congregation of whom many had come on foot long miles across the moor. So small was the space inside the church that an overflow of the pious was often crowded out into the churchyard, where the Bible was read to them by a lad put up upon a tombstone.

The most solemn and impressive of popular religious rites were the Communions, held out of doors at long tables, gatherings under the eye of summer heaven that reminded everyone present of more dangerous meetings held on the moorside in the 'killing times.' Eight or ten parishes combined to hold a communion each in turn, from June to August, and many persons attended them one after the other, thinking nothing of walking forty miles over the hills to get there.

The older Presbyterian clergy in Queen Anne's reign were men whose education had been interrupted and whose spirits had been disturbed and embittered by persecution. One who knew them in their later years described them as—

weak, half-educated men, their lives irreproachable, and their manners austere and rustic. Their prejudices coincided perfectly with their congregations who in respect of their sound fundamentals made great allowances for their foibles and weaknesses.

'Presbyterian eloquence' was a byword with English hearers for its uncouth treatment of religious mysteries, its familiar apostrophes of the Almighty, its denunciation of such harmless acts as wearing smart clothes in church or taking in the London *Spectator*. But it was an Englishman who wrote:

Were the ministerial office in England discharged as it is in Scotland, in that laborious and self-denying manner, and under such small encouragements, thousands of the clergy I daresay would wish to have been brought up mechanics rather than parsons. Here are no drones, no idle parsons, no pampered priests, no dignities or preferments to excite ambition.

Indeed, the ambition of a peasant's son, such as most of the ministers were in origin, was honourably satisfied with the leadership of a parish and the confidence of its people. Meanwhile there was growing up a younger generation, better educated in less troublous times, with more sense of proportion in thought and refinement in language, who were soon, as 'Moderates,' to be openly at odds with the older men whom Claverhouse had dragooned into bigotry.

The Kirk Session of self-important lay elders, acting conjointly with the minister, interfered in ordinary life to an excessive degree. Week in, week out, the Kirk Session and the superior court of the Presbytery were trying cases of alleged swearing, slander, quarrelling, breach of Sabbath, witchcraft and sexual offences. Some of these inquiries and judgments were properly conducted and useful, being such as were dealt with by ordinary magistrates in England. Others were intolerably vexatious, as when a woman was arraigned for carrying a pail on a Fast Day, and a crowder for fiddling at a christening feast. The adulterer or fornicator of either sex was exposed on the stool of repentance in church, to the merriment of the junior half of the congregation, to the grave reprobation of the more respectable, and to the unblushing denunciations of the minister, renewed sometimes for six, ten or twenty Sabbaths on end. There was often a long row of penitents, and the 'gowns' in which they were clad were in such constant use that they had frequently to be renewed. To avoid this intolerable humiliation, poor girls often resorted to concealment of pregnancy and sometimes to child murder. The Privy Council was constantly dealing with the question of remitting or enforcing the extreme penalty in such cases.

These activities of the Kirk Session and Presbytery had much support in public opinion or they could not have so long survived the disuse of similar Church jurisdiction in England. But they aroused deep resentment in many, not least among the upper classes. It is true that commutation of penance for fines was often allowed in the case of the gentry. But even with these mitigations, the jurisdiction over conduct claimed by low-born elders and clergymen was an offence to the proud families of lairds and nobles; it was an underlying cause of Episcopal religion and Jacobite politics in many who had otherwise no quarrel with the services and doctrines of the Presbyterian Church. Anti-clericalism strengthened the Jacobites in Scotland, as it strengthened the Whigs in England. Yet it must be remembered that the stool of repentance and the jurisdiction of Kirk Sessions had gone on even in the Episcopal days of Charles II, and had not yet ceased in those numerous parishes still ruled by Episcopalian ministers.

On the whole, the Episcopalian or Jacobite party depended on upper-class support more than the Presbyterian or Whig. The more rigorous the discipleship of Knox, the more democratic were doctrine and practice likely to be. The clash came in the appointment of ministers, which the true-blue Presbyterian claimed for the people of the parish, both on grounds of religious doctrine as to the call of pastors, and because the private patrons who claimed to appoint were often very doubtful in their Presbyterianism.

Episcopalian pamphleteers twitted the Presbyterians with their want of policy in 'constant taking part with the mob in all the disputes that happen betwixt them and the Nobility and Gentry in the choice of ministers, as if you relied upon them for the security of your establishment. . . . The Nobility and Gentry in Scotland have the commons so much under, that it argues no small stupidity in you to have blundered in so plain a case.' Even English Nonconformist visitors to Scotland were astonished and alarmed at the boldness of the Church in its dealings with 'the Great.' Whatever its other faults, the Church of John Knox raised the downtrodden people of Scotland to look its feudal masters in the face.

The position of the Episcopalians at the beginning of the Eighteenth Century was most anomalous. Their services, doctrines, organization and discipline—except for the presence of Bishops who in fact exercised small authority—differed little save in emphasis from those of the Presbyterian Establishment. Yet the greatest bitterness prevailed between the two communions, because the difference of the Churches answered to the political difference of Whig and Jacobite, behind which lay two generations of feuds and wrongs inflicted and remembered on both sides.

The Episcopalians of Scotland were at once better and worse off than the Nonconformists of England. On the one hand there was not, until 1712, any Act of Toleration to legalize their services. On the other hand, more than a sixth of the parish churches were still occupied by their ministers. In Aberdeenshire, in the High-lands and along their eastern border, Presbyterian clergymen who showed themselves were liable to be attacked by mobs as savage as those who had 'rabbled' the Episcopal 'curates' of the South-West. When in 1704 the Presbyterian minister was to be inducted at Dingwall, he was stoned, beaten and driven away by a mob of men and women crying 'King Willie is dead and our King is alive.'

The popular feeling that thus found expression in the North-East arose less from religious differences than from political feuds, regional hatred of the Whiggamores of the South-West, and per-sonal loyalty to old and tried pastors. In 1707 there were still 165 out of some 900 parishes in Scotland where the minister adhered to the Episcopal Church. But the great majority of the Episco-palian clergy had been deprived at the Revolution. In Anne's reign they were living miserably enough, the more fortunate as chaplains in some great house, too many on alms collected from their co-religionists in Scotland, or from English churchmen who regarded them as martyrs in a common cause.

I have explained in an earlier chapter how the belief in witch-craft had already so far declined in the upper strata of English society that the persecution of witches in accordance with the law and with the dictates of popular superstition was ceasing to be permitted, in a country that was then ruled according to the ideas of its educated class. In Scotland the same phenomena were repeated, a generation or two later. At the beginning of the Eighteenth Century, part of the upper class was already dubious as to the frequency of diabolic agency, but popular and clerical fanaticism was still very strong. Several supposed witches were put to death in Queen Anne's Scotland, and several more were banished forth of the realm. In the reign of George I capital punishment was inflicted on witches for the last time in this island, in the recesses of far Sutherlandshire. In 1736 the law punishing witchcraft with death was repealed for Great Britain by the Westminster Parliament. After yet another generation had passed, witches and 'the muckle black de'il' were a subject of jest rather than of dread to Burns and his farmer friends, although Presby-terians of the stricter way continued to regard disbelief in witch-craft as 'atheism' and flying in the face of God's word.

The Presbyterian Church was not the fount and origin of

popular superstitions. It fostered some kinds and discouraged others. But all had their roots far back in Popish, in pagan, in primeval instincts and customs still strong in a land of mountains, moors and yet unconquered nature, amid a population which even in the Lowlands was largely Celtic in origin and which lived under conditions in many respects little changed since the remote past. Still, when the goodman came splashing home across the ford at midnight, he heard the water kelpie roaring in the spate. Fairies still lurked in the thorn trees of the dene, known visitants to be propitiated by rites lest they should slay the cattle in the byre or take the child from the cradle. North of Tay, men lit Beltan fires and danced round them, on traditional heights, upon the first of May. Crops and cattle were defended by a number and variety of local formulas of propitiation, some dating back to the earliest times of agricultural and pastoral man,

> When holy were the haunted forest boughs,
> Holy the air, the water and the fire.

Magic wells were visited, and trees and bushes were decked with rags of tartan and offerings of the fearful and grateful. In parts of the Highlands such rites were the main religion of the people; in the Lowlands they were a subordinate but still a real part of life and belief among a nation of Christian kirk-goers.

In the absence of proper doctors for the countryside, popular medicine was traditional, and it was sometimes hard to distinguish it from a popular form of witchcraft. There were wise men and women who helped human happiness, as well as warlocks and witches who hampered it. The Church encouraged the people to destroy the latter, but could not prevent them from seeking the aid of the former. The minister was not all-powerful. How could he be, since he forbade harmless pleasures? Lads and lassies, 'danced promisky' to fiddle or pipes at every festal meeting, in spite of the Church's ban; and neither old nor young could be held back from rites older than Presbyter or Pope. There were a hundred different charms and customs to avert ill-luck, suited to every event in life—birth, marriage, death, the churning of milk, the setting forth on a journey, the sowing of a field.

Miracle was looked upon as an everyday occurrence, far more than in unimaginative, sceptical England. Ghosts, omens, apparitions were of the ordinary pattern of Scottish life; tales of living corpses taking part in the common affairs of men were told with circumstance and believed; like the Greek of Homer's time, the Scot who met a stranger on the moor might well be uncertain whether he was what he seemed to be, or was 'no that canny.' The 'muckle black de'il' was often seen waiting in the shadow at evening outside the cottage door, or slipping away over the north side of the kirkyard wall. The men who had been hunted on the moors by the dragoons, like Wodrow their historiographer, were always agape for the wonderful, moving in an element of divine and diabolic manifestations of power. Ministers encouraged such beliefs in their congregations. Shepherd lads, out alone for long hours upon the hills, had strange and sometimes beautiful fancies: Wodrow tells us in 1704 of one who declared that 'when herding in such a lee, there was a bonny man came to him, and bade him pray much and learn to read; and he supposed it was Christ.' Next year he tells us of another lad who was once drowning in a well, but 'a bonny young man pulled him out by the hand. There was nobody near by at the time, so they concluded it was no doubt ane angel.' This is an older Scotland, not the Scotland of David Hume, Adam Smith or the Edinburgh Reviewers, not even the Scotland of Burns and Walter Scott, though it supplied them with matter for their argument.

If even in the Lowlands primitive and natural conditions bred primitive belief and natural fancies, it was even more so in the Highlands, the very home of the fairies and spirits of the mountain, of the formless monster that brooded unseen in the deep water beneath the boat, of second-sight, of omens and prophecy with which the little life of man was girt round. Beyond the Highland line, seldom passed by the Lowlander, and never without those qualms which beset Bailie Nicol Jarvie on his famous expedition, lay the grim, unmapped, roadless mountains, the abode of the Celtic tribes, speaking another language; wearing another dress; living under a system of law and society a thousand years older than that of Southern Scotland; obedient neither to Kirk nor Queen, but to their own chiefs, clans, customs and superstitions. Till General Wade's work a generation later, there was no driving road through the Highlands. Nature reigned, gloomy, splendid, unchallenged—as yet unadmired—and man squatted in corners of her domain.

Far less accurate knowledge was available in London or even in Edinburgh about the state of the Highlands than can now be bought across the counter of a bookshop concerning the remotest parts of Africa. There was no tolerable book on the Highlands until Mr. Burt's letters of the following generation. A few pages at the beginning of Morer's account of Scotland told the English of Queen Anne's time almost all they cared to know about the unreclaimed northern end of the strange island they inhabited:

The Highlanders are not without considerable quantities of corn, yet have not enough to satisfie their numbers, and therefore yearly come down with their cattle, of which they have great plenty, and so traffick with the Low Landers for such proportions of oats and barly as their families or necessities call for. . . . Once or tweice a year great numbers of 'em get together and make a descent into the Low-Lands, where they plunder the inhabitants and so return back and disperse themselves. And this they are apt to do in the profoundest peace, it being natural to 'em to delight in rapine.

Defoe, writing to Harley from Edinburgh in November 1706, gives his Englishman's impression of the Highlanders:

They are formidable fellows and I only wish Her Majesty had 25,000 of them in Spain, as a nation equally proud and barbarous like themselves. They are all gentlemen, will take affront from no man, and insolent to the last degree. But certainly the absurdity is ridiculous to see a man in his mountain habit, armed with a broad-sword, target, pistol, at his girdle a dagger, and staff, walking down the High Street as upright and haughty as if he were a lord, and withal driving a cow!

What manner of life did the tribesman lead, unobserved at home, when he was not trading with the Lowlander or driving off his cattle? It is a pathetic fallacy to suppose that the tribal land was the people's, and that they lived on it in rustic felicity, until the chiefs, in a sudden access of wickedness, took if from them after the 'forty-five.' In fact, the crofter of Queen Anne's reign was fain to hire a patch of ground from the 'tacksman' or leaseholder of the chief, who sublet it on rack-rent terms that were usually most oppressive. The soil on the mountain-side was thin and stony, denuded by torrents, unimproved by manure; the agricultural implements and methods were more primitive than even in Southern Scotland; the crofts were the merest hovels. It could not be otherwise, for the scanty population was yet too large for the glens to support. As the clansmen multiplied, the little farms were divided and subdivided with disastrous results. It might easily have been prophesied that if ever the Highlands were brought into connection with the outer world by roads, or by military and political conquest, a great emigration would result as soon as the clansman had grasped the idea that change was possible in their mode of life. In Anne's reign there was only a trickle of emigration into the Lowlands for the rougher types of service, and to the Continent to join the 'Irish' regiments in French pay, which owed much to the Scottish Highlanders in their ranks.

The Chief had the power of life and death, and exercised it to the full, keeping his clan in awe, that was always strengthened by traditional loyalty and often by affection. But it depended on the uncertain personal factor whether a Chief was a tyrant or a father, or something between the two. Just as Louis XIV taxed his peasants to keep up his army, so the Chief moved about with a train of armed relations and attendants, whom he supported in idleness at the expense of the rest of the clan; but any more economical and peaceful habit of life would not have been appreciated by a race in whom personal and tribal pride was the dominant passion.

Many of the Highland Chiefs, besides the great Argyle, were also noblemen with a place in Edinburgh politics, and with something of the culture of France or of England. But always the civilized Chief and his uncivilized followers had much in common —the pride of clan, the love of the harp and of the pipes, the stories and songs in which old feuds and fancies were still being woven by tribal poets into a living Gaelic literature. If in the shadow of the glen and beside the hill-girt arms of the sea there was more of poverty and savagery than in other parts of the island, there was also more of poetry and wild imagination.

This state of things aroused the zeal of the Church Assembly and of the Society for Promoting Christian Knowledge; from 1704 onwards many thousands of pounds were raised to initiate libraries, schools and Presbyterian missions in the Highlands, where religion was divided between Presbyterian, Roman Catholic, Episcopalian and primitive Pagan, in proportions which it would be difficult to determine. Some success was achieved at once, but in some places the mission was suppressed by violence at the orders of the Chief, and in others it lapsed in the course of years. It was after the 'forty-five,' when tribalism had been effectively put down by military and political invasion from the south, that the Presbyterian missionary had his chance, and the real evangelization of the Highlands took place.

Such, in some sort, was Scotland, when the circumstances of the passing hour brought to a final issue the ever-recurring problem of the closer Union of the whole island. In that design stark King Edward had failed, and Cromwell's arm had laxed its hold in death; where force had been tried in vain, Queen Anne was to succeed by means more befitting her womanhood. The freely negotiated Treaty between the two countries, that united their Parliamentary and commercial systems, came into force in 1707 and opened the way to the movements that made modern Scotland.

Books for Further Reading

H. G. Graham, *Social Life in Scotland in the Eighteenth Century*. A number of other books on the subject are cited in the second volume of my *England under Queen Anne* (*Ramillies and the Union with Scotland*).

II

SCOTLAND AT THE END OF THE EIGHTEENTH CENTURY

George III, 1760–1820

'PROGRESS,' as we of the Twentieth Century are better aware than our Victorian ancestors, is not always change from bad to good or from good to better, and the sum total of 'progress' associated with the Industrial Revolution has not been wholly for the good of man. But the 'progress' of Scotland in the second half of the Eighteenth Century was not only very rapid but very much in the right direction. No doubt it bore in itself the seed of future evil, but Scotland in 1800 was a better place than Scotland in 1700. The lifting of the pressure of dire poverty from the bulk of the population, and of penury from the higher classes, set the Scottish spirit free for its greatest achievements.

Release from the conditions of misery described in the first part of this chapter came mainly through a revolution in agricultural methods. It was analogous to the contemporary movement in rural England, but it marked an even greater change, for Scottish agriculture had been far worse than English when the Century opened. Improvement was begun by the action of certain Scottish landlords, who introduced English ploughmen and farmers to teach their tenants new ideas from South Britain; and it culminated triumphantly during the Napoleonic Wars when stewards and ploughmen from the Lothians were taken to England to teach methods that had by that time been evolved in Scotland. Between 1760 and 1820 English agriculture had been progressing much faster than ever before or since; yet during those very years Scottish agriculture caught it up and passed it.

As in England, the first movers in the change were individual landlords with a little capital, enterprise and outside knowledge. Their success set an example which was generally followed. The first thing to be done was to break up the 'run-rig' system of common tillage (p. 132 above); it was conducted on methods more primitive than those of the English 'open fields'; it prevented individual initiative and gave neither security of tenure nor motive for exertion to the community of petty farmers, crushed under an obsolete feudalism. Unlike the old English copyholders, the Scottish tenants had no legal rights in the land, and they had short leases or none. But this system, bad as it was, had one advantage, that it could be easily terminated. There was nothing to prevent landlords bent on improvement from abolishing the 'run-rigs' and re-dividing the land in compact farms, which they let to individual farmers at long leases of nineteen years or more. By this great reform the tenant obtained for the first time a motive to exert the long dormant energy and enterprise of the Scottish race.

There was indeed an obvious danger, as in the analogous case of the English enclosures, that some of the old tenants would be turned off the land altogether, as victims of reform. For instance, where a 'run-rig' farm previously let to a community of a dozen tenants was enclosed and redivided among the half that number, what became of the rest? A few went to the now prosperous towns or to the Colonies opened by the Union to Scottish emigration. But, generally speaking, the number of people employed in Scottish agriculture increased rather than diminished, owing to the constant enlargement of the area of cultivated land. And the new acres won from the waste were often the best, being situated in the fertile valley bottom which only required artificial draining to be more valuable than the fields of older cultivation on the self-draining hillside above.

Both the old lands and the new were now enclosed with stone walls or hedges; the high 'rigs' were levelled; the fields were drained, limed, manured; one or two good horses took the place of the long train of starveling oxen at the plough; men could now afford leather harness instead of horses' hair or rushes, iron ploughs instead of wooden, carts instead of sledges. Potatoes grown in the fields and vegetables in the garden varied the food of the population, while roots and other crops fed the cattle through the winter. Plantations of trees broke the wind and served the timber-requirements of the estate; and, on a larger scale, new forests covered the hillsides in many parts of Scotland.[1]

---

[1] Dr. Johnson, who travelled in Scotland in 1773, continued to joke about its lack of trees. In fact some great plantations had already been made, but the trees were still saplings when he was there. Thirty years later the aspect of many parts of the country had been greatly changed in this respect.

After the Turnpike Act of 1751, the roads were so generally improved as to increase the marketing opportunities of farmers and industrialists alike. Agricultural prosperity supplied capital to be put back into the land. And Banks, established in Country towns early in the reign of George III, helped both lairds and farmers to finance the changes they were together carrying out. The industrial and commercial growth of Clydeside created a market for agriculture and supplied capital for further improvement of the land. Estates were bought and developed by 'tobacco-lords' of the Glasgow shipping world, and by adventurous Scots returned from British India where they had amassed fortunes. In short, there was simultaneous growth in all kinds of economic and social life, none at the expense of any other: for in that fortunate era industry and commerce were not the enemies but the allies of agriculture.

In this way the periodic famines, which had taken toll of the lives and energies of the Scottish people, lost their worst terrors. And, in ordinary years, real wages, farm profits and rents were all much higher than in former times. Potatoes, vegetables, cheese and occasionally meat were added to the porridge and milk, which was still the staple diet of the poor though the bowl was fuller than of old; in Scotland as in England the smuggler helped to bring tea and tobacco into the homes even of the poorest. Scandalous as Scottish housing remained, there was great though not universal improvement even there; in some regions solid stone farms, and cottages with one or even two rooms, with chimneys, glass windows, beds, furniture and outside privies, replaced the hovels which the peasantry used to share with their cattle. [See § 128, 129.] The sturdy Scots of the time of Burns (1759–1796) looked a different race from their grandfathers, whom want of food, clothing and warmth had too often rendered haggard, slovenly and lethargic to the view.

Moreover the Scots were now free men. The last evils of moribund feudalism, which survived in Scotland for centuries after they had ceased in England, were abolished in 1748 by the Act which put an end to 'hereditable jurisdictions.' In Lowlands and Highlands alike, the baron or chief who had his private court to try his vassals and tenants, had been able, at will or whim, to imprison the disobedient in fetid dungeons, without appeal lying to the King's tribunals. These powers, it was believed, helped

Jacobite lairds and chiefs to 'call out their men' in 1745. They were accordingly abolished three years later, and there were plenty of good reasons why they should go, apart from the political motive that hastened their end.

In the Highlands, much disappeared besides the hereditable jurisdictions. In the years following the suppression of the 'forty-five,' the whole manner of life and society, which had prevailed in the mountains of Scotland with little change since prehistoric times, was swept away at a blow. The tribal system, the kilted warrior with broadsword and target, the patriarchal rule of the chief, vanished for ever. The Highlands became, for the first time in their history, one with the rest of Scotland, so far as law, land-tenure, education and religion could make Highlander and Low-lander one. The construction of the first roads through the High-lands, effected by General Wade in the generation before 1745, had already carried Lowland influence into the hills, and prepared the way for the great change; it must have come ere long, but would have come more gradually, if the Jacobite invasion had not provoked the long-suffering South to put an end once for all to the thousand-year-old nuisance of the raiding tribes.

A population that had always lived for and by war was at last effectively disarmed; but its fighting instincts were canalized into the Highland regiments of the Crown, that did good service abroad for the Empire now common to Englishmen and Scots, to Gael and Saxon. The Chiefs were turned into landlords, like the lairds in the South. Henceforth justice and administration were royal and national, not personal and tribal any more. The acceptance of these immense changes in the structure of society indicated that the time for them was ripe. For some years after the Rebellion there was a period of tyranny and repression, the period described in Stevenson's *Kidnapped*, when the personal devotion of the clansmen to their banished chiefs was touchingly demonstrated. But there was no popular movement to restore an outworn state of society, and when the ex-Jacobite chiefs were permitted to return from abroad and their estates were restored to them under the new system of tenure, the conflict of loyalties came to an end. The tribal tartan, which had been proscribed, was again allowed to be worn, for the proud sentiments attaching to it were no longer disruptive of society and law.

Meanwhile Presbyterian missionaries and schoolmasters had been at work in the Highlands, and had from the first shown more tact and more sympathy with the Gael than the emissaries of the civil power. The imagination and intellect of the mountaineers, hitherto illiterate and poetical, had new channels opened to it by the work of the schools. Reading and writing were brought into the Highlands mainly by the Scottish Society for Propagating Christian Knowledge, which began its mission in that wild region in the reign of Anne, but was only able to succeed there on a large scale when the country was opened by the breaking of the clans after Culloden. The unity of Scottish society was achieved on the religious and educational side before the century ended, though the Highlands remained bilingual. In the glens where the Roman Catholic religion prevailed, its hold was unshaken; but the old paganism disappeared.

Closely connected with this educational movement was the great change in the economic side of Highland life. Under the tribal system, the population had been much larger than the barren mountains could maintain. The ambition of each Chieftain had been to increase not the amount of his rents but the number of his armed followers; while the tribesmen, accustomed to dire poverty and periodic famine, had neither the knowledge nor the opportunity to emigrate into the lands where Gaelic was an unknown tongue. But the new times were more favourable to emigration. The Chief, when transmuted into a peaceful landlord, wanted money more than men. And his sorely oppressed tenants became aware, by means of the new roads and schools, of a wealthier world outside the mountains and beyond the sea. The age of Highland emigration set in, very largely to Canada, while at home sheep-runs often replaced the little holdings of the crofters. In the 'seventies there were great emigrations from the Highlands and the Islands, and again in 1786–1788 as a result of the terrible famines of 1782–1783. Under the old system such famines had often taken place, but had not been followed by emigration, because the tribesmen had not known how or whither to emigrate.

Now, in some districts, the landlords themselves stimulated emigrations by evictions. But elsewhere they strove to keep people at home by the introduction of the potato, and sometimes by their opposition to the schools of the S.P.C.K. For the missionary-schoolmasters were the real promoters of emigration.

They even accused the gentry of trying 'to keep the people at home in ignorance and subjection.' The Highlander could only hope for a higher standard of living if he went oversea, or at least outside the mountain region. And as a preparation for departure, he must learn English, as he could now do at the missionary schools.

The English tongue and the Gaelic Bible suggested two ways of escape from conditions which were fast becoming intolerable. Far from undermining the characteristic independence of the Highlanders, the Charity Schools provided them with the only means of translating it into effective action. To men of vigour and courage the English language offered a new world across the seas; to those who remained behind, the schools made possible independent access to the consolations of the Bible.[1]

The Union of the political and commercial systems of England and Scotland had alone rendered possible the social revolution in the Highlands, the colonization of the British Empire by Scots, the development of Glasgow's transatlantic trade and the consequent industrialization of Clydeside. These changes, like the agricultural revolution, were mainly an affair of the last half of the Century, but during that period they were very rapid.

At the time of the Union of 1707 Glasgow was a market and University town with a population of 12,500, an outpost of Southern civilization against the Highland tribes, the capital of the Covenanting West; its inhabitants were rigid and censorious in their Presbyterian zeal, simple in manners, frugal in expense, and strictly sober; its leading citizens, such as Bailie Nicol Jarvie, lived among their fellow-citizens in modest quarters in the heart of the town. By 1800 great changes had taken place: Glasgow numbered 80,000 inhabitants, sharply divided by differences in wealth and manner of life, and no class among them was any longer famous either for church going or for abstention from drink. Well-to-do suburbs and new slum tenements had spread over the surrounding land. There were shops to suit every taste, with wares from England, Europe and America; there were sedan chairs, concerts, balls, cards and dice, punch, wine and English literature for the rich, and Highland whisky for the poor. The University had won European fame through Professor Adam Smith.

[1] Miss M. G. Jones, *The Charity School Movement of the 18th Century*, chap. VI.

These social changes had taken place, because the American and West Indian trade, chiefly in tobacco and raw cotton, had by 1800 transformed not only Glasgow but all Clydeside into a commercial and industrial district as up to date as any in England; it had already given the world James Watt, one of the lords of the new ascendant, the inventor of the modern condensing engine. Western Scotland was already beginning to suffer from the advent of Irish labourers, who made the Glasgow slums even worse than bad housing would in any case have rendered them.

In the last twenty years of the Century, cotton mills were rising in villages of Lanark, Renfrew and Ayr, with social consequences described in Galt's *Annals of the Parish*, that little story book, first published in 1821, which still remains the most intimate and human picture of Scotland during her period of change in the reign of George III.

The opening of the Scottish-American trade by the Union had naturally had less influence on the fortunes of towns upon the East Coast. Indeed, the old-established commerce of Leith and Dundee with the Baltic and German ports lost rather than gained by the British mercantilist policy of the Navigation Acts, which aimed at enlarging colonial trade with America at the expense of commerce with Europe.

On the other hand it was in the East that the first Scottish ironworks were erected. At Carron, between Stirling and Edinburgh, iron-ore, coal and water-power were found together; coal-coke was now applied to the smelting of iron. The Carron Company, founded in 1760, prospered; one of its early articles of production was the short naval gun known therefore as the 'carronade.' Such was the beginning of the Scottish iron industry that took on such great proportions in the following century.

But the only town of the Scottish East Coast that made striking advance in the Eighteenth Century was Edinburgh. No longer a political capital, it was still the legal, fashionable and intellectual capital of the country; and law, fashion and intellect were all rapidly on the upgrade in the wealthier and more active-minded Scotland of the new era. Moreover, the now famous agriculture of the Lothians had advanced even faster than the agriculture of the West. The South-Eastern Scotland of Walter Scott's youth was a land of rural wealth and mental energy centred on Edinburgh. The Scottish capital was famous throughout Europe for its 'philosophers'—Hume, Robertson and Dugald Stewart; its lawyers and academicians were men of remarkable personality and intellectual power. Joined with these professional classes, the nobles and gentry of the region, busy with the improvement of the land and the planting of forests, combined to form a splendid society, worthy of the immortality given to it by its own artist, Raeburn.

It is indeed true that, during this golden age of Scotland, her political life was dead. To use Cockburn's words, she 'had no free political institutions whatever': the absence of 'political institutions' was indeed a feature of the whole period from the Union to the Reform Bill, under Whig and Tory rule alike, but as long as Jacobitism had been active, there was a diseased kind of political life—a constant sedition. After 1746 that too had gone, till the Radical movement arose in 1790, to be at once suppressed by a harsh government persecution. Under the rule of Pitt's friend Dundas, Scotland was 'a lodge at a great man's gate,' as the Reformers bitterly said. But politics are not everything. The social, imaginative and intellectual life of the land of Burns and Scott was vigorous in inverse proportion to the political atrophy; it sprang from native sources, and though closer connection with England had given it an impulse, it paid back to England more than it borrowed. Adam Smith devised policies for the statesmen of Great Britain. And for several years at the beginning of the Nineteenth Century, while the *Lay of the Last Minstrel* and *Marmion* were initiating the 'romantic' period of letters in our island, the very unromantic *Edinburgh Review* enjoyed almost a monopoly of literary and philosophic criticism in England. The rival *Quarterly* was soon set up against it, largely by the efforts of Scotchmen. For some years Edinburgh was hardly less important than London in the British world of letters.

Physically, too, Edinburgh had grown out of her hard old shell. The insanitary warren of deep wynds and lofty tenement flats off High Street, where the greatest men in Scotland and their families had formerly consented to be cabined in darkness and dirt, were deserted for the spacious and dignified houses, built after 1780 in the region of new squares beyond Princes Street. [See § 132, 133.] The bridging of the Nor' Loch in 1767 had opened out for development this new Edinburgh. Instead of paying £15 a year for an ill-lighted flat seven storeys off the ground, persons of position could now afford to pay £100 a year for a comfortable town house. Similarly in the countryside, the tall, grim, gothic towers rising from the naked fields, that had served for the country seats of the gentry, were, at least in many cases, replaced by Georgian or classical mansions, cheerful, well lighted and sheltered by trees. [See § 127, 130, 131.] But architecture never attained in Scotland to the importance which it had for centuries had in England. In spite of much improvement, particularly the fine stone farms of the Lothians, housing north of the Tweed remained on the average below the level of South Britain. Even in the Lowlands there were still many one-roomed cottages, still in some cases shared by the cow; and the high slum tenements of Glasgow and Edinburgh were worse than ever because they had now been abandoned by the well-to-do. Nevertheless there had during the Century been great progress in housing, though less than in food, clothes and education.[1]

The rapid changes in Scottish mind and manners during the Eighteenth Century did not come into any serious collision with the influence of the Church, such as marked contemporary movements of opinion in France. For the clergy and religious laity of Scotland moved with the times towards a more tolerant and a more reasonable outlook. Presbyterian bigotry, which had been so crude in the years immediately following the Revolution of 1688, began to soften as a generation of younger clergy and elders, who knew not Claverhouse, gradually took the place of the fierce old prophets of the moss-hags. The enjoyment of toleration, better education, English influence, and the indefinable 'spirit of the age' broadened their vision as the years went by. Witch hunting died out. The latitudinarian movement prevailing in the contemporary Church of England had a close analogy in the views of the Moderates, who became the most influential section of the Scottish clergy. The sage leadership of the historian Robertson (1721–1793) guided the Church Assembly into the ways of peace.

It is possible that some of the Moderates went too far in the sweet reasonableness of their moderation, and the more zealous of their ever critical hearers had perhaps some reason in the

---

[1] An interesting comparison of Scottish and English housing of the working classes about 1820, with its local variations, will be found in Professor Clapham's *Economic History of Modern England*, I, pp. 21–41.

complaints against sermons that were 'a cauld clatter of morality,' lacking in orthodox doctrine and apostolic zeal. In due course the pendulum swung back, and in the early Nineteenth Century the Evangelical revival, connected with men like Dr. Chalmers (1780–1847), breathed fresh power into Scottish religion. But the religion of Chalmers was no longer a narrow and persecuting creed: the 'Moderates' had done their work.

The Eighteenth Century also saw great changes in the fortunes and in the spirit of the Episcopalian minority. At the time of the Union of 1707 the Episcopalians were a formidable body, practically identical with the Jacobites, and prepared to fight for a Restoration of their Church and of their King; they did not, however, use the Prayer Book, and their religion was only a milder form of that of the Presbyterian Establishment. But as the Century went on they drew nearer to the rest of the nation in politics and further from it in religion. After the death of Jacobitism they became loyal subjects of George III, while their adoption of a Prayer Book closely resembling the English divided them off from their fellow Scots as a religious community with an ethos of its own. Their numbers dwindled. In Anne's reign they had been the Church of the People in many parts of Eastern Scotland, and had as such been permitted at the Revolution to continue in occupation of parish churches and manses in spite of the law. But as that generation of incumbents died off, they were replaced by Presbyterian ministers.

On the other hand, the position of the Episcopalians was improved in one important respect. They had not, at the Revolution, been granted an Act of Toleration like the English Dissenters. Their position was in every respect anomalous, depending not on law but on local opinion and force. At length in 1712 the Tories of the Westminster Parliament passed a Toleration Act for Scotland—a first-fruit of the Union eminently right and proper, but regarded with deep suspicion by the Presbyterians as the herald of further attacks on the established order.

Indeed, there followed in a few weeks another and more questionable interference of the British Parliament in the affairs of the Scottish Church. In 1712 Patronage was restored—that is, the right of individual proprietors to appoint to livings. To an Englishman accustomed to the system in the Anglican Church this may seem a small matter, but Scottish religious and social history was profoundly affected for 150 years to come by the restoration of Patronage.

The democratic element in the appointment of ministers to parishes was regarded by orthodox Presbyterians as an essential point of religion; and apart from all theory, there was a practical danger in presentation by patrons many of whom were latitudinarians, Episcopalians or Jacobites. For these reasons Patronage had been abolished by a law of the Scottish Parliament at the Revolution: by the Act of 1690 the Protestant heritors and elders should 'name and propose' a minister to the whole congregation, which if dissatisfied might appeal to the Presbytery, whose decision should be final. But now, in 1712, the 'prelatic' Parliament of Westminster altered this law, in defiance of the spirit of the Union Treaty. The right of presentation was restored to the old patrons, unless they were Roman Catholics.

Although the new law was deeply resented, its consequences were not remarkable for the first generation after its passage. But the ultimate outcome was momentous indeed. Patronage was the root cause of a long series of secessions of Presbyterian bodies from an Established Church bound by this State-made law. For good or for evil, Scotland, hitherto inimical to Sects such as flourished in England, saw the rise of a number of Nonconformist Churches, competing with the Establishment, though differing from it in doctrine and ritual hardly at all.

The restoration of Patronage had also the effect of helping the rise of the Moderate Party in the Church. In the Eighteenth Century the rights of the patrons were often exerted to place moderate-minded ministers in parishes of zealots, who objected to their intrusion, yet benefited by their mild ministrations. Readers of Galt's *Annals of the Parish* will not forget that in the first year of George III's reign the excellent Mr. Balwhidder was thus intruded, 'for I was put in by a patron, and people knew nothing whatsoever of me, and their hearts were stirred into strife on the occasion.' Some critics of the bigotry of the older Calvinism have said in their haste that the Scots were 'a priest-ridden people.' It would be truer to say that theirs was 'a people-ridden clergy.' The zealots in the congregation kept a close eye on their minister's orthodoxy. In the Eighteenth Century many of the placed clergy did all they could to liberalize Scottish religion, often at the price of unpopularity with their lay parishioners.

In the Nineteenth Century the long-drawn-out consequences of the Patronage Act of 1712 culminated in the secession of the Free Church under Chalmers, a protest on behalf of evangelical liberty which is one of the great facts of the modern history of Scotland (1843). At length, in 1875, the measure so lightly passed in Anne's reign was reversed, with the consequence that a path was opened for the ultimate reunion of the divided parts of the Church of Scotland, which took place in our own day, after the State had still further declared the unfettered freedom of the Church over the entire field of matters spiritual by the Act of 1921.

In the course of the Eighteenth Century the inhabitants of Scotland rose in numbers from about a million to 1,652,000. This represents a natural increase, as the emigration of the Highlanders can be set against the immigration of the Irish. The rise in population, unprecedented in any previous century of Scottish history, was due, like the contemporary rise in the numbers of Englishmen, to the rapid fall of the death-rate. It was the outcome of improved conditions of life, and of better doctoring, a science in which Scots in the reign of George III were already able to instruct the English.

Rapid as was the rise of Scotland's population in the Eighteenth Century, it had not been as rapid as the increase of her wealth. The Excise revenue in 1707 was £30,000; in 1797 it was close on one million three hundred thousand. The day of small things was over.

But Scotland had still a bad hour to pass through. The Napoleonic Wars witnessed a great rise in prices of food, accompanied by much general distress. Again there were 'dear years' in 1799 and 1800, when 'oatmeal was as high as ten shillings a stone,' and Thomas Carlyle's father noticed the labourers 'retire each separately to a brook, and there drink instead of dining—without complaint, anxious only to hide it.' But they no longer died of starvation by scores and hundreds, depopulating whole clachans, as in the 'dear years' of King William a century before.[1]

---

[1] The last half of Carlyle's sketch of his father James Carlyle in the *Reminiscences* contains many vivid particulars of Scottish peasant life in the last half of the Eighteenth Century. At Langholm, James Carlyle 'once saw a heap of smuggled tobacco publicly burnt. Dragoons were ranged round it with drawn swords; some old women stretched through their old withered arms to snatch a little of it, and the dragoons did not hinder them.' The working women of those western parts, including Thomas Carlyle's mother, smoked tobacco in short clay pipes.

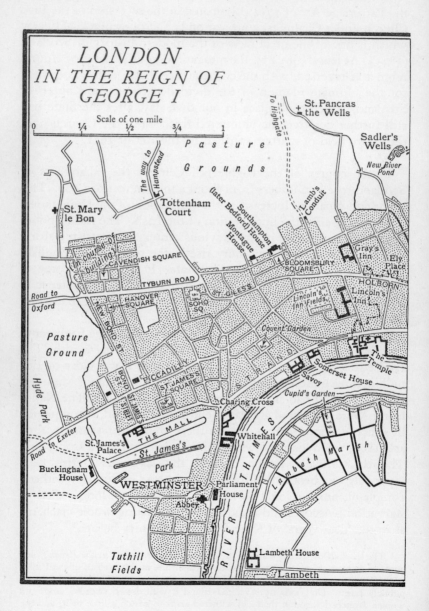

LONDON
IN THE REIGN OF
GEORGE I

Scale of one mile

0   ¼   ½   ¾   1

St. Pancras
the Wells

Sadler's
Wells

New River
Pond

P a s t u r e

G r o u n d s

The way to Hampstead

Tottenham
Court

St. Mary
le Bon

Lamb's
Conduit

To Highgate

Southampton
(later Bedford) House

Montague
House

BLOOMSBURY
SQUARE

Gray's
Inn

Ely
Place

In course of building

CAVENDISH SQUARE

TYBURN ROAD

ST. GILES

HOLBORN

Lincoln's
Inn

Road to
Oxford

HANOVER
SQUARE

SOHO
SQ.

Lincoln's
Inn Fields

Covent Garden

The
Temple

Pasture
Ground

NEW BOND ST.

CCADILLY

BOND STREET

ST. JAMES'S STREET

ST. JAMES'S
SQUARE

S T R A N D

Savoy

Somerset House

Cupid's Garden

Hyde Park

Charing Cross

THE MALL

St. James's
Palace

St. James's
Park

Whitehall

Road to Exeter

Lambeth Marsh

Buckingham
House

WESTMINSTER

Parliament
House

Abbey

R I V E R   T H A M E S

Tuthill
Fields

Lambeth House

Lambeth

162

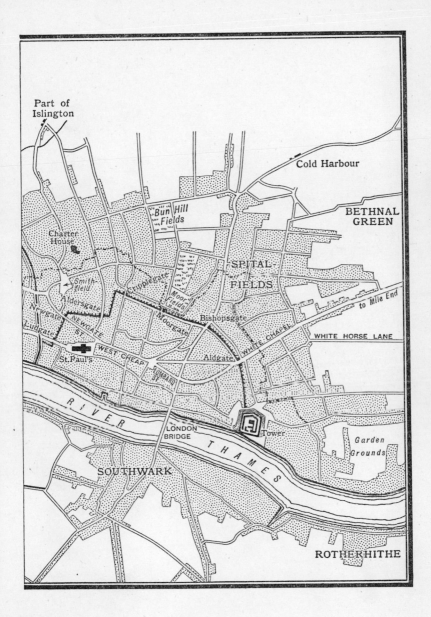

Part of
Islington

Cold Harbour

BETHNAL
GREEN

*Bun Hill
Fields*

Charter
House

SPITAL-
FIELDS

Smith-
field

Cripplegate

Aldersgate

Moor
fields

Newgate

NEWGATE ST.

Ludgate

Mooregate

Bishopsgate

to Mile End

WHITE CHAPEL

WEST CHEAP

St. Paul's

Aldgate

WHITE HORSE LANE

LOMBARD ST.

RIVER

LONDON
BRIDGE

Tower

Garden
Grounds

THAMES

SOUTHWARK

ROTHERHITHE

163

DESCRIPTIVE NOTES
TO THE ILLUSTRATIONS

These are grouped into three categories: 1. Colour Plates; 2. Gravure Plates (marked §); 3. Illustrations in the text

Colour Plate I   *Frontispiece* (cf. text p. 15)

Queen Anne and the Garter Knights. From the painting by Peter Angelis (1713) in the National Portrait Gallery.

Although the individual portraiture in this painting is not good it yet presents an interesting record of the ceremony of the Installation of the Knights of the Garter as it was held at Kensington Palace on 4 August 1713. On this occasion Robert Harley, first Earl of Oxford, together with Henry Grey, Duke of Kent, Charles Mordaunt, third Earl of Peterborough and John, Earl Poulett, were installed. Harley appears to be the Knight kneeling on the right, while the Knight with a white staff is probably Charles Talbot, Duke of Shrewsbury, the Lord Chamberlain of the Household.

Colour Plate II (cf. text p. 30)

English family at tea. From the painting (British School, *c.* 1720) in the possession of the National Gallery. At present on loan to the Victoria and Albert Museum.

In spite of the statue of Bacchus in the background the family shown here is about to take tea. The tray is set with the handleless cups and the deep saucers of the period, and the tall tea-pot can be seen behind the maid, who holds the kettle ready. The mistress of the house is measuring out the tea from one of the canisters which are kept locked in the case (in the foreground): tea and sugar were still expensive luxuries.

Colour Plate III (cf. text p. 92)

London from the terrace of Richmond House. From the painting by Canaletto in the possession of His Grace the Duke of Richmond and Gordon.

Canaletto first came to London in 1746, one of his first patrons being the Duke of Richmond, from the windows of whose town house the Venetian artist painted this view of the Thames. It is probably one of the first pictures he painted in England. It shows the busy traffic of the river and Wren's St. Paul's dominating the sky-line with the spires and towers of London's churches rising from the close-packed city.

Colour Plate IV (cf. text p. 87)

A Lady and Gentleman in a Carriage. From the painting by George Stubbs (1787) in the National Gallery.

Stubbs (1724–1806) is chiefly known for his fine studies of horses and for his *Anatomy of the Horse* (1766), but in this graceful conversation piece he conveys the whole atmosphere of this fashionable diversion: the civilized background, the consciously proud horses and the occupants of the carriage very much on view in their high curricle phaeton.

§ 1 (cf. text p. 12)

Bradbourne House, near Maidstone, Kent. From a photograph in the possession of the Central Office of Information. Crown Copyright Reserved.

Built in 1713, this house is representative of the simple yet dignified elegance of a Queen Anne country house; its town counterpart can be seen in § 2 below.

§ 2 (cf. text p. 53 note)

London street scene in 1716. From *Trivia* by John Gay (1st edition, 1716). From the copy in the Department of Printed Books, British Museum.

This little cut from the first book of John Gay's *Trivia or the Art of Walking the Streets of London*, illustrates some of the poet's descriptions of London street conditions and of the passers-by. In Book I he discusses 'Implements for walking the Streets and Signs of the Weather' and tells how 'the sturdy paver thumps the ground, Whilst ev'ry stroke his lab'ring lungs resound,' or comments

'Good housewives all the winter's rage despise,
Defended by the riding hood's disguise:
Or underneath th' umbrella's oily shed
Safe thro' the wet on clinking pattens tread.
Let Persian dames th' umbrella's ribs display,
To guard their beauties from the sunny ray
. . .
Britain in winter only knows its aid
To guard from chilly showers the walking maid.'

(*Trivia*. Bk. I, ll. 210 f.)

§ 3 (cf. text p. 7)

Model Husbandry in 1727. From Richard Bradley's *A Complete Body of Husbandry, collected from the Practice and Experience of the most considerable farmers in Britain* . . . (1727). From a copy in the Department of Printed Books, British Museum.

This work by a former Cambridge Professor of Botany, who was also a Fellow of the Royal Society, is illustrated with cuts of ploughs and farm implements, and of such subjects as 'how to make a Pot-ash-house.'

The proper drainage of land is given an important place and this plate shows a neat new house and garden with up-to-date drains for watery pastures (fig. IV), Persian wheels (figs. II and

III) to throw up water to be led by pipes to fill a pond (E) or even more ambitiously to a cistern in the house above. The crane set across the bank in the background is an ingenious contraption for draining a pool or pond, and conveying the water over a hill to a town lying lower than the source of the water.

§ 4 (cf. text p. 6)

South Prospect of Leicester in 1743 from Samuel and Nathaniel Buck's *Views of Castles, Abbeys and Towns*. From the copy in the Department of Printed Books, British Museum.

This engraving of Leicester shows in the foreground the typical wide-spreading cornlands of the Midlands at harvest time, still unenclosed in 1743. It forms one of the large series of views and prospects issued by the Buck brothers, Samuel and Nathaniel, working between 1726 and 1753.

§ 5 and 6 (cf. text pp. 12, 13)

The Radcliffe Camera at Oxford. From James Gibbs' *Bibliotheca Radcliviana* (1747). From the copy in the Department of Printed Books, British Museum.

James Gibbs (1682–1754), the architect of the Radcliffe, also built the church of St. Mary-le-Strand (cf. § 38). He was a Scotsman by birth, who had studied in Italy and had already published by 1728 his *Book of Architecture* (cf. text p. 101). These views of the exterior and interior of the Radcliffe were published in 1747 on the completion of its building. Gibbs, as Wren had done before him when planning the library of Trinity College, Cambridge, paid great attention to the fittings and interior arrangements of his library. § 6 shows the placing of bookcases and desks. The Radcliffe was built from the benefaction of Dr. John Radcliffe (*d.* 1714), an Oxford doctor of medicine who had become court physician. It was first used to house only books on Medicine, Science and Natural History.

§ 7 (cf. text p. 46)

The Mall. From the painting (British School, *c.* 1735) at Buckingham Palace. Reproduced by gracious permission of His Majesty the King.

This picture, originally from the Carlton House collection and variously attributed to Hogarth and Samuel Wale, shows an animated scene in the Mall in the thirties of the century. In the centre a fashionable group surrounds Frederick, Prince of Wales, while around can be seen family parties, soldiers, two kilted Highlanders, while on the left are benches for taking refreshment—and a cow.

§ 8 (cf. text p. 115)

A Musical Party. From the painting by William Hogarth in the Fitzwilliam Museum, Cambridge.

This was probably painted about 1731 and shows a family with some of their friends making music for themselves, for 'music was not then an affair only of listening.'

§ 9 (cf. text p. 12)

Blenheim Palace. From an air photograph by Aerofilms, Ltd. Blenheim, designed by Sir John Vanbrugh (who had been dramatist, poet and soldier before turning architect), was built for the Duke of Marlborough as a mark of national gratitude for his victory at Blenheim in 1704. Its building extended over the years 1705–27. Its exuberant baroque was to be labelled by Robert Adam as doubtful in taste and its 'barbarisms and absurdities' as weighing down and retarding its architect's admitted genius. Dr. Abel Evans' epitaph on Vanbrugh:

> 'Lie heavy on him, earth, for he
> Laid many a heavy load on thee.'

is typical of the XVIIIth century attitude to Vanbrugh's grandiose manner: the classicist distrusted the fertile invention of the baroque.

The park and grounds were later considerably altered and developed by 'Capability' Brown, who was responsible for the extended lay-out of the lake and the great hanging woods, though he was also responsible for replacing the formal parterres by the sweep of grass (in the foreground of this photograph) in his customary manner. The formal garden below the west front (on the lake side) has been reconstructed in recent years.

§ 10, 11 and 12 (cf. text p. 14)

Houghton, Norfolk. From Isaac Ware's 'The plans, etc . . . of Houghton in Norfolk' (1735). From the copy in the Department of Printed Books, British Museum.

Houghton, the seat of Sir Robert Walpole, was built between 1722 and 1725 with money made out of the South Sea Bubble. The design was Colin Campbell's (the author of the *Vitruvius Britannicus*) but was chiefly carried out by Thomas Ripley; most of the interior was William Kent's with stucco work by the Italian plasterer Artari. Isaac Ware (*d.* 1766) who published these engravings of Houghton by P. Foudrinier, also had a hand in the building of Houghton, though he is better known for his Chesterfield House.

Houghton, with its rich decoration, its statuary, its magnificent collection of pictures (sold to Catherine of Russia by Walpole's grandson for £40,000—some say £45,000) is an outstanding example of those rural palaces which were built in England in the XVIIIth century to house the treasures their owners had amassed.

§ 10 shows the main elevation, while § 11 and 12 show two sections of the interior. The richly ornamented overmantels, bas-reliefs, medallions, swags and friezes can be seen, together with the niches for statuary, the brackets for busts and (on the left side of § 12) the library fittings for books with built-in bookcases.

§ 13 (cf. text p. 101)

Interior of the Bank House, Wisbech. From a photograph by Country Life, Ltd.

Built in 1722 this elegant but modest house was decorated in its present style some thirty years later. Its builder is unknown and though there is a tradition that a Frenchman employed at Houghton was responsible for the decorative carving at the Bank House, there is nothing to support this. Note the delicacy of the rococo carving of the mirror in this photograph of the drawing room. (The curtains are in early Victorian style.)

§ 14 (cf. text p. 101)

Interior of a house at Blandford. From a photograph by Country Life, Ltd.

Built and decorated after the disastrous 1731 fire at Blandford, which destroyed half the town, this house was occupied by the Bastard brothers, who were responsible for the rebuilding of the town.

§ 15 (cf. text p. 23)

Cockfighting in 1759. From the coloured line engraving 'Pit Ticket for the Royal Sport,' by William Hogarth (published 1759). From a copy in the possession of the Parker Gallery, London.

This engraving shows a cockfight in progress before a wildly excited gathering. The central figure is a blind nobleman who is said never to have missed a main. The structure of the cockpit is clearly shown, the small circular arena in which the mains were fought out between pairs of cocks, is enclosed by a ledge forming a barrier to the audience. The steel spurs on the birds' legs can be seen and also the shadow of a man who has been 'basketed' (i.e. suspended in a basket over the arena for not paying his debts); he is offering to pledge his watch, which can be seen dangling from his hand. Cockfighting went on till the middle of the XIXth century.

§ 16 (cf. text p. 21)

The Hazard table. From the drawing by William Hogarth in the Royal Library at Windsor. By gracious permission of His Majesty the King.

This drawing illustrates the prevalence of gaming, when even the tutor (in holy orders) appears to be teaching his young charges how to play hazard. (Cf. note to § 120 on the London clubs.)

§ 17 (cf. text p. 22)

Duelling. From the pen and wash drawing (attributed to William Hogarth) in the Department of Prints and Drawings, British Museum.

This duel scene appears to be an illustration for a novel (unidentified). The 'seconds' can be seen in the background.

§ 18 and 19 (cf. text pp. 30, 31)

Joseph Addison and Richard Steele. From the Kit Cat Club portraits by Kneller in the National Portrait Gallery.

Joseph Addison (1672–1719) and Richard Steele (1672–1726) are illustrated here as reformers of morals and manners in the early XVIIIth century. Their paper *The Spectator* in its daily essays, graceful in style, half-humorous, half-didactic in content, attempted to inculcate the virtues of good breeding, courtesy and chivalric feeling, and in doing so, created the lovable figure of Sir Roger de Coverley, using club or coffee-house life as a background.

§ 20 and 21 (cf. text pp. 30, 31)

From the drawings by William Hogarth (previously known as 'Scenes in Button's Coffee House') in the Department of Prints and Drawings, British Museum.

These drawings, which belonged at one time to Samuel Ireland, were dubbed by him 'scenes in Button's Coffee House' and the various characters equated with well-known literary figures such as Pope and Arbuthnot and Addison; in spite of the fact that he dated the drawings as about 1730 he claimed that they depicted characters who frequented Button's about 1720, regardless of the fact that Addison, for instance, was dead by 1719. (Cf. L. Binyon's *Drawings by British Artists*, Vol. II, 1900.) These scenes, however, remain excellent representations of the types of people who frequented the coffee houses and of the pursuits that went on there. They probably date between 1730 and 1740. One suspects from § 20 that the club bore had already made his appearance in the coffee house.

§ 22 (cf. text p. 27)

The Newcomen Engine, from the engraving by Henry Beighton (1717) in the Science Museum, South Kensington. Crown Copyright Reserved.

As early as 1698 Thomas Savery had invented a machine for raising water by the power of steam; this was improved and developed by Thomas Newcomen to become the pumping engine illustrated here. This atmospheric steam engine was first used for pumping water out of a mine in 1712; in 1717, Henry Beighton (the editor of *The Ladies' Diary*) published this engraving. As can be seen the engine consisted of a boiler and chimney, with a great wooden beam, a cylinder, a pump and numerous pipes.

§ 23 and 24 (cf. text pp. 31, 35)

Two figures of a boy and girl in the costume of Queen Anne's reign in niches on a building formerly housing the St. Bride's and Bridewell Precinct Schools in Bride Lane, London. From a photograph by *The Times*.

§ 25 (cf. text p. 52)

Captain Thomas Coram. From the painting by William Hogarth in the Foundling Hospital.

Thomas Coram (1668?–1751) was born in Dorset and went to sea; after a period as a shipbuilder in America he returned to England as a merchant, though he kept in close touch with schemes of colonization. The rapid increase in the population, which accompanied industrial progress, was offset by such evils as the desertion of new-born (especially illegitimate) children, a practice encouraged by harsh poor laws and lack of adequate poor relief. The retired sailor, Captain Coram, often saw these wretched infants left to die by the roadside and conceived the idea of his Foundling Hospital, though it took him seventeen years to see it realized. He received a charter in 1739 and the building was opened in 1745. (Cf. § 27.)

§ 26 and 27 (cf. text p. 52)

St. Thomas's Hospital and the Foundling Hospital. From the paintings by Samuel Wale and Richard Wilson (respectively) done in 1746 and preserved in the Foundling Hospital.

These two pictures form part of a collection of eight (presented to the Foundling Hospital in the XVIIIth century) of 'the most considerable hospitals in and near London.'

The St. Thomas's illustrated here is old St. Thomas's which lay just by the present St. Thomas's Street in the Borough. Originally a hospital of Augustinian canons, it was closed at the Dissolution, but was reopened in Edward VI's reign and became known as one of the Royal Hospitals. By the late XVIIth century the place was in a poor condition and new buildings were finished by 1732. They consisted of four courtyards, one of which, the Edward Court with its open colonnade, is shown in this illustration. Thomas Guy (who founded Guy's Hospital close by St. Thomas's) was an earlier benefactor of St. Thomas's also. The statue of Edward VI in Purbeck marble by Scheemakers can be seen on a pedestal in the right corner of the courtyard where it was set up in 1737. The present buildings of St. Thomas's on the south bank of the Thames opposite the Houses of Parliament date from 1870.

When Captain Coram had secured his charter for the Foundling Hospital (cf. § 25) in 1739, he set about finding temporary quarters, and the first admittance of foundlings was in a house in Hatton Garden in 1741. The site in Bloomsbury Fields was then bought, building began in 1742 and was completed in

1747. Applications for admission grew steadily, and in 1756 Parliament was asked for assistance. This was given in the form of grants but with the proviso that all children offered must be accepted. The influx of children immediately became so great (the workhouses taking the opportunity of getting rid of their unwanted children) that the whole scheme was nearly overwhelmed through disease and overcrowding. Mortality was so high that by 1760 the grants were discontinued and an attempt made to rectify the position. After this date admissions were much fewer, through lack of funds, and it was not until 1790 that the site next the hospital was developed for building purposes to raise money to support the institution.

The building on the Bloomsbury site illustrated here was designed by Theodore Jacobsen. The west wing was finished by 1745 and the east wing by 1752. The Bloomsbury building was sold in 1926 and the children removed to new buildings in the country.

§ 28 and 29 (cf. text p. 28)

From the drawings by William Hogarth for the series of engravings representing Industry and Idleness (published 1747) in the Department of Prints and Drawings, British Museum.

The first of these two illustrations shows the idle and the industrious apprentice at work on the silk looms in Spitalfields. Their master is looking in at the door to watch their progress. The second illustration shows the triumph of the industrious apprentice, now the trusted favourite of his master, while in the background can be seen the near-factory conditions of the business. A line of spinning wheels and looms, worked by women operatives, stretches down a long bare room.

§ 30 (cf. text p. 59)

The Bench. From the painting by William Hogarth (1758) in the Fitzwilliam Museum, Cambridge.

The figures are said to represent the Earl Bathurst, the Hon. William Noel, Sir John Wilkes (Lord Chief Justice) and Sir Edward Clive, but are more probably imaginary.

§ 31 (cf. text p. 40)

Jonathan Wild in Prison. From the frontispiece of Daniel Defoe's *True and Genuine Account of the Life and Actions of Jonathan Wild* (1st edition 1725). From the copy in the Department of Printed Books, British Museum.

Jonathan Wild (1682?–1725) ran a flourishing organization of thieves under cover of great zeal in apprehending and punishing thefts. He was eventually hanged at Tyburn in 1725, having been convicted as a receiver of stolen property.

This plate is labelled 'the true Effigies' of Jonathan Wild, but whether it is, or is not, a trustworthy portrait of the man, it is a realistic enough picture of a prisoner in the condemned cell.

§ 32 (cf. text p. 53)

The Committee of the House of Commons. From the oil sketch by William Hogarth in the Fitzwilliam Museum, Cambridge.

In 1729 a committee was appointed to look into the conditions of the Fleet Prison; it is shown in the scene depicted here sitting in the prison itself questioning the Warden, Thomas Bambridge (on the extreme left), who was twice tried for the murder of a prisoner and was finally himself imprisoned in the Fleet. General Oglethorpe, who had taken the initiative in the investigation of cruelty in the treatment of prisoners, is shown in this group as chairman. In the foreground a prisoner is giving evidence.

There is an elaborated version of this in the National Portrait Gallery, in which a half-naked prisoner is shown demonstrating the kind of treatment to which prisoners were subjected.

The names on the Fitzwilliam version were added by Horace Walpole (to whom the sketch had been given by Hogarth); in this Bambridge is labelled 'Higgins the Keeper.'

§ 33 (cf. text p. 40)

Scene from *The Beggar's Opera*, by William Hogarth. From the painting in the Tate Gallery, London.

The Beggar's Opera by John Gay was first produced in 1728. Swift had suggested a Newgate pastoral 'might make an odd pretty sort of thing.' Gay's interpretation of this was an immediate success. Its hero is a highwayman; his supporting cast a warder of Newgate and his daughter, Lucy, an informer and receiver of stolen goods, Peachum, his wife and daughter, Polly. Macheath marries Polly, is informed against by her father, and, sent to Newgate, makes a conquest of the warder's daughter, Lucy. In spite of the jealous rivalry between Polly and Lucy, the latter secures his escape from prison.

§ 34 (cf. text p. 48)

Samuel Johnson. From the painting by Sir Joshua Reynolds (1756) in the National Portrait Gallery.

Samuel Johnson (1709–84) 'the great Cham of literature' was born at Lichfield, the son of a bookseller. By way of school-mastering and his pupil, David Garrick, he came to London in 1737. Employed in various literary pursuits he began work on his great *Dictionary* in 1747. This was completed in 1755 (just before Reynolds painted this portrait of him), but meanwhile *The Vanity of Human Wishes* had appeared in 1749 and the *Rambler* had run its course from 1750–2. *Rasselas* (1759), the edition of Shakespeare (1765) and the *Lives of the Poets* (1779 and 1781) were still to come. Johnson founded and ran a literary club at the Duke's Head in Gerrard Street until 1783. The friend of Dr. Burney, Oliver Goldsmith and Mrs. Thrale, his conversation, habits and beliefs have been minutely retailed for us by his companion and biographer, James Boswell.

§ 35 (cf. text p. 48)

Self portrait by William Hogarth (1758). From the painting in the National Portrait Gallery.

William Hogarth (1697–1764), is the first great satirist in painting of English manners and morals. Apprenticed to an engraver he designed and engraved many plates for book illustration. But besides this he drew and painted social scenes and conversation pieces, particularly series of sketches (later engraved) such as *The Rake's Progress* and *Industry and Idleness* (cf. § 28, 29). In this self portrait he depicts himself seated at his easel painting the comic muse; he also painted the fine portrait of *Captain Coram* (cf. § 25). Others of his paintings reproduced in this volume are *Scene from the Beggar's Opera* (§ 33), *The Bench* (§ 30), *A Musical Party* (§ 8), as well as drawings such as *Duelling* (§ 17) and engravings, *Beer Street* and *Gin Lane* (§ 36, 37) and *Pit Ticket for the Royal Sport* (§ 15).

§ 36 and 37 (cf. text pp. 49–50)

Beer Street and Gin Lane. Engravings after drawings by William Hogarth (1751). From copies in the Department of Prints and Drawings, British Museum.

The health and prosperity of a beer-drinking community as against the disease and poverty of a gin-consuming one are the contrasted lessons of these two engravings.

In Beer Street the only place which does not prosper is the closed pawnbroker's on the right, where the walls are cracking and have to be shored up with a post. In Gin Lane, however, the pawnbroker's has a handsome doorway and is in an excellent state of repair, it carries on a flourishing business, where men and women are pawning their tools and household goods. Instead of the prosperous tradesmen of Beer Street with well-rounded paunches, we see a drunken populace in the last stages of emaciation and disease; a corpse is being coffined in the background and in the house to the right a suicide can be seen hanging from a beam. In the background of Gin Lane can be seen the distinctive pyramid spire of St. George's Church, Bloomsbury, with the lion and the unicorn (since removed) at the corners.

§ 38 (cf. text p. 12)

St. Mary-le-Strand. From James Gibbs' *Book of Architecture* (1728). From the copy in the Department of Printed Books, British Museum.

St. Mary-le-Strand was the first public building (1714–17) on which Gibbs was employed after his return from Italy. (For note on Gibbs cf. note to § 5, 6.)

§ 39 (cf. text p. 44)

Covent Garden in 1749. From *The Gentleman's Magazine*, April 1749. From the copy in the Department of Printed Books, British Museum.

This view taken from the church portico shows the colonnade with the finely planned houses above, and the booths of the market in the centre of the square. Originally part of the Abbey of Westminster, Covent Garden passed after the Dissolution to John Russell, first Earl of Bedford. The market dates from the XVIIth century, the original church of St. Paul's, Covent Garden and the plan of the square being by Inigo Jones (1631–4). Its piazza was a fashionable promenade, though from contemporary references, especially in the drama, it would appear a disreputable one.

§ 40 (cf. text pp. 44, 45)

Vauxhall Gardens in 1765. From *The Gentleman's Magazine*, August 1765. From the copy in the Department of Printed Books, British Museum.

This illustration showing the Grand Walk in Vauxhall Gardens and the Orchestra gives some idea of how London amused itself in the XVIIIth century. The gardens were first laid out in Charles II's reign and called New Spring Gardens. They were not finally closed until 1859. They were the most notable of the London pleasure gardens, laid out with arbours and walks; by the early XVIIIth century, however, they had degenerated into a place of disrepute. In 1728 they came under new management and were much altered and improved. About 1737 the Orchestra was erected (with an organ) and this was replaced by a more elaborate structure later; it is this which can be seen in the present illustration. Accounts of the time speak of its shady groves and fine pavilions, its delightful walks and wonderful illuminations, its songful nightingales. The Grand Walk stretched for some 300 yards bordered by elms, and at the end stood a gilded statue of Aurora; other walks crossed this or ran parallel to it and were set with triumphal arches.

This illustration shows on either side the supper booths and pavilions; the main building of Vauxhall was, however, the Rotunda for concerts in wet weather.

(A very full description of Vauxhall may be found in W. Wroth's *The London Pleasure Gardens* (1896).)

§ 41 (cf. text p. 45)

London Bridge in the mid-XVIIIth century. From the painting by Samuel Scott in the National Gallery.

This painting of London Bridge was made before 1756, when the Act for the removal of the houses from the bridge was passed. Note the houses themselves and the jutting cut-waters of the bridge; on the right can be seen the Monument and the Church of St. Magnus the Martyr.

Samuel Scott (1702?–72) was a painter of topographical views and marine subjects, who shows the influence first of the Dutch school of painting and later of Canaletto.

§ 42 (cf. text p. 45)

The Thames near London in the mid-XVIIIth century (possibly near Deptford). From the painting by Samuel Scott in the National Gallery.

The rural environs of London in the middle of the century are well illustrated by this Thames-side scene, with small weather-boarded houses backing on to the river, a ferry and all the busy traffic of the river itself sufficiently indicated by the ships in the background. (Cf. note to § 41 above for a note on Samuel Scott.)

§ 43 (cf. text p. 61)

The Spirit of Scientific Enquiry. From the painting by Joseph Wright of Derby called 'Experiment with the Air Pump' in the Tate Gallery.

Joseph Wright of Derby (1734–97) was a painter of portraits, and (as can be seen from this illustration) delighted in depicting his sitters by candle or firelight.

This picture was painted for a Dr. Bates of Aylesbury and was exhibited at the Society of Artists in 1768. It illustrates very forcibly the new spirit of scientific enquiry that was abroad and its dramatic lit-up circle of faces achieves a vivid effect of realism in portraiture.

§ 44 (cf. text p. 61)

Edward Gibbon. From the portrait by Henry Walton in the National Portrait Gallery.

Edward Gibbon (1737–94) published the first volume of his *Decline and Fall of the Roman Empire* in 1776, further volumes followed in 1781, the work being completed in 1787; it was as great a contribution to English prose style as to historical scholarship.

§ 45 (cf. text p. 102)

Edmund Burke. From the portrait (1771) by the studio of Reynolds in the National Portrait Gallery.

Edmund Burke (1729–97), one of the foremost political figures of the later XVIIIth century, was not only a statesman and an orator but an accomplished essayist as well. His works ranged from the early *Vindication of Natural Society* to *Reflections on the French Revolution*; he was actively concerned in criticism of government policy in the war with America; in advocating the abolition of slavery he supported Wilberforce; keenly interested in Indian affairs, particularly in the investigation of the East India Company's business, he moved for the impeachment of Warren Hastings, and finally quarrelled with the Whigs over his attitude to the French Revolution and joined forces with the Tories.

§ 46 (cf. text p. 54)

'The Liberty of the Subject' (October 1779). A satire on the press-gang by James Gillray. From a print in the Department of Prints and Drawings, British Museum.

James Gillray (1757–1815) covered an extraordinarily wide range of political and social satire. Many of his caricatures are savage indictments of conditions or personalities. This print from the period of the wars with America, France and Spain, and of riots and mob violence in London, is an attack on the press-gang method of recruitment.

§ 47 (cf. text p. 54)

Sailors going aboard men-o'-war in Portsmouth Harbour. From the west prospect of Portsmouth in 1749 from Samuel and Nathaniel Buck's *Views of Castles, Abbeys and Towns.* From the copy in the Department of Printed Books, British Museum.

This engraving shows the great wooden men-o'-war lying in the harbour. The longboats, full of returning sailors, are pulling out towards them, while on the right more sailors can be seen saying good-bye to their families and sweethearts, or waiting with their bundles to be taken off.

§ 48 (cf. text p. 55)

The Soldier's Return. Water-colour by Samuel Hieronymus Grimm (1770). From the original in the Department of Prints and Drawings, British Museum.

Typical of the aftermath of war in Europe and in India is this scene of the 'missing' soldier, who returns disabled to find his wife married again, his own children having been miserably relegated to the workhouse (on the right). The setting of the scene at the Chequers and Horns Inn is thought to be in Essex. (Cf. Rotha Mary Clay's *Samuel Hieronymus Grimm* (1941).)

The Swiss artist, Grimm (1733–94), came to England in 1768, and until his death in 1794 was a tireless illustrator of English scenery and social life. He exhibited at the Royal Academy and at the Society of Artists as well as working for such patrons as Sir William Burrell the antiquary and Dr. Kaye (for whom cf. note to § 49 below), for both of whom he produced drawings of antiquities and curiosities. His work covers a wide range from a record of an Encaenia at the Sheldonian (§ 94) to that of the Durham method of roasting a baron of beef (§ 78), from an old beggar woman (§ 51) to the Pump Room of the King's Bath at Bath (§ 85). With him we can travel the roads of XVIIIth century England, visit its country houses, watch a game of cricket or attend a distribution of charity. Other examples of his work will be found below.

§ 49 (cf. text p. 58)

Distribution of charity at Durham. From the drawing by S. H. Grimm (undated) in the Kaye Collection. B.M. Add. MS. 15,539, f. 2.

Dr. Richard Kaye, Prebend of Southwell and Durham and later Dean of Lincoln, was Grimm's patron for twenty years (from 1773 to 1794). (For full note on Grimm cf. note to § 48 above.) Grimm went on a tour with Kaye about 1778 to the north of England and made many sketches in Durham. This illustration shows some of the old women receiving their bounty of clay pipes and bundles of food.

§ 50 (cf. text p. 58)

Workhouse at Birmingham, built 1733. From W. Hutton's *History of Birmingham* (1781). From a copy in the Department of Printed Books, British Museum.

The author of this history remarks that workhouses did not become general until 1730 and says that this one was erected at Birmingham in 1733 and cost £1,173.3.5, 'which' he continues, 'the stranger would rather suppose, was the residence of a gentleman, than that of 400 paupers.' The left wing was added in 1766 and served as the infirmary, the right in 1779 as 'a place for labour' costing respectively an additional £400 and £700 to build.

§ 51 and 52 (cf. text p. 58)

A beggar woman. From the drawing by S. H. Grimm (undated) in the Kaye Collection. B.M. Add. MS. 15,548, f. 140.

The disabled cobbler. From the drawing by S. H. Grimm (undated) in the Kaye Collection. B.M. Add. MS. 15,546, f.143. (For note on Grimm and his work cf. note to § 48 above.)

§ 53 (cf. text p. 62)

The good prentice at Church performing the duty of a Christian. From the drawing by William Hogarth for the series of engravings representing Industry and Idleness (1747) in the Department of Prints and Drawings, British Museum.

'The mass of the nation was either actively or passively Christian, accepting the religion that it was taught.'

Note the galleries, the high box pews and the three-decker pulpit. (For other drawings in this series cf. § 28 and 29 and for general note on Hogarth cf. note to § 35.)

§ 54 (cf. text p. 62)

Divine service in Bath Abbey. From the drawing by S. H. Grimm (undated) in the Kaye Collection. B.M. Add. MS. 15,546, f. 101.

This very detailed drawing in Indian ink depicts a late XVIIIth century congregation at prayer during service in Bath Abbey (*c.* 1788). Note how every available inch of wall space is already taken up with funeral monuments. (For general note on Grimm cf. note to § 48.)

§ 55 (cf. text p. 64)

Dr. Kaye with village children near Prior Park, Bath. From the drawing by S. H. Grimm (undated) in the Kaye Collection. B.M. Add. MS. 15,547, f. 83.

(For general note on Grimm and his relations with his patron Dr. Kaye cf. notes to § 48 and 49 above.) Grimm accompanied Dr. Kaye to Somerset and other counties in the west of England during the years 1788–90, and the then Dean is seen in this illustration in a country lane near Prior Park, Bath, with a group of children, whom he appears to be leading in prayer.

§ 56 and 57 (cf. text pp. 67, 68)

The old and new meeting houses at Birmingham in 1781. From W. Hutton's *History of Birmingham* (1781). From a copy in the Department of Printed Books, British Museum.

The author of this history says that dissenters or presbyterians had held a licence for meeting at Digbeth ('after the extinction of the Stuart Race') and that the place was still called Meeting House Yard, even though the building had become a workshop for button making; another had been erected in King William's time, and was known as 'The Old Meeting' after the erection in 1730 of 'The New Meeting.' 'This' (says Hutton) 'is in a style of elegance and has few equals. . . . In Dec. 1780, Mr. Hawkes declining the pastoral care, the congregation judiciously turned their thoughts towards the celebrated Dr. Priestly, F.R.S., one of the first philosophers of the age; whose merit seems obvious to every eye, but his own.' This is an interesting reference to the interrelation of science and dissenting religion at this period. 'Dr. Priestly' was of course the 'discoverer' of oxygen—Joseph Priestley—theologian and scientist, who had already published his *History of Electricity* and was later to publish a *General History of the Christian Church*. His opinions which included rejection of the inspiration of the text of the Bible and of the doctrine of the atonement, together with his sympathy for the French Revolution, made him unpopular and caused the wrecking of his house by a mob, which destroyed his books and papers. He retired to America in 1794.

§ 58 (cf. text p. 68)

George Whitefield. From the painting by John Wollaston (*c.* 1737) in the National Portrait Gallery.

George Whitefield (1714–70), the Methodist preacher, was famous for his extempore preachings and gained an immense popular following. He undertook missionary work in Georgia and his evangelical tours took him through Virginia and Carolina as well as to New York and Pennsylvania. In 1741, on his return to London, he set up Moorfields Tabernacle, and after preaching journeys to Scotland became Lady Huntingdon's chaplain. He finally returned to America, where he died.

§ 59 (cf. text pp. 67, 68)

John Wesley. From the portrait by Nathaniel Hone (1766) in the National Portrait Gallery.

John Wesley (1703–91), the founder of Methodism, had been ordained in 1725 and became his father's curate two years later. In 1729 he became the leader of his brother Charles's methodist society at Oxford, and then undertook the charge of the mission to Georgia. Coming under the influence of the Moravians he became, on his return to England, a member of their society and visited Count Zinzendorff. He opened a methodist chapel at Bristol in 1739 and another in London the same year. He then broke his Moravian connections and renounced Calvinism. The first Methodist conference was held in 1744 and thereafter Wesley made constant evangelical journeys throughout the British Isles; after separation from the Church of England, he spent much time in the organization of his chapels and training of lay preachers.

§ 60 (cf. text p. 78)

Derby and its silk mills in 1728. From Samuel and Nathaniel Buck's *Views of Castles, Abbeys and Towns*. From the copy in the Department of Printed Books, British Museum.

These silk mills represent the first factory proper in England, built for the Lombe brothers at Derby in 1718. Thomas Lombe sent his brother John to Italy to secure the secret of silk-throwing machinery, which was jealously guarded by the Italians. John succeeded but is said to have been murdered on his return to England by an Italian in revenge for stealing the secret. The silk mill can be seen just below and to the right of the church tower and standing directly on the river bank; in general appearance it is not unlike the Flintshire cotton mill in § 64, which was built in 1783.

§ 61 (cf. text p. 78)

View of Birmingham from W. Hutton's *History of Birmingham* (1781). From a copy in the Department of Printed Books, British Museum.

This view of Birmingham shows how even in a town of small industries of long standing, the immediate surroundings were still rural, in spite of 'Mr. Turner's Brassworks' on the right just beyond the still unbuilt-on fields. (The workhouse reproduced in § 50 may be seen in this view to the left of the brassworks.)

§ 62 (cf. text p. 99)

Colliers' houses on the road to Newcastle. From the drawing by S. H. Grimm in the Kaye Collection. B.M. Add. MS. 15,543, f. 68.

This sketch was made by Grimm on the northern tour that he took with Dr. Kaye in 1778 (cf. notes to § 48 and 49 above for general note on Grimm and his patron Kaye).

Note the outside staircases and the pig just being driven out of doors.

§ 63 (cf. text pp. 27, 99)

Colliers loading coal wagons. From the drawing by S. H. Grimm in the Kaye Collection. B.M. Add. MS. 15,548, f. 172. This sketch, made while Grimm was in Northumberland in 1778, illustrates the type of horse-drawn truck used for loading coal round about Newcastle. (For general note on Grimm and his tour in the north with his patron Dr. Kaye, cf. notes to § 48 and 49 above.)

§ 64 (cf. text p. 96)

Two cotton mills. From Thomas Pennant's *History of the Parishes of Whiteford and Holywell* (1796). From a copy in the Department of Printed Books, British Museum.

This Flintshire cotton mill (built in 1783 in six weeks) of six storeys has much in common with the Derby silk mill of 1718 (cf. § 60) or indeed with Arkwright's own cotton mill at Cromford. But it has greater architectural pretensions—it boasts a pediment on the central block, which is brought slightly forward from the rest of the building. It was lighted (Pennant tells us) by 198 sash windows 'which nightly exhibit a most glorious illumination,' and was worked by a water-wheel 20 feet high and 7 feet wide with a fall of water of 20 feet.

Pennant's description of the organization of these mills is worth quoting for the interesting light it throws on working conditions there. It was owned by the Cotton Twist Co. (founded by Mr. John Smalley of Preston) and had 300–400 apprentices, whom (says Pennant) they feed and clothe 'in commodious houses built for that purpose, the boys and girls in separate houses. These houses are white washed twice every year, are fumigated three times a week through every apartment, with smoak of tobacco, besides this the sleeping rooms are washed twice a week, and the bed stocks are frequently sprinkled with rectified oil of tar. All the windows in the sleeping rooms open at the tops, by which a thorough draft of air is admitted during the whole time the children are at work. To these and other precautions the good state of health of so many children may be justly attributed; for though the number of apprentices have not been less than 300 for these seven years past, they have only

buried seven. Their food for dinner is beef or pork and potatoes three or four times a week, the other days herrings and
potatoes, or soup and bread and cheese, as much as they please
to eat. Their breakfasts and suppers in summer is milk and
bread; in the winter, when milk cannot be had, they drink
porridge or broth, with bread and cheese. A surgeon is
appointed to superintend their health; and a Sunday school
is regularly attended by a master at each house.
'Our little children sleep three in a bed, the larger sizes only
two; and those who work in the night are so far from succeeding each other in the same beds, that they do not even sleep in
the same rooms.'
Pennant goes on to describe the process of cotton manufacture
and says that most of the cotton twist goes into ginghams and
calicoes for England and Scotland. He says that 'mules' are
used here and notes the great increase in building and the
population brought to Holywell and Greenfield by these mills.
(Cf. text illustrations for types of machinery in use in such
mills.)

§ 65 (cf. text p. 77)

Copper and Brass works in Flintshire. From Thomas Pennant's
History of the Parishes of Whiteford and Holywell (1796). From a
copy in the Department of Printed Books, British Museum.
These brass battery mills which belonged to the Greenfield
Copper and Brass Co., were originally built in 1766, but were
added to and much improved in 1786. Pennant tells us in his
history that they made kettles, rods and ornaments for Africa.
Note the still rural setting and the mill pool for water power.

§ 66 (cf. text p. 74)

Welsh cattle drovers on the road to Caernarvon. From the
water-colour by Paul Sandby (1777) in the Department of
Prints and Drawings, British Museum.
Paul Sandby (1725–1809), the water-colour painter and engraver,
drew, painted and engraved a number of topographical scenes,
which are valuable records of the countryside of his time.
After the '45 he went to Scotland to help in the survey of the
Highlands and examples of his Edinburgh sketches can be seen
at § 122–125.
This scene of Welsh cattle drovers is lively and graceful and
gives a good idea of the wild, uncultivated country of XVIIIth
century Wales. (Other Welsh subjects by Paul Sandby can be
seen below at § 67 and 69.)

§ 67 (cf. text p. 74)

A Castle in Wales. From the water-colour drawing by Paul
Sandby in the Department of Prints and Drawings, British
Museum.

(Cf. note to § 66 above for note on Paul Sandby and other Welsh subjects.) Note the bullock cart, the woman riding side saddle with a tall hat and the donkey with panniers.

§ 68 (cf. text p. 74)

The summit of Snowdon from Capel Curig. From Thomas Pennant's *Tour in Wales in 1773* (pub. 1778), Vol. II, *The Journey to Snowdon* (pub. 1781). From a copy in the Department of Printed Books, British Museum.

This illustration shows haymaking going on just below Snowdon. Note the type of carrier for the hay, which the horse draws, the rough stone wall round the haystack on the left and in the background the small houses and chapel.

Thomas Pennant (1726–98) was a naturalist as well as a traveller, and published his various tours through England, Scotland, Wales and Ireland with numerous engravings of historic castles, antiquities, and flora and fauna as well.

§ 69 (cf. text p. 74)

Welsh landscape with mine. From a water-colour drawing by Paul Sandby in the National Museum of Wales at Cardiff.

(For general note on Paul Sandby and his other Welsh illustrations, cf. § 66 above.)

The top of the shaft can be seen here with the mechanism for drawing up the coal (worked by the horse).

§ 70 and 71 (cf. text p. 83)

Two agricultural labourers. From the drawings by S. H. Grimm in the Kaye Collection. B.M. Add. MS. 15,547, ff. 54 and 123.

Two typical agricultural labourers, with two-pronged fork and staff, are sketched here by Grimm (for whom see note to § 48). Note the smock worn by the second figure.

§ 72 and 73 (cf. text p. 79)

Turnpike road near Oxford. From a drawing (1777–81) by S. H. Grimm in the Kaye Collection, B.M. Add. MS. 15,546, f. 16; and footpads attacking a traveller. From the pen and wash drawing by S. H. Grimm (1773) in the Victoria and Albert Museum, S. Kensington.

The first sketch shows a turnpike road near Oxford with gate and tollhouse, while the second depicts armed footpads attacking a lonely traveller.

§ 74 (cf. text p. 87)

Stage Coach on the Dover Road by Philip de Loutherbourg (1775). From the painting in the possession of the Parker Gallery, London.

This painting is of particular interest in that it illustrates the road surface of a main highway, as the Dover road was: one can easily understand that only a heavy fall of rain was necessary to turn it into a morass of mud. 'The humble' can be seen 'clinging to the luggage on the roof,' while three passengers ride in the boot behind. The little group in the foreground has apparently just been put down by the coach.

The painter of this scene, Philip de Loutherbourg (1740–1812) came to England in 1771 and designed scenery and costumes for Garrick. He is chiefly known as a painter of land- and sea-scapes, genre and battle pieces.

§ 75, 76 and 77 (cf. text pp. 82, 105)

The ale-bench, cowherd and milkmaid, and rabbiting. From the paintings by George Morland in the Tate Gallery, London. George Morland (1763–1804), the extraordinarily precocious boy, who exhibited at the Royal Academy at the age of ten, dissipated his undoubted talents for animal and genre painting in a life which was chiefly noted for its excesses in drink and debt. He painted an enormous number of pieces, many of which faithfully depict English rural life at the end of the XVIIIth century.

§ 78 (cf. text p. 113)

Method of roasting a baron of beef in Durham (c. 1778). From the drawing by S. H. Grimm in the Kaye Collection. B.M. Add. MS. 15,538, f. 232.

The kitchen appointments for cooking meat 'in the piece' can be studied here. The woman whose responsibility it is to see that the 'baron' is evenly and truly cooked has the protection of a screen at her task. Above the fire-place can be seen a 'spit' for roasting fowls, etc., which could be evenly cooked by turning the bar on which they were spitted (cf. method in § 34 of Volume I reproduced from the Luttrell Psalter). (For a general note on Grimm and his northern tour cf. notes to § 48 and 49.)

§ 79 (cf. text p. 85)

A Northumberland farm kitchen (1778). From the drawing by S. H. Grimm in the Kaye Collection. B.M. Add. MS. 15,543, f. 110.

The farm kitchen was the centre of life and warmth on the farm. Grimm drew here a typical room with thick walls, deep window sill, beamed ceiling and ingle-nook; the cauldron heating over the generous fire, the gun above the chimney, the rush-bottomed chair and plain table. He has noted in the corner that he sketched it at 'Grieve's farm.'

§ 80 and 81 (cf. text p. 85)

Woman burning kelp. From a drawing by S. H. Grimm in the Kaye Collection, B.M. Add. MS. 15,543, f. 108; and women cleaning fish near Bamburgh Castle, from a drawing by S. H. Grimm in the Kaye Collection, B.M. Add. MS. 15,542, f. 186. Both *c.* 1778.

These two wayside sketches observed by Grimm on his northern tour with his patron Dr. Kaye (cf. notes to § 48 and 49) show a Northumbrian peasant woman burning seaweed or kelp, which was spread on the land as a manure, and a group of Bamburgh women by a pump and trough gutting fish.

§ 82 and 83 (cf. text p. 89)

The Worsley-Manchester Canal. From Arthur Young's *Six Months' Tour through the North of England* (1770). From a copy in the Department of Printed Books, British Museum.

In Letter XIX of this book, Arthur Young (cf. note to § 107) the agriculturist, describes his visit to the Duke of Bridge-water's 'navigation'—the Worsley-Manchester canal constructed by Brindley 1760–1—and tells how the canal was carried across the River Irwell at Barton Bridge by aqueduct. § 82 shows this with a barge going over the aqueduct. § 83 shows the mouth of the subterranean tunnel at Worsley, where the canal was driven underground to the mine workings. Men are working in the neighbouring quarry and at the crane for hoist-ing the great blocks of stone into the barge.

§ 84 (cf. text p. 99)

Ironbridge, Shropshire. From a photograph by Miss M. Wight.

The first cast-iron bridge (cast in 1778 and erected 1779–80) still spans the Severn near Coalbrookdale. It was built by Abraham Darby, manager of the Coalbrookdale Ironworks, after the design by Thomas Pritchard. The use of coke for smelting iron ore was first developed by his father, Abraham Darby the second, and the iron bridge was itself cast in the foundry of the Coalbrookdale works.

The single-span bridge consists of five arches side by side, each about 2 yards from each other, forming a single roadway. The full dimensions and details are given beneath the engraving of the bridge printed by J. Edmunds of Madeley at the time of its erection; a copy can be found in the Department of Prints and Drawings, British Museum.

§ 85 (cf. text p. 88)

Entrance to the Pump Room of the King's Bath in 1789. From the drawing by S. H. Grimm in the Kaye Collection. B.M. Add. MS. 15,546, f. 118.

Grimm did a number of drawings at, and in the neighbourhood of, Bath, during his visits there with Dr. Kaye from 1788–90 (cf. note on Grimm to § 48). Here he shows the decorative fountain with a waitress (in an elaborately pleated cap) drawing the waters for visitors in the Pump Room.

§ 86 and 87 (cf. text p. 88)

Bath in 1788–90. From the pen and wash sketches by S. H. Grimm in the Kaye Collection. B.M. Add. MS. 15,546, ff. 87 and 88.

The fashionable spa of Bath was virtually created by the two John Woods (father and son), under the patronage of Ralph Allen of Prior Park. The elder Wood settled at Bath in 1727 and to him may be attributed the Circus, Queen's Square and Gay Street, while to his son belong the Upper Assembly Rooms (1771) (*not* the Old Assembly Rooms by the Abbey where Beau Nash reigned) and Royal Crescent (1769). These sketches by Grimm show Bath lying spread out on its hills in still rural surroundings. (For a note on Grimm and his patron, Dr. Kaye, cf. notes to § 48 and 49 and to § 85 above.)

§ 88 and 89 (cf. text pp. 108, 118)

Drinking posset. From the sketch by S. H. Grimm in the Kaye Collection, B.M. Add. MS. 15,537, f. 72; and Country Dancing in the servants' hall, also by S. H. Grimm. B.M. Add. MS. 15,548, f. 171.

The first sketch (possibly from Derbyshire) shows a country house party gathered round a bowl of posset, from which their host is filling their tumblers. Probably *c*. 1775.

The second sketch shows servants dancing to the fiddle and probably dates from the same year. (For general note on Grimm cf. § 48.)

§ 90 and 91 (cf. text pp. 102, 105)

Highnam Court, Gloucestershire. The music room and the dining room (decorated about 1760). From photographs by Country Life, Ltd.

Highnam Court itself, built during the Commonwealth to replace the earlier house destroyed in the Civil Wars, is not of interest in the present context—that of the XVIIIth century—but its interior was almost completely redecorated about 1760. The decorations present interesting contrasts between the rococo nature of the stucco wall decorations of the music room and the simplicity of the door-cases and chimney-piece of the dining room. The furniture in the latter is XVIIIth century but the pictures were not assembled at Highnam until much later, being part of the great collection formed by Thomas Gambier Parry, who bought Highnam in 1837. The collection consists mainly of early Italian pictures, but those in the present illustration are portraits of the Parry family; that over the mantelpiece was exhibited at the Society of Artists in 1769, and represents Thomas Parry (of the East India Company) with Admiral Cornish (whose secretary he was) and Kempenfelt (at that time the Admiral's flag-captain): it is by Tilly Kettle.

§ 92 (cf. text pp. 112, 113)

Cricket at the Artillery Ground, London. From a coloured line engraving (pub. 1750) by B. Cole. From a copy in the possession of the Parker Gallery, London.

In this illustration, the curved bat, the two low stumps and the score keeper with his tally can be seen. Note the rough ground of the pitch.

§ 93 (cf. text pp. 112, 113)

Cricket at Marylebone in 1793. From a drawing by S. H. Grimm in the Kaye Collection. B.M. Add. MS. 15,542, f. 37. This view of cricket at Marylebone was done in June 1793 from a house in Devonshire Street belonging to Lady Kaye, wife of Grimm's patron (for whom cf. note to § 48 and 49—the Dean had become a baronet in 1789 and married in 1791). The curved bat and low wicket are much the same as in the earlier scene (cf. § 92).

§ 94 (cf. text pp. 72, 73)

The interior of the Sheldonian at Oxford. From the drawing by S. H. Grimm in the Kaye Collection. B.M. Add. MS. 15,546, f. 43.

The Sheldonian Theatre had been designed by Wren and built at the cost of Archbishop Sheldon (1669) to house the University at its Encaenia, held in honour of the founders and benefactors of the University. Grimm's drawing shows such a function in progress before a fashionable gathering, with a rowdy gallery of undergraduates. This was probably drawn between 1777 and 1781; the recitation of prize poems, orations and the presentation of honorary degrees were, and are, all features of this annual commemorative gathering.

§ 95 (cf. text pp. 88, 104)

Sir William Hamilton. From the painting by the studio of Reynolds (1777) in the National Portrait Gallery.

The archaeologist and diplomat, Sir William Hamilton (1730–1803), husband of Nelson's Emma, is illustrated here as one of the XVIIIth century antiquaries and collectors, the fruits of whose works eventually enriched the national collections. As Envoy and Plenipotentiary in Naples he witnessed the eruption of Vesuvius (making many ascents of the mountain), was in close touch with the excavations at Herculaneum and Pompeii, and amassed a very fine collection of antiquities—Etruscan vases, terracottas, marbles, gems and coins, part of which he sold to the British Museum in 1772.

He is shown here (with Vesuvius in the background) surrounded by MSS., books and antique vases, illustrative of his interests.

§ 96 (cf. text p. 88)

The 'Tribuna' of the Uffizi Gallery at Florence. From the painting by Johann Zoffany at Windsor Castle. By gracious permission of His Majesty the King.

This picture was exhibited at the Royal Academy in 1780 and was painted in Florence by Zoffany in the later 1770's. It shows artists, British cognoscenti and visitors to Florence, examining the wealth of pictures and statuary in the Uffizi Gallery. It is reproduced here to give some idea of the wealth of art treasures which met the XVIIIth century follower of the Grand Tour in Italy. Small wonder that he burned to bring back something (even if it were only an inferior piece or a copy) to remind him of all these glories, to enrich his house or often to spur him on to build new rooms (or even a new house) in which to exhibit his acquisitions to the best advantage. How magnificent a result this could yield may be seen in the following illustration of Newby Hall, showing the sculpture hall as arranged by Adam.

§ 97 (cf. text p. 88)

The sculpture gallery at Newby Hall, Yorks. From a photograph by Country Life, Ltd.

This collection was made by William Weddell who visited Rome in 1765 and spent most of his leisure hours in collecting antiques. When they were brought to England they were placed in three rooms, specially built for them, and are still nearly all in their original positions. The work of adaptation and addition was designed and carried out by Robert Adam, to whom also can be assigned the decoration and arrangement, though the latter was done in conjunction with Weddell himself, the aim being to make the three rooms of the gallery a reconstruction of a Roman interior. Among Weddell's agents in collecting these antiquities was Jenkins (associated with Gavin Hamilton) who did not hesitate to 'sting' the collector, but justified himself (to himself) by providing limbs or even a head, where these were missing, without the recipient's knowledge.

§ 98 and 99 (cf. text p. 108)

Hatchlands, Surrey. From a photograph by Country Life, Ltd.; and West Wycombe Park, Bucks. From a photograph in the possession of the Central Office of Information. Crown Copyright Reserved.

'For the most part sound Georgian. . . . The more pretentious were in the Palladian or some other style that the owner had observed on his Italian tour.'

Hatchlands, built in 1759, should be contrasted with West Wycombe Park. The plain red brick exterior of the former, however, conceals Robert Adam's first recorded work of interior decoration. West Wycombe Park was built in its present form between 1735 and 1765 by the notorious 'hell fire Francis,' —Sir Francis Dashwood, 2nd Baronet. This photograph shows the south front with its great double colonnade and the east portico; the east and west porticos and the lower colonnade on the south, all had painted frescoes by an Italian artist.

§ 100 (cf. text p. 102)

Robert Adam. From the portrait by an unknown artist in the National Portrait Gallery.

Robert Adam (1728–92), son of William Adam (cf. note under § 130 and 131), like James Gibbs and Colin Campbell before him was a Scottish-born architect, who migrated to England. His travels in Italy and Dalmatia provide the key to much of the design and decoration of the houses he built, from the early interior of Hatchlands (§ 98) to the splendours of Syon (§ 102) or Kenwood (§ 101). But besides the building or decoration of country houses the Adam brothers were particularly interested in town-house building; in Adelphi Terrace (§ 103) they suffered great financial loss. This monumental scheme was a commercial failure, partly owing to the non-fulfilment of the brothers' expectation that the Government would hire the vaults under the terrace for warehouses. Robert Adam represents the break away from the Palladian of Lord Burlington and the assimilation of both Greek and Roman styles in a fresh and individual manner; his use of late Roman ornament can be seen in the reproductions of the library at Kenwood and the ante-room at Syon. His part in the planning of the sculpture gallery at Newby Hall has already been noted under § 97.

§ 101 (cf. text p. 102)

The library at Kenwood. From a photograph by Country Life, Ltd.

Kenwood, remodelled for Lord Mansfield, by Robert Adam in 1767–8, is illustrated here by this view of the library. At the end of the room can be seen one of the domed apses with which Adam terminated both ends of his library; the semi-circular effect of these is continued and repeated in the heads of the doors and bookcases. The columns, the frieze, and the wall decoration above the bookcases are all in the antique manner; note the rich variety of the barrel ceiling.

(For a general note on Adam and references to others of his works illustrated in this volume cf. the note to § 100 above.)

§ 102 (cf. text p. 102).

Syon House, the ante-room. From a photograph by Country Life, Ltd.

Here Robert Adam was faced with the problem of modernizing an existing house, consisting of the remains of the original nunnery and a Jacobean house built round them. Adam's work was concentrated in the interior. The ante-room illustrated here gives some idea of the rich inventiveness of his decoration: the colour, the rich materials, the incorporation of antique columns surmounted by sculptured figures, the reciprocity of floor and ceiling designs, all unite to give an air of magnificence and splendour. It was carried out about 1762. (For general note on Adam and other examples of his work illustrated in this volume cf. note to § 100 above.)

§ 103 (cf. text p. 102)

Adelphi Terrace in 1792. From Thomas Malton's *Picturesque Tour through London and Westminster* (1792). From a copy in the Department of Printed Books, British Museum.

Built 1768–70, Adelphi Terrace was sited on reclaimed land and was an interesting example of a terrace planned as an entity with a continuous façade. A commercial failure, it was disposed of by lottery to enable the Adam brothers to recoup themselves for their heavy losses on the project. Adelphi Terrace was demolished in the 1930's. (Cf. note on Adam and other examples of his work illustrated in this volume under § 100.)

§ 104 (cf. text p. 104)

Self portrait of Sir Joshua Reynolds. From the portrait in the National Portrait Gallery.

Sir Joshua Reynolds (1723–92), England's greatest portrait painter, first President of the Royal Academy on its foundation in 1768, devoted himself to the organizing of the Academy's schools.

§ 105 (cf. text p. 108 note)

Horace Walpole, by J. G. Eccardt (1754). From the portrait in the National Portrait Gallery.

Horace Walpole (1717–97), 4th Earl of Orford, is included here not only by reason of his Gothic interests, which found expression in the building and furnishing of Strawberry Hill and in his novel *The Castle of Otranto*, but also as a commentator in his letters on the life and manners of his times, as the author of the *Anecdotes of Painting in England*, the *Catalogue of Royal and Noble Authors* and the founder of a private press.

§ 106 (cf. text p. 104)

The Life School at the Royal Academy, by Johann Zoffany. From the painting at Windsor Castle by gracious permission of His Majesty the King.

In this picture of the life school at the Academy (exhibited in 1772) Zoffany shows all the Academicians grouped round the two models. The two female R.A.'s are (for modesty's sake) included only as portraits on the wall!

§ 107, 108 and 109 (cf. text p. 108)

Arthur Young. From the portrait by G. Dance (1794) in the National Portrait Gallery, and his idea of the picturesque as sketched by himself in his *Six Months' Tour through the North of England* (1770). From a copy in the Department of Printed Books, British Museum.

Arthur Young (1741–1820), the agriculturist, whose work has already been touched on (cf. note to § 82–3), also had his ideas on picturesque scenery and architecture, and these he slips in between his more technical passages on the prices of oats and barley or the best kinds of farming implements. In Vol. II of his *Six Months' Tour through the North of England* he describes a visit to Raby Castle, the seat of the Earl of Darlington, and highly extols the farm buildings (§ 109) which, says Young, 'shew how much beauty and utility may be united in these kind of edifices.' (Letter XIV.) Looking at its crenellated outline, its ecclesiastical windows and central tower, we fail to find the 'beauty' and are inclined to doubt the 'utility.' In Vol. III Young rather spreads himself on the picturesque beauties of the Lake District and ventures to reproduce a sketch or two of his own to show its wilder attractions. On the waterfall (reproduced in § 108) with its fearfully poised rocks, which may be either the result of poor drawing or a desire to exaggerate the picturesque disorder, Young comments: 'Nothing can be fancied more grand, more beautiful or romantic. The sketch . . . will give you but an imperfect idea of it.'

§ 110 (cf. text p. 106)

William Kent. From the portrait by B. Dandridge in the National Portrait Gallery.

William Kent (1684–1748), landscape gardener and architect, Burlington's protégé, may be said to have initiated the 'landscape' fashion in gardening. Instead of formal alleys and artificial shapes in flower beds or hedges, his aim was to give a 'natural' appearance; in fact Horace Walpole said of him that he was ruled by the principle that 'Nature abhors a straight line.' His interests were directed towards the grouped effect of water, trees and grassland to achieve an appearance of irregular nature, which should in its variety conceal surprises as well, such as a 'hermitage' (complete with hermit), a grotto or a temple as additional garden attractions, thus giving an early start to the fashion which culminated in every kind of 'folly' and 'conceit,' the last of which to linger on is probably the rustic summer house.

§ 111 (cf. text p. 106)

'Capability' Brown. From the portrait by N. Dance in the National Portrait Gallery.

With Lancelot Brown (1715–83), better known as 'Capability' Brown, the garden became even more romantically wild. The unmown grass of the park came up to the very walls of the house, gently winding paths meandered past clumps of trees, cunningly planted to diversify the softly undulating landscape in an artfully natural manner, assisted by skilfully controlled stretches of water.

§ 112 (cf. text p. 106)

Stourhead, Wiltshire. From the pen and wash drawing by S. H. Grimm in the Kaye Collection. B.M. Add. MS. 15,547, f. 210.

Stourhead, is chosen here to illustrate a mid-XVIIIth century landscape garden with lake and clumps of trees, green grassy slopes, temples and ornamental bridge. These gardens were planned and laid out by Henry Hoare, whose father had bought Stourhead in 1720. Here may be found Temples of Flora and of the Sun, a Grotto and a Rustic Cottage and the much later 'folly' of Alfred's Tower (1772). Grimm's sketch was probably done between 1788 and 1790. (For general note on Grimm cf. § 48.)

§ 113 (cf. text p. 108)

Mow Cop Folly, Cheshire. From a photograph in the possession of the Central Office of Information. Crown Copyright Reserved.

The vogue of the 'folly' or artificial ruin grew with the century. Partly due to the revival of interest in the mediaeval and gothic, it also grew out of the desire to crown a hill top or end a vista with an object of interest or surprise.

Mow Cop thus tops a rocky hill with its tower and pointed arch (suitably ruined) and was built by Randle Wilbraham of Rode Hall in 1750.

§ 114 and 115 (cf. text p. 106)

A picnic on Pinnacle Island. From the pen and wash drawings by S. H. Grimm in the Kaye Collection. B.M. Add. MS. 15,543, ff. 106, 107.

The delight in natural scenery of a wilder kind is well evidenced by these delightfully intimate sketches by Grimm of his visit, with his patron Dr. Kaye and his house party, to Pinnacle Island in the Farne Islands, c. 1778. (For a general note on Grimm and his patron cf. notes to § 48 and 49.)

In the foreground of § 114 can be seen Dr. Kaye (with his carving knife) and on the left the artist busily sketching. § 115 shows the servants on a lower spit of land also having their picnic meal. Besides the opportunity of visiting picturesque scenery this expedition was also undertaken for antiquarian reasons, for it was on the Farne Islands that St. Cuthbert had had his cell.

§ 116 (cf. text p. 107)

Bathing at Scarborough in 1745. From the engraving by Samuel and Nathaniel Buck in *Views of Castles, Abbeys and Towns*. From a copy in the Department of Printed Books, British Museum.

In this illustration of a watering place in 1745 can be seen the bathing machines with swimmers striking out from their shelter, while on the beach itself are the coaches of those who have come to take the waters at the Spa well. The 'rooms' connected with this can be seen on the left just above the beach.

§ 117 (cf. text pp. 82, 111)

Hunting scene. From a coloured line engraving by D. Lerpinière (pub. 1778) after the painting by John Wootton at Houghton, Norfolk. From a copy in the possession of the Parker Gallery, London.

This engraving after Wootton's picture at Houghton (in which figure Sir Robert Walpole and his huntsman Thomas Turner) conveys a pleasant sense of English country within sight of the sea, and the Englishman's delight in horses and hounds.

§ 118 (cf. text p. 82)

A country race-course. Aquatint (pub. 20 May 1786 by J. Phillips and R. Pollard). From a copy in the possession of the Parker Gallery, London.

Interest in the horse was not confined to hunting among country gentlemen (§ 117) or racing with a fashionable party (§ 119) but as this animated scene shows was lively and whole-hearted among all classes. The horses are shown lining up for the start: in the foreground one of the jockeys is being given last minute instructions, while his horse is being given a swig from the bottle. In the background can be seen early examples of the grandstand, the one in the middle being labelled 'Red Lyon' and that beyond 'Ladies Booth.'

It is described as being a view taken on the spot.

§ 119 (cf. text p. 82)

The Prince of Wales (afterwards the Prince Regent) at Newmarket. From a coloured aquatint (pub. 1791) by J. Collyer after E. F. Burney in the possession of the Parker Gallery, London.

Described as a 'View of the Noblemen's and Gentlemen's Trains of Running Horses taking their exercise up the Warren Hill east of Newmarket,' this print shows the Prince of Wales as the centre of an admiring group, with horses being exercised on all sides, while in the middle distance lies the town of Newmarket.

§ 120 (cf. text p. 109)

London Clubs. St. James's Street in 1792. From Thomas Malton's *Picturesque Tour through London and Westminster* (1792). From a copy in the Department of Printed Books, British Museum.

The English club may be said to have had its first origin in that Elizabethan society of poets and playwrights, which met at the Mermaid Tavern. The coffee-house and the tavern carried on and enlarged the tradition in the XVIIIth century, especially in its political and literary associations. The Club, as we know it to-day, grew partly from these, partly from the fashionable gaming club which was the outcome of an age addicted to gaming in all its forms from wagers and cards to lotteries. Almack's, White's and Boodle's were three of the most fashionable of the century. White's itself developed from White's Chocolate House (established in 1697-8), which in 1736 ceased to be a public chocolate house, and became instead an exclusive gambling club and moved to its present site in St. James's Street in 1755. Almack's, Pall Mall (founded in 1764) was the most notorious for high play but is not to be confused with Almack's Rooms, the fashionable and exclusive assembly rooms in King Street, St. James's, whose social life was ruled by Lady Jersey. Almack's Club passed into the hands of Brooks (a wine merchant and money lender) in 1778 and thereupon removed to St. James's Street, becoming known as Brooks's Club. It can be seen in the right foreground of the present illustration.

§ 121 (cf. text pp. 97, 98)

Wedgwood's shop in St. James's. From Rudolph Ackerman's *Repository of the Arts* (1809). From the copy in the Department of Printed Books, British Museum.

The demand for Wedgwood's wares is well illustrated by this early XIXth century print.

Josiah Wedgwood (1730–95), the potter, with his cousin Thomas Wedgwood, evolved a great variety of wares, which were in world-wide demand. He built a factory at Etruria, and a model village for his work-people. Besides making many technical improvements in the production of pottery, Wedgwood, by his introduction of an imaginative range of colours, from black basalt to cream, from jasper to lustreware, and by his imitations of Greek and Etruscan vases (in making which he employed Flaxman to design the figures), altered the whole status of pottery and created an eager demand for his wares.

§ 122 (cf. text p. 126)

Playing golf below Edinburgh Castle. From a water-colour by Paul Sandby (1745) in the Department of Prints and Drawings, British Museum.

Paul Sandby (1725–1809), assisted in a survey of the Highlands

between 1745 and 1751, and most of his water-colours and drawings of Scotland date from this period.
In this early view of golf the players and their caddies can be clearly seen, and even the shape of their clubs made out.

§ 123, 124 and 125 (cf. text pp. 137–140)
Edinburgh in 1750. High Street, a butcher's shop and a street scene. From water-colour drawings by Paul Sandby in the Department of Prints and Drawings, British Museum.
These sketches by Paul Sandby (cf. note to § 122 above) show Edinburgh and its townspeople in 1750. In § 123 a notice in the High Street reads 'Good eating down this close,' while in § 125 people are shown supping broth at a wayside stall.

§ 126 (cf. text pp. 137–140)
Edinburgh Castle, by J. Elphinstone (c. 1746). King's Maps, XLIX. 74. c. From the Map Room, Department of Printed Books, British Museum.
This engraving shows the fortress-like aspect of the Castle and the castle esplanade in front of it, obviously used at this date as a promenade as well as a parade ground. It succeeds in conveying a lively picture of the contemporary scene.

§ 127 (cf. text pp. 125, 158)
Hawthornden Castle. Engraving from Francis Grose's *Antiquities of Scotland* (1789). From the copy in the Department of Printed Books, British Museum.
This illustration is given to show an example of a Scottish country house which had grown up 'by additions to the war towers of former days,' the front door abutting on the farm buildings. Hawthornden Castle, well known as the poet William Drummond of Hawthornden's house, consisted of the old tower and the more modern house built by Drummond c. 1638. It should be contrasted with the first truly classical house to be built in Scotland (cf. § 130 and 131 below).

§ 128 and 129 (cf text pp. 131, 132, 152)
Scottish cottager spinning and a Scottish interior. From Allan Ramsay's *Gentle Shepherd* (1788 ed.) From a copy in the Department of Printed Books, British Museum.
Allan Ramsay's pastoral drama *The Gentle Shepherd* had been written in 1725, but this 1788 edition gives a vivid idea of XVIIIth-century Scottish life. § 128 shows a typical housewife spinning by the door of her stone and thatch cottage, while in § 129 one sees the arrangements within. We see a room which serves for the whole family to live and sleep in, along with the chickens roosting in the roof and pecking on the earthen floor. In the back right corner can be seen the box bed, while slung from the rafters are hams curing and a string of onions.

§ 130 and 131 (cf. text pp. 157, 158)

The Drum, Midlothian. From photographs by Country Life, Ltd.

Though an earlier house stood here in the XVIth and XVIIth centuries and though part of this was cased up by William Adam when he came to build the new house, it is essentially the first evidence of the new spirit in Scottish building, with nothing traditional about it. William Adam (the father of the more famous brothers Robert and James) had worked with Sir William Bruce of Kinross and completed Hopetoun House in 1710. The Drum was probably built between 1724 and 1734, though some of the interior work is possibly rather later than this. (For a full discussion on this *v.* Arthur T. Bolton's article in *Country Life*, 9 October 1915.)

§ 132 and 133 (cf. text p. 157)

The old and the new town, Edinburgh. From two air views by Aerofilms, Ltd.

These two modern air views of present-day Edinburgh are used here to illustrate the essential difference (still visible to-day) between the old city and the 'new town' of the XVIIIth and early XIXth centuries. In the first can be seen the tall houses, the haphazard grouping, while the second shows the crescents and squares of a planned and harmonious lay-out.

§ 134 (cf. text p. 137)

The Tron Church, Edinburgh High Street. From an engraving by J. Elphinstone, King's Maps XLIX. 68. e. 8, in the Map Room, Department of Printed Books, British Museum.

The Tron Church (1637–63) owes its name to a nearby 'tron' or weighing beam. This engraving shows the old high buildings of the High Street crowded in between the church and a newer block. In the street can be seen a busy throng of townspeople and coaches. (For a view of the interior cf. § 135 below.)

§ 135 (cf. text p. 137)

The General Assembly of the Kirk of Scotland (1787). Interior of the Tron Church, Edinburgh. From a drawing by D. Allen, King's Maps, XLIX. 68. g. 2, in the Map Room, Department of Printed Books, British Museum.

Protestantism became the official religion of Scotland in 1560, the General Assembly being its governing body. There was a modified revival of episcopacy in the XVIIth century, but the Church of Scotland was Presbyterian in organization again by 1689 and this was confirmed in 1707 at the Union. The General Assembly meets annually in Edinburgh, and consists of both ministers and laymen, each presbytery sending its delegates; it is presided over by a moderator, who holds office for one year; the King's representative is also present as well as members of the Scottish universities. This illustration shows the Assembly in session in 1787.

Text illustration, pp. 32, 33

A Weekly Review of the Affairs of France. First page of the first issue 19 February 1704, and one from the third number of 4 March 1704, showing the section called the 'Mercure Scandale.' Daniel Defoe's *Review* ran from 19 February 1704 to 11 June 1713, and therefore covers nearly the whole of Queen Anne's reign. It began as an eight-page weekly issued on Saturdays, but this was soon reduced to four pages, and a little later a Tuesday issue and then a Thursday issue were introduced as well: thereafter the *Review* came out three times a week. It changed its title from time to time; beginning as *A Weekly Review of the Affairs of France* it later added to its title the words: 'with some observations on Transactions at home.' It became with Volume III *Review of the state of the English Nation* and (after the Union) *A Review of the State of the British Nation* until finally abbreviated in Volume IX to *Review*. It consisted of an essay followed by answers to correspondents and social criticism—the 'Mercure Scandale: or Advice from the Scandalous Club. Translated out of French' and later 'Advice from the Scandal Club.' Later this became a monthly supplement and then a separate publication *The Little Review*. Defoe is thought to have written the entire paper himself without any help from correspondents. It covered politics, economics, trade and social life. Its circulation was probably never above 1,000, possibly only some 400 to begin with, but it must be remembered that it would be read in the coffee-houses, rather than be bought personally and individually. The page of the first issue here reproduced sets out the aims of honest journalism and soundly trounces the inaccurate English and muddled writing of the press.

Text illustration, p. 36

A Short Warning or Reproof to all Desperate and Profane Swearers, Cursers, Damners &c . . . by Philaretus. London. Printed and sold by T. Sowle in White-Hart Court in Gracious St., 1702. B.M. Add. MS. 19,752, f. 131.

Text illustration, pp. 93, 95

Arkwright's original spinning machine (1769) and his improved spinning machine (1775). Hargreaves' spinning jenny (from a replica), (patented 1770 but designed 1764-67). Crompton's 'mule' (1774-9), (from a replica). Drawings by W. Savage from photographs supplied by the Science Museum, S. Kensington. These pioneer machines increased the amount of yarn that could be spun per person and steadily increased the fineness and strength of the spun yarn. After carding, the cotton was made into yarn by attenuating the thickish cord (or 'roving') and spinning. The principles of Arkwright's spinning machine and Hargreaves' jenny were combined by Crompton in his 'mule' to produce a smoother yarn of higher count than had been possible before.

(A full description of the beginnings of the cotton industry and of the differences in action between these early machines will be found in *The Early English Cotton Industry* by G. W. Daniels (1920).) The 'mule' was first worked by hand (like the 'jenny') but was later used with water power to give it greater power. The kind of factory in which this type of 'mule' was being used can be seen at § 64.

INDEX

INDEX

Edinburgh Privy Council, 119, 120, 140, 142

Edinburgh Review, the, 157

Education, 16-19, 34-5, 69-73; Eighteenth Century, 16-19; common schooling of upper and middle class, 17; classical curriculum, 17-18; secondary education, 364-5, 367; *and see Subject Headings*

Education (Scotland), 18, 35

Edward I, 119, 149

Elizabeth, Queen, 312

Empire, the, 102-3

Enclosure, 6-8, 80-5; the age of enclosure, 80-5; economic effects of 80-1, 84; expense of, 84*n*.; and draining, 84*n*.; of commons, 7, 81, 84; lands of old enclosure, 8, 74, 80, 81

Enclosure Acts, 80, 81, 84, 111; area seriously affected by, 81

'Enthusiasm,' 62

Episcopalians, Scottish, 126-7, 142-4, 159-60; Jacobite politics of, 126, 142-3, 159-60; bitterness with Presbyterians, 142; comparison with Presbyterians, 126, 143, 160; dependence on upper class support, 143; and the Kirk Session, 127, 142; anomalous position after (1688), 126, 143, 160; in Anne's reign, 143; in North-East Scotland, 144

Eton College, 16, 19

Evangelical revival, 159

Exeter, 39

Exmoor, 110

Factories, employment in, 28

Fairies and Fairy Tales, 25 *and n.*

Fallodon, 11

'Fanatics,' 3

Farm animals, feeding of, 82

Farm labourer. *See* Agricultural labourer

Farquhar, George, 17, 19; *Beaux' Stratagem*, 115

Field-sports, 23-4. *See also* Shooting *and* Hunting

Fielding, Henry, 48, 55*n*., 59

Fielding, Sir John, 40, 55 *and n.*

Fishing industry, 26

Flaxman, John, sculptor, 104

Fleet prison, the, 53

Fletcher of Saltoun, 135, 136

Flodden, 124

Football, 23, 24

Forbes of Culloden, 126, 128

Foundling Hospital, the, 52-3

Fowey, 78

Fox, Charles James, 42, 54, 108-9

Foxe, John: *Book of Martyrs*, 13

Foxhunting. *See* Hunting

France, 61; *noblesse*, the, 112; of Louis XIV, 104

Free Church of Scotland, 161

French privateers, 5

French Revolution, 47, 70

Fuel, 97

Furniture, Eighteenth Century, 12

'Gaberlunzies,' 135

Gainsborough, Thomas, 88, 102, 104, 105

Galloway, 129, 134

Galt's *Annals of the Parish*, 156, 160

Gambling, 19, 20-21

Game, Game laws, 24, 111; poaching war, the, 112

Garbage, 138-9

Gardens: Dutch gardens, 106; landscape gardening, 106-7

Garrick, David, 115

Gentry. *See* Country gentleman

George II, 104

Georgia, Colony of, 54

Germany, scholarship in, 17-18

Gibbon, Edward, 48, 61, 65, 71-2, 88, 104; *Decline and Fall*, 58, 104; *Autobiography*, 65

Gibbons, Grinling, 12

Gibbs, James, 12, 101

Gibraltar, 29

Gibson, Edmund, Bishop of London, 62

Gideon, Sampson, 100

Gilbert and Sullivan, 115

Gin drinking, 49, 50; and death rate, 49; Hogarth's 'Gin Lane,' 21, 49

Girtin, Thomas, 105

Glasgow, 137, 155-6, 158; Clydeside, 152, 155-6

Glasgow University, 137, 156

Gloucestershire coal trade revolt, 5-6

Godmanchester, 6

Godolphin, Earl, 24